Doc Holliday

DOC HOLLIDAY

by
John Myers Myers

UNIVERSITY OF NEBRASKA PRESS
LINCOLN AND LONDON

Library of Congress Catalog Card Number 55-5528
International Standard Book Number 0-8032-5781-3

First Bison Book printing: August 1973
Most recent printing shown by the first digit below:
15   16   17   18   19   20

Doc Holliday was first published by Little, Brown and
Company in 1955. The Bison Book edition, published by
arrangement with the author, is reproduced from the
1957 edition published by Jarrolds Publishers (London)
Limited.

Manufactured in the United States of America

∞

To Two Fellow Clansmen
KENT deGRAFFENRIED
and
JOHN MARTIN MYERS
this chronicle of a man
as a slight token
of avuncular esteem

CONTENTS

PART I

The Western Progress
of a Georgia Gentleman

CHAPTER I

THE story of John Henry Holliday does not add up to stock biographical fare. He was martyr to no cause and served no nation. He was far from being the victim of social oppression or the world's neglect. He created neither empires, business corporations nor works of art. His life was not such as to mark him a model for future generations.

He was one of the coolest killers ever to snatch gun from hiding. He was a gambler of enough parts to make two. He was a con man to match tricks with old George Peele or Simon Suggs, and equally deft at dodging the passes which the law often made in his direction. He drank enough liquor to earn a place on John Barleycorn's calendar of saints.

For these and other reasons it has been freely remarked of him that he was not a good man. It is not the purpose of the ensuing chronicle either to refute or press such a charge against this Southern dentist who turned Western adventurer. It is rather the plan here to report what it is still possible to learn about an invalid whose name grew to be a byword for frontier prowess during the 1870s and '80s.

In line with this aim it is fitting to state that if he was not a good man, he was yet a man who was good at a number of things. The list includes a duke's mixture of characteristics as well as his assortment of skills. As to some of his bents, it might be conceded that they let criticism in at the front door. Others must be reckoned admirable.

He was, for instance, good at making his own way under circumstances that would have excused dependence. He was good at following his own course, unswayed by public attitudes. He was good at keeping faith with such friends as he saw fit to make. He was good both at keeping his own counsel and respecting the privacy of others. He was good at accepting facts without flinching. He was good at facing death, both as an ever-present threat to a victim of consumption and a special menace in the many gun- and knife-fights in which he engaged.

By contrast, he was not good at winning the regard of society's moral leaders, wherever found. Many not so marked for grace shared this distaste for him, generating a hatred which has filtered down through a couple of succeeding generations. Among divers other things, these said that he was not good at distinguishing between his own and another's property. That case will be tried in subsequent chapters as well as the remaining evidence allows. Meanwhile it is enough to say that he was never at any time good at keeping out of hot water.

Some asserted that he sought it as his natural element, and this may have been so. At any rate he was up to his ears in it for most of the fifteen years he spent in Texas, Kansas, Oklahoma, Wyoming, New Mexico, Arizona, South Dakota and Colorado. By the time he finally had to wait and face death with his hands down, he had achieved what many a more ambitious man had vainly attempted. Thousands of once celebrated names have all but faded from the record, but the West has not forgotten Doc Holliday.

That his life is, nevertheless, worth reporting may be doubted —but only by people who hold that history is properly a study of social and economic forces. Contradicting them and not begging their pardon, history is also a study of men; and in the history of the Wild West Doc has the distinction of playing a unique part.

One of the shadow shapes which has delighted mankind since Robin Hood was made one and the same with the noble Earl of Huntington is the idea of the gentleman rogue. This fancy has been especially popular in the United States, where any mildly housebroken killer is apt to wind up with the subtitle, "aristocrat and man of culture rare". But if specimens of the type abound in Western myth, only one is to be found on the hoof, complete with a background which can be documented. This is John Henry Holliday, who was undoubtedly the product of an organized, patrician society, so recognized by itself and so rated by those not encompassed in its circle.

Unless some fellow craftsman produces a book on the subject before this chronicle gets into print, or unless some long-buried manuscript comes to light meanwhile, this will be the first effort at a full-length presentation of Doc's hectic career. Such being the case, a brief discussion of the sources on which it is based will follow.

He did not live, as did his associates Wyatt Earp and Bat Masterson, to hand down any comments or to confide his recollections to a biographer. Unlike Bill Tilghman, whom he also knew, he was not survived by a widow who could give an intimate picture of his private life. He left no body of letters, or at least the one group known to have existed has not been located, and it might not be very informative if found. It is doubtful if he would have confided much about his frontier activities to a nun.

But if he did not write of himself, other men did him that sometimes dubious service. Chief among these could be cited Wyatt Earp, who was fond of him; Bat Masterson, who did not like him, although he usually found himself an ally of Doc's; and William Breakenridge, who lived to become the spokesman of a highly hostile faction. He was also cited in the memoirs of Bob Wright, anecdotal historian, and Eddie Foy, the actor, who were entertained by him at Dodge City; Miguel Otero, later governor of New Mexico, who enjoyed his company at Las Vegas; John Clum, the Indian agent and editor, who disapproved of him at Tombstone; plus a few others who unquestionably had some acquaintance with him.

In addition to the above there are the statements and comments of sundry old-timers who speak with an authority to which they may or may not be entitled. That is to say, there is nothing to prove that their assertions were based on first-hand knowledge. In certain instances the odds favour it, while in as many cases these reports sound like the windjamming of old codgers who have used their imaginations to build good stories out of vaguely-remembered rumours.

Next come the contemporary newspaper accounts, in so far as it has been possible to hunt them down. Missing or sketchy in several States, these achieve respectable bulk in Arizona and Colorado. By kind they fall into several groups. In a solitary case the name of the reporter is known and a personal acquaintance asserted. In two other instances Doc was actually interviewed and quoted. In one series the objectivity at which newspapers for ever shoot and miss was attained in the reprinting of actual court records. A fourth category is composed of items mailed to papers by correspondents, one or two of whom may have known Doc, although this is not implicit in the accounts. A fifth class consists of items picked up and re-written—in the days before press services broadcast standard reports—for papers in towns where Doc had ceased to live or was known only by repute. A sixth is made up of obituary notices, ranging in tone from *de mortuis nil nisi bonum* piety to a gleeful realization that, dead or alive, John H. Holliday was good copy.

Twentieth-century references have been more remarkable for their frequency than for the information offered. Those that go further than a general recognition of Doc's standing as a first line Western character are mostly based on the statements of Earp, Masterson and Breakenridge, singly or in combination. Three articles, all brief but each demonstrating that the author had done a small amount of independent research, have made a show of being more comprehensive. Father Stanley Crocchiola, while doing research for his book on New Mexico outlaws, unearthed some long-buried data from deed and criminal records. The rest seem to have picked up some unnamed old-timer's recollection or to have sliced a chunk from the steadily growing body of the Holliday legend.

The fact that myth has adhered to him is a point of which due note should be taken. No such thing happened to such men of frontier mark as the afore-mentioned Tilghman and Masterson. Men of remarkable achievement though they were, they did not stir creative fancy. They were in such and such places at established periods and participated in events firmly anchored in documented history. There may be widely different interpretations of the record; but the record is there, and they are never found far away from it.

Doc Holliday's ghost has shown no more respect for the proprieties of history than Doc in the flesh did for the canon law of Mrs. Grundy. Even before he was lowered into his grave he showed a tendency to turn up in places where he probably never set foot, and to do things probably wrought by other men, if at all.

It is not easy to fix the qualities which draw cycles of stories around certain men, for those who share this property—witness Abraham Lincoln and Billy the Kid—may not belong to the same lodge at all. Greatness is not the criterion, for many of the greatest men have been totally without it. What was the poacher

Robin Hood, that he should have songs and books without end for his epitaph while all the mighty barons of his day have been sloughed off with a line or so? There is no answer for that question at this remove of time; but a few reasons why American imagination has been tempted to weave tales around Doc Holliday can be confidently set down.

One is the anomaly which enabled a man who belonged in a wheel chair by every right—except that of his bitter determination—to hold his own among as hardy a tribe of desperadoes as the world has ever seen. Another, already discussed, is the fact that he was blue blood fallen from grace. Allied to the foregoing is the fact that he was a professional man and, by all accounts, one whose mental attainments went beyond the ordinary. Lastly, he had a raffish sense of humour, giving him a dimension that many of his compeers were utterly without.

Commentators are fond of remarking that this or that fellow was a product of his times. To some degree that is true of everyone, but in the case of complex personalities it is often hard to say whether the life made the man or the man made the life. The people who are typical of a given period would probably be typical of any period, and most of the rest wind up trying to blend with the scenery. Chameleonism is a principle of life to which not many are heretic, but having acquired them, Doc was one of the rare birds who stuck to his different feathers.

Certain of his qualities lurk in the never-never land of hereditary and variant types, where those can wander who want to. Such star-gazing will not be undertaken here. Nonetheless, a reasonable amount can be learned about Doc by taking a short look at the society which helped to produce him. High among the contradictions of which he was composed stands the fact that he was a man of tradition who clung to a few handholds on that rock, no matter what seas washed over him.

John Henry Holliday was born near Griffin, a town then in Henry County, Georgia, instead of Spalding County as is now the case. The record of his birthday was one of the numberless victims of Sherman's passion for arson, but the baptismal docket of the Presbyterian Church in Griffin shows that he was baptized there on March 21, 1852. As "infant" baptism is specified, it is reasonable to assume that he was born in '52, during either February or the latter part of January.

Henry County, old style, was a large one lying south and east of Atlanta in the new Piedmont section of Georgia which was challenging the coastal region for economic dominance. The State was then the richest in the nation, and its wealth was almost entirely agricultural. Fortunes were to be made by those with the capital, which is to say the slaves, to develop large holdings. Within a few decades, therefore, this frontier had been woven into the classic social pattern of the Southern coastal plains.

It was a highly stratified society. At the top were the few dozen clans with slaves enough to man large-scale operations. Their power was bulwarked by their blood ties with other clans so situated, both throughout the State and Jefferson's agrarian empire generally. Not capitalists only, they accepted as a right, and undertook as an obligation, political, social and cultural leadership.

The benefits conferred at birth to one born of this order were universal in one sense. Nothing but the heavens and those who might abide there was reckoned above him. There were also local advantages.

It was a time and a place where cities and most of those who dwelt in them were not held in esteem. The emphasis was on regional identification, taking the form of county pride. The feeling towards this native territory was that of the Frenchman who reverently calls everything he can see from his town on a pocket-size hill "my country". Nowadays if a man from a rural section is asked where he hails from he is apt to mumble something about "a little place in the sticks you never heard of", or else he will give its geographical relationship to the nearest metropolis. But in the South before the American Civil War, a man native or naturalized to any locality would stick out his chest and tell you about it. If he belonged, as Doc Holliday did, to one of the county's leading families, he would expect you to know something of his standing as well as the special virtues of the clan stamping ground.

The class which rejoiced in wealth and social dignity peopled the professions and supplied officers to the army, in addition to running the great plantations. Doc's father was typical in all these respects. Major Henry B. Holliday was a lawyer as well as a planter. Nor was Major a courtesy title. Fifteen years before he

entered the Confederate service he led troops carrying the United
States flag into Mexico during the war of 1846-48. His unit
was a body of volunteers calling themselves Fannin's Avengers,
in recognition of the Georgia origin of Fannin, who was murdered
with most of his command, following his surrender in the Texas
war of independence.

It was shortly after returning from Mexico that he married
Alice Jane McKey, the event taking place on January 8, 1849.
A tribe of large-scale planters, the McKeys, had moved from
South Carolina to claim their share of Georgia's phenomenal
prosperity. They had come in clan strength, but not all to
Henry County. A couple of McKey brothers had elected to push
on to Lowndes County in the southern part of the State. A two-
wheel town called Troupeville was the metropolis when Doc
used to go there to visit his cousins. As this region was later to be
his home and the place he said he hailed from—on the rare
occasions when he gave out any reliable information on that
subject—a word about it belongs in the story.

More recently chopped out of the wilderness than any other
part of Georgia, Lowndes County pressed upon the Florida
border. Pine country in its native condition, it proved exceedingly rich when ploughed. Troupeville might have been expected
to prosper accordingly, but it wasn't gaited that way. Serving as a
trading post and a county seat, it had useful functions but few
civic ambitions. A couple of times a year it waked up for court
sessions and the accompanying horse racing and cock fighting.
The rest of the time it basked dormant in the fork of the
Withlacoochee and Little Rivers.

A strange fate befell Troupeville, however. Even before the
war of 1861-65 it felt the blight of changing times and was
literally pushed off the map. The force that accomplished this
was the first railroad to serve that part of the State, which
legged it south from Savannah in 1859. In spite of protests from
Troupeville's leading citizens, the railroad persisted in by-
passing the town.

If the people of Lowndes County didn't think much of
cities, they could see the value of a shipping point for cotton
very plainly. When the railroad refused to recognize the importance of their county seat, they shrugged and moved the
town four miles to where the stage road crossed the tracks.

B

They didn't take the name along with it, though, considering that bad luck. At the same time they didn't want to hurt the feelings of the popular Governor George M. Troupe, in whose honour the deserted village had been christened.

From this dilemma the citizenry were rescued by the genius of Leonoreon de Lyon, editor of the *South Georgia Watchman*. Noting that the plantation home of Governor Troupe was called Val de Osta, he suggested the elision, Valdosta.

While all this was going on, Doc was growing up as the only child of Henry B. Holliday, late of Fannin's Avengers, and his beautiful young wife, who is said to have been possessed of considerable talent as a musician. There had been one other child, a girl, but she had died in infancy.

Beyond her comeliness and musical ability, not much is remembered of Doc's mother. Concerning the Major a little more data is available. One of the early settlers of the region around Griffin, he carved himself a holding in what is now known as the C. J. Manley sub-division. When Spalding County was formed and Griffin made its seat, he was elected clerk of the Superior Court.

There are differences of opinion between sources in Spalding and Lowndes County as to just when he left the first and came to the other. One school holds that he made the shift before the war and another that he moved as a result of Sherman's destructive progress. In any case he was an early volunteer, serving, as Confederate records show, first as Regimental Quartermaster and then as a line Major of the Twenty-seventh Georgia Infantry. After the conflict, he resumed his career as a planter and dabbled mildly in politics. For one thing, he served a term as Mayor of Valdosta, where Holliday Street now bears his name. He is also credited by the *History of Lowndes County* with being the first to launch Georgia's vast pecan industry in that part of the State. This he did in 1876, the year when his son John made the first of many extraordinary wilderness flights to escape the clutch of the law.

In such a picture of a local man of mark there is little that hints of the fire which ran in Doc's veins. Fortunately, however, a man known only by his surname of Moore has left in the Arizona Pioneers Historical Library a report of a meeting he had with Major Holliday in 1881. A surveyor at the time,

Mr. Moore found his work routine until he was ordered by the city fathers to take sights along a certain alley.

"When I reached the alley," so reads this deposition, "I was confronted with a rather dignified, irascible old man with a double-barrel shot-gun. He asked what I was doing and I told him that the Mayor had sent me down to survey the alley. 'Hum,' he grunted, 'that old rascal wants you to get shot.' I told him I had no desire to get shot and left. I do not know whether that alley is surveyed yet or not."

Moore did not indicate whether or not this well-guarded way is the one which now carries the Holliday name. He did go on to say that he later got to know Doc's father and found that "He seems to be very much respected and pretty well liked."

As to how Doc himself stood in the community which fostered him there is little on which to base any report. His exploits were achieved afar, and it is doubtful that much in the way of news trickled back. In general, all that Lowndes County could have known about its most famous citizen during his lifetime was that he had gone West and wasn't expected to return.

Yet something about his boyhood can be learned from kinsmen who received first-hand information from the generation old enough to remember Doc. More can be guessed through appraising the impact of war, military occupation and the bitter period of reconstruction on a youth born with more than his share of red pepper.

In Valdosta and the vicinity Doc is remembered as a clever youngster with the excellent manners bred in the bone of the small fry belonging to his kind and time. Until comparatively recent years, in fact, there were a few old ladies who cherished recollections of his courtly airs and his grace as a dancing partner.

Yet it is also remembered of him that he had his coat-tails dragging, and that when his dander was up all men looked the same size to him. Altogether he was, to use the old phrase, quick at his books and did a considerable amount of reading, though the outdoors called to him with equally persuasive force. Riding and shooting were his pet enthusiasms, and it was well for him that it was so. In after years his ability to aim with accuracy and to gallop away from the wrath that followed saved his life on more occasions than a cat could afford.

When it came to drawing a bead, he developed a skill that

opened the eyes of war veterans, themselves bred to hunting from early years. One such told a now surviving relative of Doc's that "John was the best pistol or rifle shot I ever saw, and could shoot the eyes out of a rabbit when the rabbit would look at you before he started running."

Only two actual incidents connected with his days in Valdosta have been accorded a place on the record. One will be dealt with presently. The other takes the form of a recollection that at the close of the war Doc rode to meet his uncle, Captain T. S. McKey. That reads like a simple gesture of greeting; but it was a great deal more. One of Sherman's mad-elephant accomplishments had been to rip up the railroad tracks. The Georgia soldiers mustered out after Appomattox had to make it home on foot, some from Savannah, some all the way from Virginia.

What Doc as a thirteen-year-old boy had undertaken to do was to ride until he had somehow managed to pick his uncle up. In so doing he had to make his way along roads crowded with hard-pressed veterans, many of whom might have figured that they needed a horse more than he did. It was alike typical of Doc that he was confident of being able to take care of himself, in the face of the circumstances, and that he returned with both horse and uncle in due time.

Meanwhile the war had run its course, wreaking certain temporary changes in Lowndes County and other, more sweeping ones, that would never be eradicated. South Georgia was never the scene of combat, although there was infrequent excitement as troops rolled through to repel Federal thrusts at nearby points in Florida. Nevertheless, and especially from late in 1863 on, the war was an ever-present reality.

By then the blockade had operated to cut off the supplies of a pleasure-loving people who were accustomed to import all their luxuries. A prosperous class who took pride in dressing well could no longer buy clothes. Homespun drabness descended on a community which took to drinking strange bark concoctions in place of tea, coffee and wine. Towards the end, the order of the day was pinched rations, boding no good for boys rounding into the ravenous years of adolescence.

It is unquestionably the case that the high incidence of tuberculosis among the Southerners of Doc's generation was

owing to the unbalanced or starvation diets of the war years
and the equally lean ones of the reconstruction era. Those youths
and girls were battle casualties as surely as were their fathers and
uncles who lost arms and legs at Shiloh or Chancellorsville.
Young John H. Holliday, it is hardly possible to doubt, was a war
victim of this category.

Undermining his health was by no means all that war wrought
upon him. The society to which he was born was destroyed. Its
forms and ceremonies survived for some decades, but its bullet-
riddled ranks never regained their intellectual and political
dominance. The postwar emphasis on cities and the growth of
commerce created a new scale of values, epitomized in Georgia
by the rise of hustling Atlanta. However he might regard himself,
the plantation owner was no longer a baron in his hall. He had
been relegated to the position of a farmer, while leadership was
assumed by those engaged in turning county towns into cities.

This was not only war, it was revolution, generating a restlessness to which youth is bound to respond, even if older people
manage to ignore it. These hectic impulses, plus all the feuds and
hatreds caused by the reconstruction programme, worked on the
young in direct proportion to the warmth of their blood. How
those who smoke easily shape up depends on how well their
energies have been channelled by discipline.

During the War between the States all the men of Henry
and Lowndes Counties agile enough to catch whippersnappers
and belt them into an appreciation of moral beauty were at the
front. Only women and old men remained, and for colts given
to bucking that isn't enough. No longer ago than World War II
many families discovered to their grief that a high-spirited kid—
without a father around to kick his behind when needed—may get
so out of hand that he never really respects any whims but his own.

Another circumstance aided this trend in John H. Holliday.
In 1866 Alice Jane Holliday died. Major Holliday promptly
found another wife, and thereby lost a son. There was more to
this than the natural attachment of an only man-child for a
devoted mother, and the consequent distaste for the speedy
intrusion of a step-parent. The action outraged Doc's sense of
loyalty, which was the driving force of his being. To all intents
and purposes he seems to have been through with his father from
that time on and went his own way more than ever.

Those were some of the factors that conditioned him—nine years old when the war began, and an independent citizen, ready four years later to take the risky journey referred to above. A good part of the time it was literally true that school did not keep, either. There was no public-school system, and the private academies folded up when their staffs marched off to the front. Intermittently a few of the older men, Colonel Leonoreon de Lyon of the *South Georgia Watchman* for one, stepped into the educational breach, but these seem to have been short-term efforts.

By a year or so after the war Doc was probably freed from the restraints of even this spotty tutelage. Commencement, if so his separation from schooling could be called, offered none of those shining prospects with which speakers at graduation ceremonies try to dazzle the young. There was a Federal garrison at Valdosta to ride herd on a defeated and disfranchised people. The freeing of the slaves had wrecked the old economy and the new one had not yet been fairly launched. For experienced men there was little work and next to nothing in the way of pay if it could be found. For half-grown boys like Doc the prospects were even narrower.

What Doc did with himself most of the rest of the time cannot now be discovered, but on a certain day in the late '60s he went to a swimming-hole in the Withlacoochee, hard by where the stage road used to cross to old Troupeville, and fired shots in the direction of human targets for the first recorded time.

Those he fired upon were Negro youths, age and size unspecified but plainly big enough to have challenged the teen-age white boys for the use of Valdosta's bathing beach of the period. This was enough of an institution to win mention in the *History of Lowndes County*, which furnishes the information that it was then used by the girls as well as the boys.

That fact may or may not have had a bearing on the case. All that is told is that young Holliday ordered the Negroes to swim elsewhere, changed their refusal to acceptance at pistol point, and slung shots towards their retreating forms.

Doc has been indignantly condemned for this incident in various references, none made by witnesses or by people with any knowledge of the circumstances. Their fury is possibly justified, but there are things to be said which have not been offered by Doc's detractors.

For an act to be fairly appraised it must be seen in the light of the times in which it took place. Reconstruction was a time of vicious madness, with the pace set by a Federal government which had come to secure and had remained to prey. A dazed people who thought the fight was to make them come into the Union found themselves thrust out of it. Looting them while they were in this state of disinheritance were two kinds of agencies. One was frankly predatory, seizing for northern capital. The other was inexpensively charitable, snatching property from the legal owners and handing it over to the manumitted slaves.

Of these, because of the social complications, the latter was the harder to take. It has been said that there was a Federal garrison at Valdosta. It was a Negro garrison. Under its protection the local Negroes started sporadic reigns of terror. This was natural enough, on the part of newly freed men, but that fact added no sweetening.

Violence, where military authorities were indifferent to chaos, or were even conspiring to stir it up, found its only curb in civilian ire. Those stirred to action by this wrath were not Quakers but veterans with the smell of battle smoke still in their nostrils. In the end, what had to be done was accomplished, but it was not at all points wrought with measure, or by keeping the niceties carefully in mind. It was, in fact, the most infernal period in the history of this nation. Youth with the boldness to become precociously involved was bound to suck poison from it. That lads like John Holliday would sometimes do senselessly what their elders were doing to gain a definite end is not to be wondered at.

Just what did happen as a result of Doc's sending bullets across the Withlacoochee is debatable. In certain Western narratives, it is turned into a minor massacre. Several were dead, by those accounts, and as many more lay writhing on the ground by the time the maniacal young killer had gleefully emptied one pistol. That would have represented excellent shooting, but it is doubtful that Doc should be credited with it. When Moore, the surveyor, ran lines along all Valdosta streets but one, the reported tally was more modest. A single Negro lad was supposed to have been killed, and Lowndes County opinion was divided as to whether even he had been hit intentionally.

Family spokesmen, to give the active defence a hearing it
has not before had, claim that Doc killed nobody. In view of
Moore's testimony this can hardly be allowed, although by
1881 gossip could conceivably have made manslaughter out of
a mere wounding. The further statement that Doc did not leave
Valdosta while under a cloud of any sort can be accepted unre-
servedly. Due to the general public attitude, or perhaps to
special circumstances, no consequent stigma need have clung to
young Holliday. Beyond argument, in spite of statements made
by Masterton and his echoes, the incident had nothing to do with
urging Doc to go West.

What it did bring about, in all likelihood, was to make the
Hollidays and McKeys take a closer look at just what they had
on their hands. Here was an alert, restless youth with not enough
occupation to take up the slack of his energies. Something had to
be done with him before he got into real trouble. He did not seem
to be of the temperament for agriculture, and class tradition outlawed a mercantile career. In former years the military services
would have been the answer, but war bitterness forbade that,
even if West Point and Annapolis had been open to Southerners.
The only other allowable refuge for gentlemen was the professions. Doc's family packed him off to Baltimore to study
dentistry.

Whether this was Doc's own choice or that of his people
cannot be ascertained. The chief reason for favouring the former
notion is that dentistry puts a premium on good hands. Doc's
were preternaturally strong and deft. In later life this was the
one factor which compensated for his general bodily weakness.
It was his hands which made him quick on the draw and slippy
with the cards. Whatever involved their use, tooth pulling and
patching included, he could be confident of doing well.

As to Baltimore, it had been the dental capital of the nation
since the 1840s. At that time the first school of dentistry in the
world had been established there, as the initial step in doing away
with the old method of learning through apprenticeship. This
was the Baltimore College of Dental Surgery, which gave a
two-year course of lectures and application. It was not that
institution which Doc attended, according to the findings of a
dental historian named Dunn, but an imitator and would-be
rival called the Baltimore Dental College. Presumably it gave

about the same course as the more famous school, which has survived through being incorporated into the University of Maryland.

One thing which can be taken for granted is that Doc learned things in Baltimore, dentistry aside, which could not be easily studied in the Lowndes County of the sombre reconstruction era. The Maryland metropolis had itself fallen on evil days, following the outbreak of war and Federal occupation. Yet it was still one of the nation's largest cities, out-ranked in the East only by New York, Brooklyn (which was then a separate entity), Philadelphia and Boston. It was one of the great ports of the country, too, being a favourite of the clipper ships, which rode towards it on the winds of the Chesapeake and the tides of the Patapsco estuary from all the ports of the world.

Then there is the special quality of the place to be considered. Some cities, like some houses, give out the feeling that nobody has ever had much of a good time there and that no nonsense will be expected or tolerated. Baltimore is just the opposite in this respect. It invites belief in the presence of good living, which may, in fact, be enjoyed there on a variety of levels.

Those investigated by John Henry Holliday can be defined within whisper range of exactitude. A single young man of good address can usually find a welcome where he wants it, and in this case the network of cousin connections which linked Southern society could have been counted on to help out. But that was one phase only. Some youthful bachelors, drawn to cities for work or study, can be relied upon to seek no more than proper circles, which they frequent until marriage offers them the haven of permanent chaperonage. Others gravitate towards robust entertainment as naturally as eels seek the Sargasso Sea.

Doc Holliday, it need hardly be remarked, was of this exploratory cast. He was the sort of fellow who could walk blindfolded in any direction in the confidence that he would end up where something was going on. It is said in Valdosta that he did not drink to speak of while there. It can be taken on faith that he had learned what to do when the cork was out of the bottle, as well as something about the art of playing cards, by the time he left Baltimore.

The face that he then turned to the world was that of a man just reaching his maturity. It was, as a picture taken some years

later testifies, an extraordinarily striking face. Even from a
faded camera shot the eyes look out with challenging force.
They were blue eyes. In the fashion of the times a walrus-tusk
moustache cut between a well-formed nose and a mouth at once
strong and suggestive of emotional capacity. His hair was blond.
He was five-feet ten-inches tall, but his spare frame made him
look taller. It was a well-adorned frame, for he was fond of good
clothes.

Such was the appearance of the professional gentleman who
headed South in, as nearly as can be determined, the summer
of 1872. Atlanta was the city where he decided to hang out his
name-plate as a dentist, and the choice was a good one. Growing rapidly, it was already passing Savannah, to become the
metropolis of Georgia. Trained dental surgeons were not
numerous, and the chances of building up a good practice were
excellent. He loved his profession, moreover, and had a strong
competitive instinct which should have sufficed to push him
forward. With work to anchor him, there was an even chance
that his wild streak would remain more or less in hand. Everything indicated that Dr. John H. Holliday was on his way to
becoming a successful Georgia citizen.

This is not what happened, although Doc gave it a try. He
had been in Atlanta only a few months when his health showed
signs of letting him down.

Hopeful apparently that he would do better in a smaller
town, where the peace of life was not so hard on the system, he
moved his practice to Griffin, near which he had been born. The
tradition of him to be traced there is that he was a quiet, even a
subdued young man; and there was plenty of reason for this to
be so. Whether or not he had guessed what was the matter with
him, the doctor of dental surgery eventually called in a doctor of
medicine, who gave it to him straight. John Holliday had
consumption, and had had it for a long while. It had reached such
an advanced state that no cure could be expected. If he stayed
where he was, he'd die in short order. If he wanted to take the
trouble to put death off for a year or so, he could seek a drier
climate.

CHAPTER II

THE cheerless presciption handed Doc Holliday was his signal to move westward. He promptly did so, though on the first leg of his journey he did not quite leave the South. In 1873, as now, Dallas stood where one region ended and another had not quite begun.

Why he chose a city in Texas no one that knew ever said. Colorado would have seemed a more logical selection, but at that time it may have seemed too much like enemy territory for a young partisan to consider. Among Southern States Texas was the most westerly and, to speak in terms of railroads, Dallas was then the end of the line.

Actually that town is not as high as Atlanta and squats in a river bottom where the Georgia city stands upon the hills. This fact may not have been clearly understood. People from the Atlantic seaboard have only vague notions about the West today, and there is no reason to believe that they were any better informed in the 1870s. At a certain remove beyond the Mississippi all cities were doubtless envisioned as either on the high plains or in the Rockies, and all were alike supposedly blessed with bracing elements.

But whether through bias, instinct, his physician's ignorance or the fact that the railroads couldn't take him any farther, Doc made an excellent choice. Dallas, as any denizen of that ebullient city will tell you, *has* got an invigorating climate; and its artesian water, although it does villainous things to whiskey when mixed in a highball, is apparently beneficial to the human system. At the time Doc reached it, moreover, Dallas was in a most interesting state of development.

The transition through which it was going had so many points in common with the changes of Doc's way of life while there that it seems like a conspiracy of symbolism. And though Dallas later cooled down, while Doc went on to places that made it seem like a New England finishing school, neither was ever the same again.

It so happened that in 1872 Dallas got its first view of railroad tracks. These were laid by the Houston and Texas Central, which wasn't sufficiently impressed with the town to deviate from its chosen line north. The best the city's anxious merchants could obtain was a terminal a mile east of town. This, combining with the fact that Dallas stood at the head of Trinity River navigation, gave the city a boom which had by no means settled when the next year brought the Texas and Pacific. Crossing the Houston and Texas Central tracks, this road drove through Dallas and built a station right in town.

What that did to a quiet southern village was a caution. Its population early in 1872 was about three thousand, mostly living in a cluster of streets around the courthouse square. Before the second railroad showed up, more than nine hundred new buildings had been erected. When the Texas and Pacific hove into town, this frenzy of construction was multiplied.

The dazzling speed with which boom towns grew during the nineteenth century has been exaggerated in some cases. It is almost impossible to exaggerate it in others. The key to the difference was a railroad or the lack of one. Towns like Tombstone, which weren't served by tracks, were put together with relative slowness. Many a railroad town literally rose up over the week-end because of the use of prefabricated houses. These were packed up and moved as matter-of-factly as personal luggage, as soon as any given place seemed in danger of losing its boom-time prosperity.

Just what happened, and what the buildings looked like, was clearly described by J. H. Beadle, whose book *Western Wilds* has the copyright date of 1877. "Transactions in real estate in all these [railroad] towns were, of course, most uncertain; and everything that looked solid was a sham. Red brick fronts, brown stone fronts, and stuccoed walls were found to have been made to order in Chicago, and shipped West in sections. Ready-made houses were finally sent out in lots, boxed, marked and numbered; half a dozen men could erect a block in one day, and two boys with screwdrivers put up a habitable dwelling in three hours. A very good grey-stone stucco front, with plain sides, twenty by forty, could be had for three hundred dollars; and if a man's business happened to desert him, or the town moved on, he had only to take the store to pieces, ship it on a platform car to the next city, and set up shop again."

That this gives an accurate picture of what took place in Dallas in 1872 is shown by an entry from the journal of a young Texan who was there to see. Referring to the crowd of new settlers brought in by the Houston and Texas Central, he noted that they "began to set up their portable houses which in sections they had brought from Corsicana".

Among those who threw their shanties together on arrival many were either welcomed or feared as competitors, depending on the point of view. These belonged to a class of opportunists who had earned separate recognition under the name of "terminus merchants".

The phrase is apt enough to tell of their calling and vagabond habits in one breath. They moved with the railroads to keep the trade of the construction crews—said to number five thousand in the case of Dallas. In so doing they were able to take advantage of a moving belt of inflation, creating a seller's market in every new section reached by the tracks.

Railroad crews were not the only sudden arrivals. A terminus town drew additional thousands, all hopeful of making a killing. Nothing was nailed down on the frontier, least of all the people. Even if they were doing fairly well with one enterprise, they were always ready to abandon the whole works for a pig in a shinier poke.

The capable and enterprising poured into the new towns along with drifters, hopeful that their luck would change. Swelling these ranks and the confusion were the new chums from assorted regions back East. Southerners, recruited from war-ravaged regions or places where reconstruction had stopped the clock of opportunity, swarmed over Texas. But the North sent its quota, too. Vermont, along with Georgia, had discovered that agriculture was playing a smaller part in the new economy which followed the conflict between the States. Finding no place for themselves as they left the service or reached beyond high school, young men cleared out. So did lads from the midland States. The latter were not yet crowded, but it was the American fashion to move; and the West had been an irresistible lure since before Daniel Boone's time.

The West was still, too, a place where anything could happen; a place where a bonanza could be laid like an egg in your hat while you were sleeping off a drunk in somebody's barn. It was a place where all the previous wrongs of fortune could be righted in a moment through a man's sheer willingness to try anything.

This exuberant will to believe, which was perhaps the most noteworthy fact about the frontier, fostered the sucker and fed the opportunist. In a terminus city real-estate prices took off from the floor and found no ceiling. Horn-mad speculators saw New York and Philadelphia eclipsed within the year. They bought, built and equipped, not only for the present but to meet the luxuriant expectations of the future.

On all this optimism the terminus merchant smiled, as well he might. He had seen it go on in other towns, now returned to the rural graves from which they had briefly risen, and expected to see it at the next headquarters of the railroad construction crews.

How complete the exodus from a terminus city could be as soon as it lost that status is graphically described by Beadle. He tells of railroad towns which grew from a crossroads settlement to cities of about ten thousand within six months. But by their anniversary—the terminus buck having been passed to the next point on the line—they were reduced to a matter of a couple of hundred inhabitants.

Allowing for the fact that it was a more solid community to begin with, some such fate might have overtaken Dallas while Doc Holliday was there. It did not. Flush times gave the city their feverish blessing throughout his stay.

When the Houston and Texas Central pushed north across the Trinity River, it took some terminus merchants with it. By then, however, the Texas and Pacific was expected. Still Dallas would in the nature of things have lost many of its busiest citizens to Fort Worth when the El Paso-bound railroad moved its construction crews there.

Having reached Dallas in June of 1873, the line could reasonably have counted on covering the thirty-odd miles to Fort Worth before another summer rolled around. It was giving it a try and getting good results when the depression of 1873 scrambled all plans. The economic paralysis was second to none in the nation's history. Further railroad construction was out of the question. Eight miles west along the Trinity from Dallas the tracks of the Texas and Pacific ended. It was nearly three years before any further spikes were driven.

The depression which ruined so many communities fattened Dallas. Its terminus merchants stayed and dug in perforce, nor had they cause to regret it. By virtue of its two railroads and its river connections with the Gulf of Mexico, the city thrived as the supply point for an immense frontier empire. To the north and north-east were the many thousands of Indians whom the the Federal government had herded into what is now Oklahoma, and whom it had to somehow feed and clothe. West, beyond Fort Worth, was one line of military posts garrisoned against the untamed tribes. Hundreds of miles west again another line of forts stretched along the Pecos in New Mexico. Scattered over the vast intervening region were the trading posts for ranchers and buffalo hunters, which also looked to Dallas for all or much of the merchandise they sold.

As the starting or finishing point for expeditions in and out of this wild half-continent, Dallas was familiar to the region's prominent characters. Plainsmen, tycoons on the make, Indian fighters and outlaws, these were a varied lot; but Doc Holliday was not yet one of them.

He had come there to stretch out his time on earth by a few months at most. To others the West might stand for hope unlimited. To Doc Holliday it meant only a place where he could survive for a while if he was careful.

Something of the grimness with which he faced his trip to Texas may be read into the fact that he apparently did not visit Valdosta before leaving. As far as can be determined, he simply took off, upon receipt of his physician's findings. If this was the act of a dying man, turning his face to the wall, it also stood for pride bitterly injured. To an active male, accustomed to draw on bodily strength in all emergencies, nothing is more crushing than to learn that his forces will not again respond to his marshalling.

It was typical, nevertheless, of Doc Holliday's self-reliance that he did not go to Dallas as a patient, helpless in the face of circumstance. He went there as a self-supporting citizen, prepared to keep his feet under him while they would still hold him up. As soon as he had found suitable quarters in the hustling terminus city, he let it be known that J. H. Holliday was ready to work on teeth.

The gesture might have been his final one had time run out on him as swiftly as Georgia medical opinion believed it would. The first norther season would have laid him flat, and he would have been put in a box shortly thereafter.

As it turned out, his physician had given him better advice than he knew in urging him to go West. It took a while for Doc to find this out, according to his own intimations, but the climate pulled him more or less together. He never regained his strength. The face of death was what he always saw when looking in the mirror. He was never confident of surviving any of the dreadful coughing spells with which his disease wracks a man. But within those limits he was able to carry on.

In large measure this was due to a discovery which not everybody has the quality to make. He learned that where the body fails, the spirit can be its demonic substitute. In Doc Holliday's case, it enabled him to endure physical hardships of a type to test the sticking powers of healthy men, hardened to the country.

Meanwhile, being the sort he was, he had not neglected to take in the town. As has previously been remarked, Dallas was a lively city. What has not so far been pointed out is that all that went on didn't meet with the approval of its own civic leaders. For the furious enterprise of the terminus merchant was matched by that of the terminus outlaw.

He came with the railroad, and for the same reason as the business opportunist. Inflation and the madness of flush times, which unloosed the fountains of capital from their bed in the bowels of bank vaults, were his meat, too. If men expecting easy fortunes were suckers such as merchants dream on when they think of paradise, they were likewise the answer to other prayers. The card-sharper and the con man came to share the wealth, and so did the whore and the pimp.

When the railroads caused Dallas to mushroom, a whole new section of the city was developed by what today would be called the underworld. A term suggesting secrecy would not be appropriate for what then went on in Dallas, though. In Doc's day a section of Main Street was lined with gambling dens. Whore-houses and part-time brothels called dance-halls dominated another block or so.

In themselves these establishments were not illegal. Certain restrictions were forced on brothels and their inmates by custom, but the whore houses did not operate in defiance of authority. As to gambling, only the straight-laced frowned upon it. Where most citizens were concerned it was reckoned a business, and by no means one of the least respectable. The fellow who made his living by dealing cards was accorded the status of any other businessman. The fact that he was ready to answer querulous customers with gun and knife, if need be, served but to increase his standing.

In their purest form those attitudes belonged to the frontier proper. In Dallas, during its day as a terminus city, feelings were mixed in this respect. Its civic leaders were bent on turning the town into the great market city it has since become. Merchants, real-estate dealers and bankers have always been the arch-enemies of gambling, as a pursuit which milked suckers before they could get to them.

Public opinion was not all on the side of trade, though. Secure in this knowledge the gamblers fought back. Histories of Dallas relate that in the middle 1870s they banded under arms and forced civil authorities to back down from efforts to impose restrictive regulations.

Yet the term "outlaw" was applicable, beyond any possible questioning, to many who walked the streets of Dallas, bought chips in its gambling-halls, or—like Cole Younger and his two surviving brothers—sang in its churches. This section of the James gang had come to Dallas when Jesse had given the word to scatter, following a bank robbery in Missouri.

Arriving in Dallas early in 1874, they were there during quite a few months of Doc's own sojourn. They did not leave until the James brothers themselves showed up. The robbery of the San Antonio stage was then planned and successfully executed before they all swung north to Missouri again.

Throughout their visit the presence of the Younger trio was known to the authorities of Dallas County. The latter deputized the visitors to hunt Texas law-breakers and otherwise helped them over the hump with public employment. The gangsters played ball by being model citizens while in Dallas.

Pinkerton detectives, who knew of their whereabouts all this while, couldn't get to the bandits, because local authorities

blocked the way. Solid Texas satisfactions in the thought that
the Missourians had looted Yankee banks was partly responsible.
The fact that the brigands had served in the Confederate Army
was also a strong count in their favour.

If the Youngers had the keys to Dallas, so, too, at such times
as he wanted them, did Sam Bass. Where the great outlaws
walked freefooted, the lesser ones did not fear to tread. It was a
wide-open town in which a man who knew how to look after
himself could stretch without feeling crowded.

In more ways than miles it was a long way from Valdosta.
Instead of being a place where people could trace their family
trees back to when they had been used as rubbing-posts by
dinosaurs, it was one where tradition was in swaddling clothes.
A citizen started from scratch when he came to Dallas. He was
welcome to find his own level, with his natural leanings as sole
sponsor.

The qualities of mind which spurred Doc along his own
chosen course need a little further consideration here. He was
one of those men with a gamey taste in excitement. For such
fellows the quieter social pleasures are not enough. Neither do
the ordinary problems of living suffice to meet their gluttony
for drama. Only a way of life which gives them a continual
sense of action can keep them in good running order. If they
can't find it, they degenerate into great lovers or some other
form of artificially compensated nonsense.

This that is the seed material of piracy was part of Doc at
birth, yet it was only one part of his complex personality. He
had a good mind and had braced it with exercise. His formal
education may have been sketchy; but he liked to read, and it
is clear that he had done so to considerable advantage. One
after another of such frontier contemporaries as were equipped
to appreciate the fact, spoke admiringly of his breadth of background. This was the side of him that urged him to become a
doctor of dental surgery and to take his work seriously. He is
said to have been a good dentist, and as he had the hands and
the intelligence, that can be believed. The work absorbed him,
moreover. He once made the curious confession to Wyatt
Earp that only when he was in a fight or working on teeth did he
cease to be nervous.

Fascination with a particular line of work is the only thing which can keep the changelings of piracy within the bounds of normal social living. So ballasted, and with outdoor sports and gambling to work off their excess energy, they may wheel along with only an occasional big drunk or scrape over a woman to mark the restraint they are using. In not a few cases this bottled dynamite drives them to unusual eminence in their chosen professional fields.

In the instance of John H. Holliday, D.D.S., the one balance wheel which could be counted on to steady a man with his temperament was missing from the moment he hit the West. He had no apparent future, and he was aggravated by at least one facet of his past.

After returning to Georgia from Baltimore he had renewed his boyhood acquaintance with his cousin, Miss Mattie Holliday. Just what his feelings came to be for her is something that can't be examined without danger of leaving history for fiction. Nevertheless, here are the facts. She was the only known link between his life in the South and that new one he made for himself in the West. A revelation made at the time of Doc's death indicated his unwavering esteem for her. What he then did will be taken up in its proper place. In the meantime it is enough to say that he never ceased to correspond with her, notwithstanding her immurement in a nunnery.

For not long after John Henry Holliday was given his medical sentence of banishment, Miss Mattie Holliday also left the world they were born to, taking the veil as a Sister of Charity in an Atlanta convent. If there was anything connected with their relationship in that circumstance—of which Doc must have learned while at Dallas—it was but one more monkey-wrench tossed into the gears of an already disorganized existence.

An additional factor was that trade was not brisk. Doc had the skill, but people do not like to have their teeth fixed by a man with a consumptive's chronic cough.

Some commentators have asserted that Doc lost his practice because he spent too much time at gambling-joints. Others claimed that his failure to keep clients made some new source of income mandatory. As his health would not stand up to the demands of most frontier pursuits, gambling was more or less the only pastime left for him.

The truth here is probably of the hen and egg variety. Doc

was bound to see the sights, and he had even less respect for curfew than the amorous girl who muzzled the bell. It was inevitable that he would gamble and take aboard hard liquor, for he had genes that put those things in his destiny. To the question, did he indulge in them at the expense of his dental practice? the answer is probably, yes. A man whose closest companion is his ghost might naturally feel that he had better do what he felt like while he could. If any blame attaches to him for that, let those bestow it who have been in Doc's boots.

In any case Doc came to spend less and less time with a probe in his hands, and more and more of it with a duke full of cards. When the changeover was complete, gambling became the sole source of his income.

This adjustment, which seemingly began in 1873, was not complete until some time in '74. A professional gambler, like a professional artist, does not spring into being by a declaration of intent. Requisite in both cases is the ability to hold one's own in the face of competition. Granted there's some native talent as a basis, only experience can bring success with enough regularity to count.

Doc saw this clearly, if not from the outset, at least after a few disastrous experiences. Playing a friendly game with other gentlemen, no matter how expert they might be considered, was not the same thing as playing for a living. The spirit of the former was that it really didn't matter who won. The necessity of the latter instance was that the gambler had to win more often than he lost, or he didn't eat. The amateur player who didn't want to lose face had to pretend indifference to losses, whether he felt that way or not. The man who dropped his sack to a professional gambler was under no such compulsion to be casual. Often enough he gave up his chips with a growl in his throat, and where he couldn't get them back by cards he might try to do so by force of arms.

His pretext for going over the heads of the cards was that he had been cheated. In most instances the indignant player was merely out-cheated. Giving the odds a helping hand was so common a practice as to be standard.

A stock character of not only Western novels but non-fiction chronicles is the crooked professional dealer. The impression given by much of this literature is that he was a hawk among game-cocks, if not exactly among doves. The further inference is that when he resorted to gun-play it was to defend himself against righteous men who had discovered his deceit.

That happened, of course. But the dealer had to realize that if five people were bucking his game, at least three, and probably more, were trying to out-manoeuvre him in ways not countenanced by Hoyle. To stay in the business, he had to be prepared to call these fellows to account, and to stay alive, he had to be able to cope with those who resented it.

As the recognized objective was to end up with more money than a player had started with, cards were not the only things juggled. It was more directly profitable to steal chips, and for one player to do so while the dealer's attention was held by a confederate was often attempted. In faro and other games where bets were placed on fixed cards in a layout, some became adept at nudging stacks of chips from a losing to a winning ticket. Going further than that, in dives which permitted such freedom of action, they might rough the dealer and make off with his bank.

The professional gambler of the West had to have several perfections. He had to be better than good at cards. He had to have a comprehensive knowledge of cheating, for protection against others, as well as for his own use. He had to be swift, accurate and of sure purpose with a gun. As an emergency precaution, he also had to be handy with a sheath-knife.

By Doc Holliday's own report, he put himself through a rigorous schooling in the use of weapons. He had always been a remarkably good shot, but the quick draw was not prized in Valdosta. He practised this methodically for months until he felt sure of his competence. He needed that certainty more than most, aware as he was of his physical handicap.

When it came to cards, he was born to be good, provided he bent his mind in that direction. He had a cool, analytical brain of the type which figures percentages swiftly and accurately and doesn't get rattled under fire. As to cheating, he had the quick eye for catching his opponents in skulduggery and the hands to act in kind, when, as and if needed.

One other attribute of the gambler deserves consideration. He had to school himself to keep alert through periods of wakefulness that the ordinary citizen could hardly endure at all. Many gambling-houses were open on a twenty-four-hour basis. When riding with a streak of luck, or while sticking with a crew from which he could not conveniently withdraw, a dealer might see the clock around twice, or even more than that. Seventy-two-hour poker sessions didn't turn up every week, but they were not unheard of then any more than they are today.

These are not the hours recommended for tubercular invalids. Their regimen calls for long and regular sleeping hours, dodging smoke-filled rooms in favour of sun-purified fresh air. There are dietary requirements, too, which would be ill-met by midnight snacks, wolfed between deals in a saloon.

The question is, how did Doc stand the pace? The answer is, nobody knows; but he somehow did. It can be added that he not only survived but thrived. By the time the two years of his death sentence were up, he had found new sources of vigour. At least one of these was whiskey. Doc warmed himself at this fire with amazing results. It was his primer when he rose and his staff of life throughout the hours that followed. He developed a capacity for holding it that startled the hard-drinking West. According to the prophets of science and the Koran of their textbooks, it should have killed him out of hand. Actually it did wonders for him. Not that he had fully developed this talent by the time he had taken up professional gambling. He was still short of being notable in any respect. He was not yet a frontiersman, as the true frontier had moved beyond Dallas long before he got there. He was not a full-fledged Westerner, for in its core Dallas is Southern rather than Western. The most that he had accomplished in the way of his new career was to move from Dallas, the solid city of commerce, to Dallas, the citadel of the terminus outlaw.

To this order Doc himself did not belong. He was no more than an apprentice gambler, in itself a legal occupation. The term "outlaw" was never employed there and then in any loose, general sense. It was used rather to describe the exact civil status of one or more citizens. A man was only called "outlaw" if he was believed to be wanted by peace officers who charged him with some major felony.

Yet if Doc was not a qualified outlaw, he may have let his new associates think he was. This raises the query as to just who could have brought the story of the Valdosta swimming-hole incident to Texas. An obscure dentist, even one who moves in on the night life of a terminus city, is not going to meet more than a few hundred people in the course of a couple of years. One that Doc Holliday encountered might have come from Lowndes County, but the odds against it are enormous.

The incident of the shots fired over the Withlacoochee became known while Doc was in Dallas, nevertheless. And the killing or wounding of one Negro, which Valdosta regarded as the half-accidental act of a hot-headed boy, became enlarged to the deliberate massacre of several Negroes.

Who brought the news in this magnified version to the western terminus of the Texas and Pacific? Harry Van Denmark, who published a recension of Bat Masterson's appraisal of Holliday some years ago, supported Bat's conclusion that Doc himself did. There is every reason for believing that this judgment was correct.

It was the last time Doc's criminal record needed any artificial padding, but it can be granted as useful to him at the moment. An invalid, he had stepped into social circles where weakness invited scorn and disaster. The only thing which could take the place of rugged manhood was skill with a Colt or Smith and Wesson equalizer. Doc had not yet furnished proof that he had this; but by claiming he had come to Texas a jump ahead of the law he could make roughnecks wary of trying to shove him around.

There was a second practical aspect. A man who desired to deal cards in a terminus city gambling-house had to convince the management that he could look after himself before he got the job. A consumptive with no better credentials than experience as a dentist would have a hard time in doing this. If it was noised around that this frail-looking young fellow was on the dodge for murder, he might be taken on.

What Doc did, if this theory is accepted, is exactly what a young chap who had come West to work in a store or on a newspaper would do. He told the boss man that he'd picked up the necessary experience back East, and trusted to luck that nobody would check on him.

In just what Dallas establishment he was licensed for his new profession is something that forms one of many blank spots in the record. By the summer or fall of 1874 he had become accredited as what was known in the trade as an "artist". In chief, that meant he dealt faro. The only other game in high standing throughout the West generally was poker, although Spanish monte was not beneath a high roller's dignity in certain sections. This is not to be confused with three-card monte, which is no more than a pasteboard version of thimble-rig.

The emoluments of dealing, though high in a rich terminus city, were not out of proportion to the risk involved. Inevitably the time came when Doc's vague reputation as a man with a record was not enough.

There might have been earlier incidents, but the first recorded one is Doc's encounter with a man named Austin, which earned jocular recognition in the *Dallas Weekly Herald* of January 2, 1875. The mention of firecrackers is not, incidentally, mere journalistic nonsense. As a town of Southern instincts Dallas was faithful to the custom of shooting off fireworks during the Christmas season.

It is probable that Holliday's soubriquet of "Doc" dates from the time when Dallas gamblers were astonished to find a professional gentleman in their midst, but the *Herald* is evidence that the famous nickname had not yet been picked up by the press. "Dr. Holliday and Mr. Austin, a saloon keeper, relieved the monotony of the noise of fire-crackers by taking a couple of shots at each other yesterday afternoon. The cheerful note of the six-shooter is heard once more among us. Both shooters were arrested."

This New Year's Day engagement was apparently bloodless and the law did not take it seriously. Released, Doc stayed on in Dallas for several months before—his speed and co-ordination no longer something for a reporter to joke about—he once more drew and fired at a fellow gambler.

PART II

A Texas Outlaw
on the Gambler's Circuit

CHAPTER III

THE man he faced on this occasion was described in contemporary accounts as a prominent citizen of Dallas. That seems likely in view of the furore churned by the outcome. A terminus city did not get worked up over the fate of casuals, of whose existence the steady residents were not previously aware.

The fellow in question, although not named, was said to have been an excellent gunman. He wasn't good enough. Doc put holes in him that couldn't be corked, then started looking for the nearest exit.

Being often so employed by Dallas Counter, Cole Younger and his brothers could have been among those deputized to ride in Doc's wake. The roster of the posse has unfortunately been lost, and Doc himself did not pause to identify its members.

In terms of distance and the difficulty of the terrain this was not one of his major rides on the dodge, but in some ways it was the most significant. When he rode out of Dallas he left more than that city behind. He left the last fringe of the South to enter the West. He left the rim of settled country in favour of the full frontier. He moved from the comparative shelter of legal respectability into the wilderness warrens of the outlaw.

Journey's end was in Jack County, west a hundred miles or so, but he did not go there directly. "He went first, it is presumed, to that paradise of tough characters, the Indian territory," one news-paperman wrote, following conversation with several of Doc's associates.

One of the advantages in this move was that the Indian Territory was also United States Government Territory, where county sheriffs were without legal jurisdiction. The other advantage was not immediately apparent; but Doc got experience in living off the country as a plainsman which was to serve him well before the rounding out of another twelve months.

There was at that time no settlement in what later became
Oklahoma which offered much to a man who fancied himself as a high-rolling gambler. At a respectful distance from
Dallas County, Doc recrossed the Red River and again made
his stand in Texas. The place he picked, which was not so far
south of the boundary that he couldn't swim back over it if the
situation called for such action, was Jacksboro.

This at last was the unadulterated West, as the preserve of
misplaced nations in the Indian Territory was not. It was, moreover, the West in full dress.

The Red River war to put the remaining Comanches and
Kiowas on their allotted reservation was just reaching its final
stages. Fort Richardson, just a couple of miles away from Jacksboro on Lost Creek, was one of the key posts in this horse-back
war. Camped near it was the attached band of Tonkawa scouts,
hereditary enemies of the Comanches, who scorned them as
cannibals.

The county seat of Jack County, Jacksboro was within the
battle zone. One of the duties of the garrison was to furnish
escorts for the mail stages as they galloped in from Fort Worth
and dusted on towards El Paso. Soldiers also guarded the cattle
herds which trudged up the Chisholm Trail within short range of
the town.

Jacksboro was not one of the showcase boom towns of the
West. The pickings were, however, good enough to attract
ranking gamblers. One a frontier rarity—was a woman, Lottie
Deno by name. A cultured and attractive red-head, she was off-
brand in her habits as well as in her profession. Bafflingly crooked
at cards and disappointingly straight in more personal matters,
she left everybody guessing as to where she had come from. They
knew why she was there, though, after they had gambled with
her. If tales be true, she was a daring and usually successful
plunger.

If she was atypical of the dealers who roved, or were chased,
from one to another of the towns in their vast domain, the men
in competition with her were not. Whatever their differences of
mind, features, habits and attitudes, they were alike in one thing.
They rode out of the wilderness into ramshackle Western camps
with the cool assurance that they would be able to live by their
wits. Often they had no capital, and usually no credentials. Their

only standard equipment was a gun and the knowledge that they would use it as occasion required.

This was what Doc Holliday had when he came out of the Indian Territory to unsaddle at Jacksboro. Otherwise he was no more than a frail young man in a region that put a premium on robust health. His name did not carry the weight it would pack in years to come. He was as yet of small reckoning both as an outlaw and a dealer.

As he stayed in Jacksboro for about a year, his confidence in his ability to hold his own there was not misplaced. The life he led meanwhile can best be glimpsed by taking a closer look at his occupation.

Gambling has its snobberies, like every other trade. Its patricians of the period, as has earlier been remarked, played only two or three games. They loved and played poker, but the caste mark of a professional was his proficiency at banking or bucking faro.

Played by the rules, this game made no demands on either the intellect or manual skill. That was true alike of the dealer and the player. In this respect it resembled roulette, if the existence of an honest wheel is supposed. Its immense popularity was also owing to a quality it shared with roulette. It was a colourful spectacle and part of the entertainment came from being able to watch the moves of other players.

There was a layout of thirteen spades on which bets were placed; but suit did not count, and the deuce rated even Steven with the king. A card, that is to say, had no more value than the amount bet on or against it.

The dealer shoved the cards one at a time out the side of a box, open-face to show the pips. Soda, the card showing before the deal began, and hock, at the bottom, were dead, although the latter functioned when bets were made on the order of the last three tickets. The other fifty were dealt in pairs called "turns". The first card in each of these was a loser, the second a winner. The dealer collected and paid off after each turn. There was a house percentage only when a turn consisted of two of a kind, in which case the bank claimed a half of the stakes.

Betting could take the form of complex combinations for or against, and the player had to keep an eye on a device called the case, whose keeper was supposed to indicate just how many cards of any kind had been played. This, of course, was the key to the odds in betting.

In the bigger establishments there was a lookout, a house employee charged with following the play and seeing that there was no mix-up in the paying off of bets. But the dealer, be it noted, theoretically did nothing but reach for chips or shove them towards the winners. He had nothing to do with the betting, which was left to the discretion or whims of the players. His rule-book function when dealing was merely to lay the cards down in the order in which they appeared.

Yet for doing this that any boy could do, gambling-houses paid men a hundred or so dollars a week, at a time when the sum was worth six times what it is now. Furthermore they were paid this to deal a game in which the house percentage is so small as to be inconsiderable.

In part he was paid for the occupational hazards. Boom-town dealers were not what insurance men would call sound policy risks. Mostly, though, they were paid to see that the house showed a consistent profit.

Experts on cards doubt the historic existence of an honest faro game. The universality of sharp dealing was no secret from Western players, who took it for granted. This poses the query as to why certain professional gamblers were respected as honest. The distinction was one of methods. A gambler who relied on his skill at manipulation was respected. One who worked in cahoots with the casekeeper and lookout, to confuse the players as to what cards had been played and to shortchange them on bets, was a tinhorn.

These were ruses that a true high roller would scorn; but his pride in his craft could, and often did, lead to defeat. Opposing him might be men who had been playing faro on every possible occasion for years. They knew what it was possible for the dealer to do as well as he did. By figuring how the artist was likely to stack the deck, in view of the circumstances and the betting idiosyncrasies of the other players, they could outguess him and break the house. Many professional gamblers, including Doc himself in later years, found it as profitable to buck the tiger as to bank.

The dealer was therefore seldom free to abolish chance. Just how far he could go depended on the quality of the opposition. Ringing in a prepared deck, or using one that was stripped, pricked or otherwise marked, could not be safely done under the eyes of experts. Then the most that could be accomplished was to build up the house percentage by second dealing, the frisking in of a palmed card, and so forth.

So far faro was like the prohibition era. It had rules which everybody agreed should be broken in the name of practicality. Nobody blamed the dealer for protecting the bank by any sleight of hand he could master. The anomaly attached to this spirit of tolerance was that it was a shooting offence to be caught.

Jacksboro was hardly Monaco, nor were its shanty saloons Monte Carlo. Gentlemanly decorum—which most had never heard of, while the rest didn't care—was scarcely expected of the clientele. Hard-bitten mavericks, they were barely housebroke, let alone schooled to the amenities. Of a lot of them it could justly be said that they were wilder than Comanches, as the latter accepted the disciplines and obligations of tribal life.

Such were the men that the ailing doctor of dental surgery had to force terms upon when performing as a dealer. Off duty, he had quarters in a bare-plank hotel, furnished with a bunk, a chair and a washstand. He ate in a boarding establishment where tin plates rattled under the onslaught of knives wielded by rough-necks, ten or a dozen to the bench. His diet, which would have horrified his Georgia physician but which was probably good for him, consisted largely of buffalo meat and other game of the prairies.

The habits and attitudes that he developed on the frontier can be gathered, in part at least, from the comments of those who knew him. If some of this testimony is contradictory, that is small cause for either astonishment or doubting the sincerity of the commentators. Most men with enough personality to create strong impressions will set up a chain of reactions ranging from positive admiration to equally strong distaste.

He started and ended his day with hard liquor. "Perhaps Doc's strong outstanding peculiarity," Wyatt Earp said of him, "was the enormous amount of whiskey he could punish. Two and three quarts of liquor a day was not unusual for him, yet I never saw him stagger with intoxication. At times when his tuberculosis was worse than ordinary, or he was under a long-continued physical strain, it would take a pint of whiskey to get him going in the morning."

By the time he had so primed himself, he had also adorned his person. All accounts agree that Doc was fond of good clothes but E. D. Cowen, who knew him both in Denver and Leadville, dissents from the opinion that he was a flashy dresser. "He was scrupulously neat and precise in his attire, but neither a lady's man nor a dandy." Others bring out the point that he avoided the traditional gambler's combination of black and white, affecting coloured shirts and often wearing a grey suit, as he did at the O. K. Corral engagement.

For a frontier gambler a part of the business of getting dressed for the day consisted in strapping on and tucking away weapons of one sort or another. Some gamblers are asserted to have carried as many as eleven six-shooters, derringers and knives, racked in tiers from the hideaways in boot tops to the bowie knife dangling down the back of the neck. Doc seems to have carried no more than three weapons, these being a gun in a hip holster worn under the right-hand flap of his jacket, another in a shoulder holster under his left arm and a sheath-knife in his breast pocket.

One point under dispute is Doc's feeling about a shot-gun. Those who asserted that it was his favourite killing instrument probably had his use of it at the O. K. Corral in mind. Wyatt Earp, who had reason to know, said that he disliked the weapon. This is reasonable in view of his frail physique. A double-barrelled shot-gun charged with black powder had a terrific kick, and one that he could hardly have been expected to control with ease.

But, to return to his daily routine, noon was his sunrise. It might be two o'clock by the time he'd finished his antelope steak and buckwheat cakes. From that time on the pace of life in the saloons picked up until it reached a furious climax in the zone of midnight and faded away with the promise of dawn.

How John Holliday faced the perils of his profession is a point concerning which there is general unanimity of opinion. "Doc Holliday," a veteran plainsman named C. P. Thomas reminisced to a reporter of the *Washington Post* in 1906, "was a native of Georgia and take him all in all, he was possessed of the most daredevil and reckless bravery of any of his associates." "As far as I can recall, Doc had but three redeeming traits," Bat Masterson reported. "One was his courage; he was afraid of nothing on earth." Doc was "the nerviest, speediest, deadliest man with a six-gun I ever knew," according to Wyatt Earp. E. D. Cowen of the *Denver Tribune* and the *Leadville Democrat* concurred. "His nerve and eye, victorious in more than thirty duels to the death, were the admiration and envy of all the fighters of the time."

There was much less agreement as to whether he sought out combat or waited for it to become inevitable. He went looking for it, according to Masterson and others, goading men into challenging him by his nasty manner. He gambled with an air of moo-cow innocence which led other players into believing he could be pushed around, declared an unidentified Denver newspaperman who wrote a profile of him shortly after his death. Doc was a merry devil who fought for the fun of it, Wyatt Earp declared in an article signed with his name. He was a saturnine fellow who fought with fatalistic detachment, according to the Wyatt Earp of Stuart Lake's biography. "The doctor was a peculiar one and deceptive in his methods," said Colonel John T. Deweese, an attorney who defended him on divers occasions. "He would seem to back out and hesitate as if afraid, then suddenly he would rush on his antagonist and before the latter knew what was coming he would be laid out stiff with one of the doctor's bullets in his carcase." He was mild mannered up to the crucial moment but direct and quietly confident when it arrived, according to Cowen.

But whether he hotly sought, cheerfully invited or coolly accepted combat—and it can be assumed that he did all three at different times and under various circumstances—he was not stinted of blood during the fall, winter and spring of 1875–76. Contemporary report allowed him three fights with civilians while in Jacksboro. No details have come down with this tradition except that in each case the cause was gambling. Of only one man was it specifically said that he was killed, so it can be taken for granted that the others were only wounded. In Western pistol battles as in other wars the dead were far outnumbered by the casualties who recovered. A study of the method of fighting furnishes sufficient explanation. At the same time it increases the respect for old-time Western marksmanship. The wonder is not that so many survived, but that hits were scored with such frequency.

The Western *code duello*, like everything else created by the

D

Anglo-American of the Great Plains and the Rockies, was for everyday use. It was as practical and as bare of concessions to ornament as a pair of jeans.

When a man considered that he had cause to fight, he did not send his seconds around to make a date for a future engagement. If he had checked his heater at some saloon, he went and got it at once. Otherwise he simply jerked his weapon out of its harness. The most he might do, if he didn't want his favourite bar shot up, was to suggest settling the matter out in the street. Under such circumstances the principals did not start from a back to back position, prepared to take twenty steps before they fired. On rare occasions they moved towards each other from agreed points, but the only rules were to come afogging black powder.

Above all the Western gun fighter was under no moral compulsion to stand fast and stoically await his opponent's shot. The understood object was to kill while avoiding return fire. Formality and even dignity were not in the reckoning. As for the quick draw, it was decisive only if it prevented the other man from having a chance to fire. After that, leg work and the ability to shoot while on the dodge were what counted.

Black powder was another obstacle to accuracy which the Westerner overcame with remarkable success. This explosive threw up a heavy smoke which was no friend to the eyes. When confined indoors it could offer a good imitation of a London pea-soup fog, laced with a strong admixture of tear gas. Further agility was thus necessary, in order to avoid its hampering effects.

Such was the type of warfare, carried on by lamp or candle-light, in which Doc several times proved his mastery over various teamsters, trail drivers, buffalo hunters or fellow gamblers of the Texas frontier. His gun-fights there did not raise up the law against him, as his one serious encounter in Dallas had done. Of more importance, in Jack County of the period, they did not stir up any vigilante action.

That is as much as to say that he didn't shock regional prejudices governing assaults at arms. For there really was a *code duello*, even if it didn't extend to cover forms and ceremonies. A man could not shoot an unarmed opponent, or an armed one who was not on his guard. This rule might be ignored in the absence of witnesses. It was rarely overlooked in public for the very good reason that it was suicidal to do so. The impulsiveness of citizen justice was something that a man who knew his way around bore steadily in mind. In report after report of Western gun-fights it is stated that the challenger asked whether his enemy was heeled before making a move to draw. It was frequently remarked of Doc that he was careful in this matter, and a newspaper account of one of his battles describes him in the act of taking this precaution.

Another mistake was for a transient or newcomer to shoot faster and straighter than a well-liked local citizen. The vigilante viewpoint was then apt to be tribal. The foreigner had killed one of the clan, and no matter what the rights and wrongs of the case, vengeance was in order.

As Doc stayed on in Jacksboro, it is evident that he did not —as he had done in Dallas and was later to do in one other Texas town—commit this solecism. But although there was no reason why he had to leave, it is a matter for some wonder that he stayed so long. The Red River war had ended in breaking the back of the Kawahadi Comanches. When these diehards were moved to the reservation already occupied by the rest of the tribe, the frontier was ready to push forward. The importance of Fort Richardson declined. The Chisholm Trail to Ellsworth and Wichita surrendered its feature spot to the Western Trail, leading to Dodge City.

Other gamblers reacted to this decline in liveliness by drifting south and west to Fort Griffin, but Doc stayed on in Jacksboro. As this was foreign to the restlessness he evinced in the years to come, it can be judged that he had his reasons. It may be that he had no intention of going any deeper into the frontier. Possibly he was only marking time in Jacksboro until he felt that it would be safe for him to move back into East Texas, perhaps even Dallas itself. In those days of ill-kept records, a man could often return with impunity to the scene of the crime if only he waited long enough for a stockpile of new felonies to bury the memory of his old one.

In the upshot, however, he did leave Jacksboro and was not making easting when he went. As the finale of a gambling game in May or June 1876, Doc killed his second man in that town. Dead, with a bullet or so in him, was a member of the Sixth Cavalry Regiment, United States Army, on pass from neighbouring Fort Richardson.

This earned him no civilian enmity. The residents of towns like Jacksboro were not inclined to take sides between the blood-eyed transients and the soldiers, equally hard-case, who jingled spurs along their streets. A trooper or an outlaw drilled and planted was one less rascal to interfere with the orderly development of their community.

But if the people of Jack County took no active interest in Doc's latest feat of arms, the United States Government did. What's more, it enlisted the support of the sovereign State of Texas. Sought by the peace officers of both these political agencies, Doc was in about all the trouble one citizen can find for just one killing.

The Indian Territory, standard refuge for outlaws fleeing a county sheriff, was no hiding place. United States Marshals, aided by troops who would break their necks to find the slayer of a fellow soldier, would have hunted him down. He couldn't leave one county of the State and ease into another, there to live unmolested, as he had previously done. Not with Texas Rangers alerted to pick him up and turn him over to the Federal authorities. If arrested, there was small doubt that he would be convicted. Doc could have been entirely in the right according to the code of frontier gambling, and he would still have no defence which the government would recognize as an excuse for slaying a fellow trained at great cost to die in a different cause.

To avoid certain hanging Doc had to go from that place. What he did do was, all circumstances considered, an amazing thing. Bat Masterson, a notable plainsman himself, appreciated the magnitude of the exploit and summed it up in a grudging tribute to a man he didn't like. "Then he killed a soldier and to avoid being caught by the military authorities made a desperate flight to Denver across eight hundred miles of waterless, Indian-infested desert."

Before discussing this adventure in detail, it is important to give a word as to just why he felt impelled to undertake it. For reasons already presented, most points of the compass were closed to him. To head south-west would have taken him past the whole series of military posts which stretched in a vast semi-circle around Comanche land. Starting with Fort Dodge in Kansas, they swept south to the Big Bend country and then by

way of El Paso up to Fort Union in northern New Mexico. The
same chain of strongholds argued against the use of the shortest
route out of Texas, due west across the Staked Plains. The only
way out of the military cul-de-sac was to gallop north-west
through the Texas Panhandle and the strip of Oklahoma—then
called No Man's Land—which sits on top of it.

As far back as 1859 Oliver Loving had driven cattle from
Jack County to Colorado; but the trail had long been tracked
over by buffalo. The great hunt which was to destroy the bison
herds was still rising to its climax. Elsewhere most of the hunters
were white or had some partial claim to it. In the Panhandle they
were apt to be roving Indians, ready to turn a hunting party into
a war party at a moment's notice.

Re-horsed and resurgent after their defeat of the previous
year, the Comanches and Kiowas were off the reservation in
constant relays. The base of the Panhandle was adjacent to their
allotment of land in the Indian Territory; the crown of it was
handy for the equally warlike Arapahoes and Cheyennes. All
four tribes were supplied with arms by the industrious Coman-
cheros and renegade white traders. As commander in chief of the
United States Army, William T. Sherman could proudly report
to Congress in 1876 that the wild tribes of that area were peaceful
reservation residents. The official records of the Military Department of Texas show that forty-six palefaces were killed by
Indians that year. That figure includes only the ones actually
found in a vast, unmapped wilderness.

It was a country where a man could find ample game and
enough water to keep him going, if he went to the right places.
It was likewise a region where a man who didn't know his way
around could starve to death in short order. To die of thirst
could be even quicker of accomplishment.

It is difficult to say whether the journey was more remarkable as the forced march of a novice plainsman or as the endurance
feat of an invalid taking a rest cure. Doc's judgment of horse-
flesh, incidentally, must have been remarkably sound. Just how
he came by the mounts that took service under him at moments
of extreme need is a subject for guesswork only; but steeds to
match Bucephalus were found between his knees, whenever the
blindfold of Justice slipped enough to show the deadly gleam in
her eye. These horses, in turn, had no cause to complain of their

rider. He knew how to get the best out of them in any type of terrain and leave pursuit behind. He did so now.

Bat Masterson's summary of his ride was good but not quite accurate. Pueblo came before Denver, and it was there that he changed from the duds of a Western range rider back to the trim town clothes of a first-line faro dealer.

Pueblo, like so many other points and parts of the region, was responding robustly to the changes brought about that year. The *annus mirabilis* of the inland Far West was 1876. The depression which had slowed development for three years had ended. The march of the Texas frontier, with the Texas and Pacific railroad pushing from behind, has already been referred to. In the north the winding up of the Sioux wars cleared the way for a similar advance. The rise to eminence of Deadwood and Dodge City date from 1876. In that year Colorado became the first Western territory to become a State since the war of 1861–65. Denver took a new lease on life in consequence; while Pueblo did so for a different reason. The extension west of the Atchison, Topeka and Santa Fe railroad had given it the status of a terminus city.

This was where Doc—bearing Dallas in mind—had come in. There was a great deal of difference, though, between the doomed young doctor who had arrived by train in Texas and the fellow who trotted into Colorado three years later. The cough was about the same, but his profession and his point of view were radically different. A terminus outlaw himself, he was now a rider in good standing of the gambler's circuit.

That Western phenomenon is worth a book in itself. Nothing like this Hanseatic League of boom-town havens for faro dealers has ever existed before or since. In its full flowering it lasted for the years inclusive of 1876 to 1883. Doc, who came to be one of the best-known citizens of its far-flung and garish capital cities, was one that survived to stay with it throughout its classic era.

Great travellers though its paladins were, none of them saw the circuit in full. In extent it was larger than all of the United States east of the Mississippi. From South Texas it swept all the way to South Dakota—then known only as part of Dakota Territory—and from camps in Idaho to camps in Arizona.

Some were more lucrative than others, but they were all good towns, taking the dealer's viewpoint as opposed to that of the moralist. Money was free and in possession of a bachelor population. Usually they didn't have self-improvement in mind; but even for addicts of such art forms as music, the drama and the dance, to go forth of an evening meant to head for a saloon. They had money to get rid of and nothing to worry about if they lost their last cent. They tossed it on the layouts, sometimes to bring returns but generally to make a quick bounce into the gambler's pocket.

During the great days of the circuit that was apt to be bulging in any case. The master craftsmen carried huge rolls around with them, prepared to bank games of any size. They might, as did Doc himself now and again, own or have a piece of the saloon where they held forth. On the side they might be peace officers, prospectors with a few likely claims to work or salt, real-estate dealers, whore-masters, bankers, entertainment brokers, freight-line operators, detectives, smugglers or anything else which promised quick and easy profits.

None of these pursuits, taken singly or in the mass, was ever enough to hold them anywhere. When the camp they were in grew stale or too hot for comfort, or when a newly found one beckoned, they unloaded—or simply dropped every-thing—and were off. Their only constant interest was in gamb-ling, and their only patriotism was to the circuit. It can be said with certainty that money for itself was not important to them. What they thrived on were the peculiar excitements native to new settlements in an unorganized land.

Once he had been thrown in the swim, by courtesy of the United States Government, Doc became as bound to the circuit as all the others. Here at last he had found his true career, nor can he be accused of sparing any effort to make good.

During the months following his flight from Texas he hit a number of towns in rapid succession. Denver came after Pueblo, but the names of the others can't be called with confidence. Leadville and other silver towns of Colorado were a couple of years in the future, and many of the ageing gold towns had lost their lustre. Retaining glitter enough to catch a gambler's eye were Central City, together with its Black Hawk twin, George-town, Rosita and Boulder. These were near enough together for Doc to have tried them all before he followed the circuit north to Wyoming.

By the time he had done so, he had found it necessary to shoot down two, or as some sources would have it, three more men. Wyoming didn't want him, witness the findings of a Cheyenne historian named John Charles Thompson; but nobody felt quite like mentioning the subject to Doc.

To quote from one of Thompson's reports on the Cheyenne of the period and certain of its visitors: "Yet another was Dr. John H. Holliday . . . Run out of Texas because of his lethal propensities, this platinum blond desperado tried Colorado, extinguished several gunmen there, came to Cheyenne and did right well at gambling. The reputation of this dour misanthrope with death gnawing on his lungs caused him to be unchallenged here. Jeff Carter, the town marshal, regarded him dourly, but, courageous though the big officer was, he didn't choose to take on a killer of Holliday's ruthless character."

It was at this period, if the undocumented murmurings of a few real or self-styled old-timers can be believed, that Doc first began to practice that other ruthlessness peculiar to the con man. In view of his subsequent mastery of the art of evading issues, the stories cannot safely be challenged. At the same time their basis is so shadowy that they will be treated in the chapter of this chronicle reserved for maverick legend.

But to pick up the continuity, the fall of 1876 found Doc in Cheyenne. It was a promising town itself, but at that time there were pulls in two directions from places that took an even better shine. North and east, Deadwood was the focal point of the Black Hills gold rush. As Cheyenne was the rail-head for the western half of Dakota, it would have been natural for Doc to have joined the stampede. He might well have done so, if a circus of a different sort was not then holding forth in Denver.

Touched on once before here, Colorado's dream of Statehood became a reality in August of 1876. As the capital, Denver broke out in a rash of new Federal offices and their staffs. Other carpet-baggers swarmed in to profit by the expanded market and the mark-up of real-estate values. If Denver had outgrown the days when it could be overwhelmed by terminus outlaws, it was still a boom town, and one of excellent repute among gamblers.

Doc decided to winter there, or rather a man did who resembled him in every particular except one. Finding Denver full of Federal representatives—some of whom might have been urged to keep an eye peeled for a fellow named Holliday—Doc did what he could to avoid unpleasantness by changing his name. It was as Tom Mackey that he was known in Colorado's capital, that being the only time when the record shows him to have used an alias. At least Mackey was the name preserved in print. What Doc no doubt actually used was his mother's family name of McKey.

During the winter, as he later recalled, he "dealt cards for Charley Foster in Babbitt's house". This establishment, as he also said, was located at a site later occupied by the more famous gambling premises of Ed Chase. What finally happened to remove his anonymity is best told by quoting from the *Denver Republican*. "The Doc had taken the name of Tom Mackey. He was a quiet, modest man, with a smile that was childlike and bland; he was generally regarded as very inoffensive, but one night he electrified the town by nearly cutting off the head of Budd Ryan, a well-known Denver gambler. 'Doc' Holliday, alias Tom Mackey, was a little better known in Denver after that."

The reason for Doc's use of the knife on this occasion is given by Masterson, Earp and others. Denver, which was already leaving its salad days as a frontier town behind, had strict ordinances against carrying guns, and Doc kept his nose technically clean by only carrying a shiv. Normally, as has elsewhere been stated, he carried his knife in the breast pocket of his jacket, but for better concealment in Denver he is said to have worn it dangling from a lanyard around his neck.

Now what is true of sundry other places today was the case in Denver, A.D. 1876. Laws enforced upon transients were not necessarily mandatory for home-town boys on friendly terms with the cops. Belonging to this privileged class, Ryan carried a rod as a matter of course, though not, as it turned out, with impunity. When he tried to use it to over-awe or extinguish his frail-looking opponent, he wasn't quick enough. As he was to prove once more before that year was out, Doc was speedier and deadlier with a knife than most men were with a pistol.

Ryan survived this encounter, but Doc didn't wait around to send flowers. He left for Pueblo and from there took horse for other points on the circuit.

CHAPTER IV

ALTHOUGH repeatedly published during his lifetime, the report that Doc went to California—in the summer of 1877 —must be included in the Holliday legends. What he did do was to drift down along the Pecos Valley in New Mexico.

From men that moved back and forth across the plains he was there able to learn how he stood in Texas. The statute of limitations in the West was already operative where he and the Lone-Star State were concerned. Hundreds of other crimes of violence had been committed in the fifteen months since he had galloped away from Jacksboro. If anything remained of the reward bills posted for him, they were covered by layers of notices, calling for the arrest of men more recently in the news. Not then having any national law enforcement body, dedicated to following such matters up, the Federal Government had lost interest in him. Doc was free to return to Texas, and to reside there as long as he did not advertise his presence.

What drew him east along the Goodnight-Loving Trail was the resounding reputation of the Flat below Fort Griffin. Along with Deadwood and Dodge City it was then one of the prize towns of the circuit, and for pure rugged wildness it had them both skinned off the map. The elephant might be seen in other camps of the West; here was the habitat of the mammoth. Doc rode to make its acquaintance, and in so doing added new wrinkles to his destiny.

Since leaving Atlanta his life had had nothing but gambling to give it a sense of continuity. Each town was an episode more or less distinct from anything in his past or future. He carried no luggage in the form of associations that meant anything to him. His activities were not conditioned by anybody that he felt bound to.

But no man can thus deal in the marts of free trade for ever. Sooner or later the slipperiest fish feels the gaff of human ties.

For John Holliday, the place where this happened was Fort Griffin, and lightning struck twice.

The now vanished fort was one of the chain set up to contain the Comanches. To quote Edgar Rye on the subject of its founding, "where the McKenzie Trail crossed the Clear Fork of the Brazos River, near the confluence of Collins Creek, Major George H. Thomas established an army post on the top of a low, flat hill, and named it Fort Griffin". On the south side of the stream, the place was reached by crossing on a causeway of rocks. Those who had business there ascended Griffin Avenue to the post on Government Hill. Doc, who decidedly did not have business with any military establishment and didn't want any, stayed in the settlement below.

This, too, has been sufficiently described by Rye, a man who was in and out of it before, during and after Doc's arrival, and departure. "The town known as the Flat surrounded the base of Government Hill and was the central trading point for the cattlemen two hundred miles west. It was also the headquarters for an army of buffalo hunters and the intermediate supply point on the overland cattle trail between Southern Texas and Kansas feeding-pens. . . . The jumble of houses on either side of the street could not be dignified by the name of town, but should more properly be designated as a temporary group of houses to meet the emergency of a demand for shelter for the men who made the Flat a resort. . . . All the space not occupied by houses was covered with ricks of buffalo hides, representing the winter's hunt, ready to be transported to Dallas, Denison or Fort Worth, 150 to 200 miles distant."

Just outside the town was the encampment of the post's Tonkawa Scouts, for Comanches and Kiowas still swooped over the region on moonlight raids. Cow-hands from local ranches, or those bound up the Western Trail to Dodge City, rode in to hoorah the town. Buffalo hunters and teamsters swarmed in and out of the place; but wild though they were, they for once found their match in the local citizenry.

Typical of social life on the Flat, was the interchange between a saloon keeper named Mike O'Brien and the well-known Hurricane Bill, himself a former buffalo hunter and scout. Bill, however, was only armed with a Winchester when O'Brien besieged him and his consort, Hurricane Minnie, in their shack on Griffin Avenue. O'Brien, who had seated himself in the middle of that thoroughfare, was the one firing a heavy-duty buffalo gun. With this weapon he was sending slugs through the porthole of the Hurricane residence when an Irish friend named Bill Campbell sauntered by with a jug under his arm and a kindly feeling towards all humanity in his heart. Observing that Mike was hot, dusty and without refreshment, he offered him a drink of "the critter". Giving Hurricane Bill and his Winchester liberty to do their worst, O'Brien had a snort of whiskey on the spot, and then went on firing.

John Selman, later the assassin of John Wesley Hardin, had left town before Doc arrived, when it was discovered that he was one of Shackelford County's leading stock thieves as well as a deputy sheriff; but Lottie Deno, who had abandoned Jacks-boro for its more exciting and prosperous counterpart, had not yet made the disappearance which remains one of the mysteries of the old West. It was during the time she was dealing faro in the Flat that a couple of tinhorn gamblers, known respectively as Monte Bill and Smoky Joe, quarrelled over a short card game. Each accused the other of cheating, and each was probably right. Each thought he could beat the other to the draw, and each was only half right. There were two corpses on the floor when Sheriff Bill Cruger rushed in to take charge. Everybody that could had made tracks, with the exception of the red-headed Lottie, who was coolly counting her chips as the sheriff arrived. When the baffled officer stared at her, she calmly stared back. When the sheriff said that he couldn't understand why she had remained on the scene, she merely murmured, "But then you have never been a desperate woman."

There were other desperate women on the Flat, even though most lacked Miss Deno's poise and air of aloof refinement. Doc, as he had occasion both to thank and curse his stars, took up with one of the boldest. She was to save his neck and to come near getting him hanged. In between these times she stormed in and out of his life for four tempestuous years. Her moniker was Big Nose Kate.

What her last name was is a matter of some debate. Wyatt Earp, speaking decades later, when his memory may have tricked him, said it was Fisher. Others claim it was Elder. It is possible she used both names at various times, though there

is newspaper evidence to the effect that "Elder" was the name
she was using while in Tombstone. Not that it was a matter of
importance in the communities she frequented. Nicknames
were in general use throughout the West, and this was particularly true of red-light girls. Most of them, for all the record
shows to the contrary, had no surnames. They weren't needed.
The denizens of a dozen or so camps knew who Big Nose Kate
was. Such were the niceties of nomenclature, they also knew that
she was not to be confused with Nosey Kate. A madam, the
latter ran a trust, while Miss Elder—or was it Fisher?—was a free-
lance advocate of individual enterprise.

Early in the fall of 1877 Doc met this young woman where
her kind made their social contacts, in one of Fort Griffin's
saloons. It was owned by John Shanssey, himself a Western
character of some repute. As a youthful teamster he had proved a
good man with his hands in many a frontier rough and tumble, and
some promoter talked him into believing he was ready for the
championship ring. He learned that he was not the hard way,
when he took on Mike Donovan in Cheyenne back in 1867.
Tough, game, but ignorant, young Shanssey absorbed a beating
that turned his thoughts in other directions. Later he was to settle
in Yuma and be mayor of that Colorado River town. Meanwhile
he had become a follower of the circuit, and was prospering
thereby. In Fort Griffin, though he sometimes had to address his
patrons shot-gun in hand, he was doing very well as proprietor
of a combination bar, restaurant, dance-hall and gambling-joint.

Doc, who had become friendly with Shanssey, dealt cards
there and in general made it his headquarters. It was a ramshackle
barn of a place, with appointments to match, but the great
southern buffalo hunt was pouring money through the pockets
of the hunters and into the night spots of the Flat. According to
Rye, the gamblers of Fort Griffin lived as lords would like to do
if they could only afford it. According to Rye, also, each high-
rolling princeling of chance had a madcap wench, as reckless
and as scaled to the Devil as himself, to help him circulate
currency.

Big Nose Kate performed this service for Doc, as well as the
more personal ones expected of a concubine; but there is no
reason to believe that Holliday took the affair more seriously
than the situation called for. It was just one of those things,

destined to run a short course and then blow away, if an untoward development hadn't taken place.

As for Kate herself, the record puts the spotlight on her a few times, and that is all. Many documents refer to her, but what they tell is disappointingly little. Her prominent nose was one of a bold but comely set of features and her proportions, though good, were generous. That and the fact that she was flamboyantly tough and as fearless and hot-headed as Doc himself make up the bulk of her dossier. What else there is to be told must be read between the lines that relate her always impetuous comings and goings.

Nothing is known about her background, but legend has rushed in where history hasn't bothered to tread. According to this myth she was a girl Doc had married, after first snatching her from a Saint Louis finishing school. If such was her education, the young ladies of her era got a training in the useful arts that is begrudged finishing-school girls today. She habitually carried a gun and was adept in its use. She was a whore by preference, sticking to her trade even when she didn't have to, with the determination of a skilled craftsman. She was a plainswoman, competent to negotiate the great distances that separated Western towns. She was also a town girl, willing and able to make her own way upon reaching civilization. Most remarkable of all, perhaps, she seems to have been one of the frontier prostitutes who operated on her own, without paying tribute to any madams or macs.

With Kate for company Doc weathered the rugged social currents of the Flat a couple of months before anything else worth noting took place. Even violence and dissipation have their routines. The music may be loud, fast and furious, but it still has rhythms which come to be taken for granted by those who move in time to it.

Life on the Flat began with vague stirrings in the early afternoon. Only merchants and transient customers were earlier astir. The community's élite did not show themselves before the fashionable hour of four to five. From that time on the place was a volcano of action that roared and fired sparks until dawn brought quiescence and pin-drop silence to Griffin Avenue.

That was the way of it until the man of Doc Holliday's

destiny rode across the clear fork of the Brazos and on to the Flat. His name was Wyatt Earp.

Already one of its famous characters, Earp was eating the space and dust of the circuit inquest of a wily bandit killer named Dave Rudabaugh. In Kansas the latter had engineered a successful robbery of a Santa Fe train, and the railroad company wanted his blood. A veteran plainsman and a peace officer with a record of sitting on the lid of several tough towns, Wyatt had been set on Dave's trail.

It was a cold trail by the time the Santa Fe had put him on it, but Earp knew his country too well to bother with tracks at that late stage in the game. Learning that Rudabaugh had ridden on south through the Indian Territory, Wyatt made for Fort Griffin. Dave had come and gone by then but that didn't especially matter. The Flat was the headquarters for more outlaws than any other town on the southern plains. They knew, as the world of roguery always knows, what was going on along the byways of crime; and anything they didn't know they could find out, if it was at all discoverable.

Of course, a man who set out to get such information from them had to move with caution. Earp did so, but while moseying around the Flat he ran into a piece of luck in the form of John Shanssey. It so happened that Wyatt had acted as referee of Shanssey's ill-fated fight with Donovan in Cheyenne. Earp's handling of the matter must have been satisfactory to John. The latter was cordial, so much so that the railroad detective was encouraged to put his problem before him.

"Your best bet in this camp," Shanssey said, "is Doc Holliday."

His remark was a recognition of several things. Among them was the fact that Doc had attained major status along the circuit, and was thoroughly informed as to its inner workings. He took it for granted that Wyatt knew who Doc was, even though they hadn't met. Implicit, in addition to the inference that Holliday could keep his mouth closed, was that Doc was a free agent, bound by no underworld ties.

Wyatt *had* heard of Doc, but he wasn't favourably impressed with Shanssey's advice. "I wouldn't figure him to be friendly towards a peace officer. He's the killer, isn't he?"

"He's killed some," Shanssey conceded.

Then with his next remark he put his finger on the salient feature of Doc's character. "Doc's in my debt for some favours and will help you if I say so."

Wyatt described to his biographer the meeting that then followed. At Shanssey's call a slim man in his middle twenties rose from a table and joined them. His face was haggard but illuminated by brilliant, steadfast eyes. The other features were handsome, particularly his nose and mouth. Incongruously, in view of his reputation, they spoke to Earp of breeding and education. Doc had to pause to cough before acknowledging the introduction; but when he took Wyatt's hand he astonished Earp by the strength of his grip.

Earp was four years older than Doc and twenty-nine at this time. He was six feet tall and weighed one hundred and fifty. Not so fair as Doc, Wyatt was still blond, with blue eyes. He, too, was handsome, though with cold regular features, where Doc's showed the heat within. Like Doc, and in the fashion of the period, he sported the full sweeping moustache known as leonine.

Having introduced this pair in mid-November of 1877, Shanssey broached Wyatt's problem and asked Doc to help the railroad sleuth out. In return for the unspecified favours to which the saloon keeper had referred, Doc agreed to find out where Rudabaugh and his gang were hanging out; but he warned Earp that it might take some days. Having no other lead to his man, Earp consented to wait around.

The casual acquaintance was thus prolonged, but to Earp, as he subsequently declared, it was strictly a business connection at this time. He made himself agreeable to Doc, in order to avail himself of the latter's good offices. Yet he had no intention of allying himself with a man as notorious as Holliday had become.

Unlike Doc, Wyatt belonged to the respectable order of circuit paladins. Albeit later accused of malfeasance—with what justice will be argued further on in this chronicle—he had been unswervingly on the side of law and order up to this time. A gun slinger of enormous reputation, he had been temperate in the use of the weapon regarded as a firearm. His dexterity in using the barrel as a club when subduing roisterers bent on shooting up a town had made him enemies along the cow trails, and understandably. To be buffaloed, as this was called, could not have been pleasant, and Wyatt's own words support the accusation that he delighted in the practice of the art. In part this was vanity, but it was merciful in its workings. He had not fired his six-gun at times when most other town marshals would have felt called upon to do so. As far as can be determined, therefore, he had not killed a man up to the time he arrived at Fort Griffin.

A plainsman while still in his teens, Wyatt had run the Western gamut as teamster, buffalo hunter, prospector and odd-job man. He had been marshal of the uproarious cow towns of Ellsworth, Wichita and Dodge City. He was a gambler like all riders of the circuit, and by the standards of the profession an honest one.

Perforce a frequenter of saloons, he did not drink, except for beer and wine, which were not always available on the frontier. In the absence of any statement of his own, it can be guessed that this abstemiousness was due to pride in his competitive efficiency. Sobriety stepped up his winning percentage in gambling and at gun-play, and he always figured percentage. He liked to win and usually did. He was a cool, aggravatingly self-assured man. He had been shaken once, by the loss of his wife in a youthful marriage, but the cracks in the ice had closed again.

That's the picture presented by a study of his life, but it fails to explain the two most noteworthy things about him. One was that he came to have the most virulent set of enemies that ever carried hate to the grave with them and passed on necrophobia to faithful and still-living descendants. The second was that he had more friends, ready to go to bat for him under any and all circumstances, than the law of human averages allows.

Whatever the spell was, Doc fell under it. Wyatt may not have been much interested in him, but with all the fabled attraction of a man towards his opposites, Holliday was drawn to Earp. Where his personal life was concerned Doc ordinarily said nothing at all. On the rare occasions when he felt that some sort of comment was necessary, he told whatever outrageous fiction he thought his inquisitor was gullible enough to believe. Few people, however, go through life without at some time or other finding someone they elect as father confessor. For Doc Holliday Wyatt stood in this position, and he talked to him as he did to no one else whom he met in the West.

E

Part of the explanation undoubtedly lay in the fact that Earp was better qualified to understand what Doc was talking about than the general run of men encountered on the circuit. His people on both sides were Virginia gentry, though Wyatt Stanley Earp had been born in the course of various moves through the Middle West. There was a lawyer tradition in the family, which had led Wyatt himself to read for the law at two different times during his young manhood before the pull of the plains had induced him to abandon it. He had, in short, a good, incisive mind, and it had been trained to follow other trails, in addition to the ones left by desperadoes or big game.

Beginning by paying a debt to John Shanssey, Doc ended by working to oblige Wyatt Earp. While he dealt faro, played poker or lounged at the bar, he listened for the talk of newcomers from points West or asked casual questions concerning news of the outlaw world. He had to move with great care. Then, as now, the business of putting the finger on a gangster chief was apt to be attended by fatal consequences.

That was particularly so in the case of the bandit he was trying to locate. Rudabaugh was one of the slipperiest and most lethal-minded thieves in all the wide marches between Sedalia and Hangtown. Both characteristics made it risky to have anything to do with his arrest. He could be and was caught on divers occasions, but it was bad luck to try to hold him. Adobe walls did not a prison make for Dave very long, and he customarily left a dead jailer or so behind as he fled.

Later he joined forces with Billy the Kid, but as an ally not a follower. He is said to have been the one gunman who made young Bonney nervous.

Neither Rudabaugh nor anybody else made Doc nervous. He persisted with his risky assignment, and in just short of a week he had pinpointed his quarry. Dave, together with his band, had holed up in Fort Davis, a Texas post west of the Pecos River.

Having received this information, Wyatt saddled up for his long ride. Doc was left to the society of Big Nose Kate. In the natural order of things, he might run into Earp in some one or another of the circuit's camps; but nothing more permanent seemed likely to come of their acquaintance. Seen in retrospect it was an interval of good conversation, ballasting the dynamic eroticism of Kate and the generally explosive life on the Flat.

Nevertheless, as such matters are relative, Doc had had a peaceful sojourn at Fort Griffin. When Wyatt Earp had referred to him as a killer, Shanssey had offered the defence that Holliday hadn't killed anybody thereabouts. Like Kipling's Diego Valdez, Doc was getting to be the victim of his own success. It was no longer easy for him to find fights.

Even on the circuit he had become notorious for a willingness to carry all quarrels to the limit. His efficiency had also been noted. As Cowen reported of him: "He was incredibly swift and accurate with the six-shooter. Given two men for objects, anywhere within the semi-circle he could hit both at the first discharge."

It was said of him that he liked to kill. More disturbing yet was the assertion that he sought gun-play in utter unconcern as to whether or not he himself might be the victim. True or not, such tales were daunting. A man as ready to die as he is to live has a psychological edge over the bravest of warriors with a healthy concern for their own future well-being.

Wherefore men normally refrained from stepping on Doc's toes, and when that didn't happen he was the soul of an almost self-effacing politeness. When it is said of him that he went looking for quarrels, it should not be understood that he made himself obnoxious in the way of a camp bully. Until he conceived that he had reason to act otherwise, he gave men their decent due. Trouble started when he thought his own rights and dignity were being lightly considered. Once he judged that to be the case, he was literally up in arms, and the fellow suspected of slighting him, or trying to put something over on him, had the choice of making himself scarce or of trying to shoot faster and straighter.

By the fall of 1877 the average gunman did not think he could. The better than average gunman had different ideas, of course. One of the qualities which made an expert gun slinger was the deep-seated notion that when it came to the clutch, nobody could beat him. Fort Griffin had its share of such self-confident men, and early in December, Doc ran afoul of one.

Ed Bailey had the status of an old resident of the Flat. A cock of the local walk, he was popular and used to having his own way. Like any long-term citizen of Fort Griffin, he had seen his share of bad men, and he figured on being able to hold his own with any of them. Doc's reputation didn't impress him. He sat down to play with no intention of minding his poker manners.

This is the first of Doc's fights of which a play-by-play description can be given. The necessary information is available because Wyatt Earp, who returned to Fort Griffin and later got Doc's own account, picked up the story from both ends of the line.

Bailey started the quarrel by sneaking looks at the discard, then usually called the "deadwood". The practice was in bad taste, if the offender was caught at it. Although he was not actually looking into the other fellow's hand, he was doing the next best thing. If he didn't see what his opponents had, he could see what they didn't have, thereby amplifying his knowledge of the odds. The rule-book penalty for being detected was to lose the pot.

There were certain tricks that professional gamblers might successfully pull on each other, but this was not one of them. It was the sort of thing that would normally be tried against greenhorns, or those afraid to object. Unless a man was actually looking for trouble, notice that he was being observed was all that should have been necessary. Doc gave such notice, pointedly but mildly.

To quote an article printed above Wyatt S. Earp's name in the *San Francisco Weekly Examiner* of August 8, 1896: "The trouble began, as it was related to me afterwards, by Ed Bailey monkeying with the deadwood. . . . Doc Holliday admonished him once or twice to 'play poker'—which is your seasoned gambler's method of cautioning a friend against cheating—but the misguided Bailey persisted in his furtive attentions to the deadwood. Finally having detected him again, Holliday pulled down a pot without showing his hand, which he had a perfect right to do. Thereupon Bailey started to throw his gun around on Holliday, as might have been expected. But before he could pull the trigger Doc Holliday had jerked a knife out of his breast pocket and with one sideways sweep had caught Bailey just below the brisket."

Why Doc used a knife instead of a gun on this occasion

nobody who was not there can say for certain. It was probably
a matter of position and timing, with the knife in his breast
pocket nearer to his left hand than either of his guns was to his
right. However that may be, a knife was what Doc used on
Bailey, who was less fortunate than Budd Ryan of Denver.
Eviscerated, the Fort Griffin gunman collapsed and therewith
died.

By all the laws of the circuit's Medes and Persians, Doc was
in the right; and it was this consciousness of rectitude which
kept him from clearing out with usual celerity. It was Bailey
who had forced the quarrel, and Bailey who had first gone for
his weapon. That added up to an open-and-shut case of self-
defence, which the courts of the frontier could be counted on to
recognize. Doc, therefore, stood his ground and submitted to
arrest by the town marshal.

It wasn't until after he was in custody that his mistake became
apparent. The real menace was not the law itself, though. The
true danger came from the popular Mr. Bailey's friends. They
started howling for vengeance; and instead of taking their
prisoner to the county seat at Albany, the officers had to hustle
Doc into a hotel to protect him from the crowd that gathered.

The lynch mob, as it chanced, was the lesser of two worries.
More dire was the threat of the local vigilantes, who were as
tough as everything else in and around Fort Griffin. If repute
does justice to them, they were readier to hang, and did so more
frequently, than any other group of citizen executioners on the
frontier. Moreover, they made a practice of taking prisoners out
of jail, to forestall any possibility of foolish lenience on the part of
justice.

Edgar Rye, who himself held court in Albany at this period,
wrote that in spite of all the rambunctiousness which habitually
shattered the peace of Shackleford County, he almost never
had any but civil cases brought before him. His explanation
was that the vigilantes handled the criminal end of justice. He
also made it plain that they would trample over a peace officer
who might elect to stand between them and a malefactor.

The ticklish situation in which Doc found himself was that
if the marshals moved him outside, the mob would get him,
and if they waited around long enough for the vigilantes to
catch hold of the excitement of the moment, the latter would

break in and take their customary reprisal for the death of a well-liked local figure. Of all this Doc himself was acutely aware. He was, perhaps, exaggerating when he later told a newspaperman that the vigilantes had hanged twenty-four outlaws from their favourite tree while he was in Fort Griffin; but it must have been kissing kin to fact. No doubt he thought of these others, hanging limply and with their heads cocked to one side, as he made shift to chat offhandedly with his guards.

That was how he was engaged when Big Nose Kate worked her way down an alley and peeked through a side window of the hotel. Her scouting trip served to confirm what she had heard in the saloons, where members of the mob spent such time as they were not occupied in watching for the officers to try to make a break for it. Doc was the man they were waiting to see; and the word was going around that some of Bailey's friends were stirring the vigilantes to action.

Kate had been at Fort Griffin too long to take the threats for bluster. She figured, as Wyatt Earp remarked, that Doc's life wasn't worth a plugged nickel. She was aware, too, that there was no one to whom it would do any good to appeal. Outside of herself, Holliday's only friend there was John Shanssey, who could hardly be expected to take on the camp single-handed. If anything was to be done, she had to do it.

Fortunately for Doc she saw the problem with clarity. She couldn't overpower the embattled citizens of the Flat any more than Shanssey could. That being the case, the thing to do was to arrange for the mob members to go elsewhere.

Her first move was to borrow, as Earp declared, "a six-shooter from a friend down the street, which with the one she always carried, made two". With this same friend or another she made arrangements for a pair of horses to be brought down to the bosky along Collins Creek at dawn.

Having accomplished that much, Kate dashed back towards the hotel. To quote Earp again, "There was a shack at the back of the lot, and a horse stabled in it." For all her frantic haste, Kate took the trouble of leading this nag into the alley and hitching it where it would be safe, before she returned to the makeshift barn. To this she then set fire.

It made a good blaze, and it got results. As Kate knew, fire was the abiding dread of all matchwood camps in dry country.

If not checked at the source it could destroy an entire settlement in the length of time it would take a nervous man to smoke a cigar. There was no fire-fighting equipment, and no organization of smoke eaters in a place like Fort Griffin Flat. Fighting fire was everybody's business.

Everybody went to this crackling conflagration. It was a form of excitement, mixed with the urgency of self-preservation, with which even a lynching couldn't compete. The saloons lost their customers, and the bartenders followed. Two of the officers guarding Doc trailed along, to give police supervision to fire-fighting operations.

Leaving out a few conscientious drunks who had already passed out at that early hour, only three Flatites didn't rally to the fine blaze Kate had made out of hay and a weather-board shanty. One was Doc, one was the deputy town marshal, left in charge of the prisoner, and the third was Kate herself. As soon as his colleagues had left, she bounced into the hotel, got the drop on the flabbergasted officer with one of her six-shooters and handed her lover the other.

"Come on, Doc," she laughed.

"All that night," as Earp went on to state in his narrative, "they hid among the willows down by the creek and early next morning a friend of Kate's brought them two horses and some of Doc Holliday's clothes from his room. Kate dressed up in a pair of pants, a pair of boots, a shirt and a hat, and the pair of them got away safely and rode the four hundred miles to Dodge City, where they were installed in great style when I got back home."

CHAPTER V

THAT was another great dash for freedom; yet it was the one time that Doc didn't make his point. Although he got away geographically, he was shaking off one set of trammels to tie on a different kind. If he wasn't bothered by matrimonial bonds, then, or in the future, he was no longer singlefooting it. By the terms of his streamlined but inflexible code, he was bound to Big Nose Kate.

But that no doubt seemed joyously fitting, as they shook off the Shackleford County vigilantes and sped up the Western Trail towards the Indian Territory. It was a great journey for a man and his girl, both full of a mirthful triumph and a fine lust for each other to fortify them against the rough going. And it *was* rough. There are mild winter days in Texas, but others are awfully hard on male brass monkeys. This was the norther season. The nights were all cold, and the pair were camping out.

The elements were only one tough aspect among many. After Doane's trading post and the crossing of the Red River, the trail skirted the reservations of the Comanches and the Cheyennes before it cut through the Cherokee Strip. More dangerous than the wild tribes were such white men as they would meet. Not many cattlemen would be shuttling back and forth between Texas and Kansas at this time of the year. The probable trade of anybody they might meet would be cutting throats to get whiskey money.

There were four hundred miles of hard pushing, but they made it, and told of it with gusto later. The end of their road, as Earp declared in his article, was Dodge City.

Wyatt himself, who made this town his headquarters, was one explanation for the choice. Geography was another. The straightest way out of Texas was the Western Trail, and unless a man had his reasons for staying in the Indian Territory, he would go through to the railhead terminus.

All the great camps had one particular year when they out shone their rivals in dynamic pageantry and the quality of the acting cast. In 1878 it was Dodge City's year to be the capital of the circuit. Most of the events for which the town is celebrated in frontier saga took place then. As for the personnel, it can be safely said that never before or since did so many of the circuit's top hands make one town their headquarters at the same time.

Doc was now a celebrity, second to none in renown, albeit ranked with the darker stars. It was not in his character as an outlaw that he first moved into Kansas, however. When he ensconced Kate and himself in the finest rooms that Deacon Cox's boarding-house had to offer it was as Dr. and Mrs. John H. Holliday.

The words had not been said over them, but as far as Doc was concerned, the bargain had been sealed when Kate threw down on the officer who was guarding him at Fort Griffin. Just why they didn't go through with the form of getting married was no doubt a matter of circumstances. They were anxious, or at least Doc was, to start out right in Dodge City, and the simplest way to avoid scandal in a town they had hit together was to claim that they were wed. Once having made that announcement, they couldn't very well ask any third party to legalize the union. As that was the only good luck Doc was to have out of this mating, it shouldn't be begrudged him.

In December of 1877, though, he was brimful of intentions to give Kate the sort of life he then thought she deserved. As for Doc himself he resigned his commission as a bad man. Having no other dentist, Dodge could not be as choosy about its tooth repairers as was Dallas. Out went the Holliday name-plate again.

His arrival was not totally in the character of a determined young professional gentleman, however. This is shown by an episode culled from Dodge City annals by dental historian Dunn.

While Kate was revelling in a chance to get the Indian Territory out of her ears, Doc went in quest of what he himself wanted most, and made port at the Alhambra. Dog-tired, dust-covered and needing a shave, he looked more like a seedy tramp than a high roller just about to reform. His woebegone appearance amused a group of transient cow-hands, in Dodge out of season and unhappy about the quietness of the town. They had emptied one of the bottles on their table but hadn't done much with the other when Doc strode into the saloon.

One of the bored steer chasers gave him a long once-over. "Have a snort," he finally barked.

Doc's answer was prompted by his normal resentment of arrogance, but only in part. With a con man's trained instinct for such things, he smelled sucker. Wherefore he drew himself up and slid a note of primness into his voice.

"I don't drink that stuff."

"You don't, eh?" This was better than the cow-hand had hoped for. He picked a tumbler from the table, filled it and held it out to Doc. "It's time you learned, son," he said, drawing his gun with his free hand. "Tip her down."

Sighing and making awful faces, Doc did as he was told. Seeing that his companions were as entertained by the spectacle as he himself, the cow-hand filled the tumbler again. Under protest, but over-awed by the gun each time he begged to be let off, his victim made away with it. He was still on his feet, but then the liquor had not had much time to hit him. Figuring that one more would be like pulling the rug out from under the leaning tower of Pisa, the bully got another bottle from the bar and filled a third glass. Beginning to feel the strain themselves, the watchers saw Doc polish it off. He was starting on the fourth when it finally dawned on the range riders that they were being had.

Yet aside from that one exploit, Doc started in by settling down, as per excellent resolution. He was still Dr. John H. Holliday, in domicile with his good wife while not working teeth over, when Wyatt Earp returned for a brief visit early in February. In the meantime Earp had ridden a couple of thousand miles on the trail of the elusive Rudabaugh. The information Doc had secured for Wyatt at Fort Griffin had been accurate. Dave and his gang had hung out at Fort Davis for a while but after moving their headquarters several times had ended by returning to Kansas for another crack at the Santa Fe. Still a few days behind them, Earp had followed them back through Texas.

It was while spending a night on the Flat that Wyatt got a message which Holliday had sent him, care of John Shanssey, when he arranged for his hastily abandoned belongings to be forwarded by freight to Dodge City. In this note Doc had told Earp that he would see him in Dodge, though it did not turn out to be much of reunion. By the time Wyatt returned, Bat Masterson had scooped up Rudabaugh, but one of the latter's associates, Mike Roarke by name, had slipped out of the bag. The Santa Fe wanted him and Wyatt was put on a trail which he followed for three more months.

Doc meanwhile plugged doggedly ahead at the business of building up his status as a professional man and generally establishing his position as a pillar of a somewhat dubious better element. As far as dentistry was concerned, at least, he was getting along all right. He knew what he was doing and liked doing it. Just how well he might have succeeded in giving Big Nose Kate the position in life which he felt that he owed her is something that will never be known. This was a noble experiment that did not get far beyond the planning stage.

The person who smashed the test-tubes and threw the chemicals in the sink was Kate herself. She stood being the respectable spouse of a solid citizen for a couple of months and then told Doc she had had enough of that nonsense. She was going back to the nights of dancing and gambling in saloons, and he could either come along or not as he saw fit.

That was the first of many bitter quarrels with her and himself which ended in the surrender of Doc's great personal pride to his even greater sense of the importance of making good on an obligation. He could either trail with her, to extend some powers of chaperonage over the woman he had called "Mrs. Holliday", or repudiate her. No doubt he was still bound to her, emotionally and in the way of the flesh, but there was a stronger tie. This was the rope which had not fitted around his neck, because of Kate's boldness and quick thinking.

It was not long, of course, before his dental instruments were lying idle. Always in his blood, the pull of night life had been strengthened by years of addiction. In short order it was apparent that he could not see the dawn in and then go on to keep appointments with patients all day. The name-plate was scrapped, and Doc took his rightful place among the élite of Dodge City characters.

At that time the Mastersons had a corner on the law enforcement market. Ed was marshal of Dodge City and Bat was sheriff

of Ford County. The latter, as had been said, arrested Dave
Rudabaugh, trespassing on a neighbouring county to do so. A
member of Bat's posse on this occasion is worthy of note. This
was John Joshua Webb, whom Rudabaugh was later to spring
from jail in New Mexico. Doc was subsequently to be associated
with him in a historic undertaking.

With Bat himself, whom Doc first met at this time, Holliday
was to have a curious relationship. Bat is certainly responsible
for the fact that Doc is dismissed as a fellow with no redeeming characteristics except his courage and his loyalty to Wyatt
Earp in most chronicles that mention him. It is by now traditional to follow the Masterson lead in saying that Doc was a
sour misanthrope whom nobody but Wyatt could stand. The
testimony of other contemporaries who found Doc a pleasing
and witty companion has been overshadowed by Bat's voice of
authority.

Yet if Bat, with qualifications, blackened Doc's reputation
after his death, he is on record as giving a fulsome account of
Doc's noble inclinations to a newspaper of the day. At the time,
too, as shall later be seen, he was working hard and effectively to
save Doc's skin. Nevertheless, Bat was to claim that he never
liked Doc, and that is a subject on which he should be reckoned
the ultimate authority. What the quarrel between them was,
Masterson never indicated. He seems to have liked most
other people, including that senseless wild-dog of a killer, Ben
Thompson.

The latter was at Dodge at the time. So was Mysterious
Dave Mather, a bird whose devious path has not yet been well
followed. With Thompson, Doc was to be briefly associated
in Colorado. There seems to be nothing which ties him to the
most interesting if not the most venerated member of the Boston
Mather clan, from which Dave reputedly stemmed. With Luke
Short, who had the gambling concession at the famous Long
Branch Saloon, Doc was on very good terms, as he was with
Cockeyed Frank Loving. Other famous circuit figures that he
now met included Virgil and Morgan Earp, Charlie Bassett,
Shot-gun Collins, Dog Kelley and Bill Tilghman, as well as Bill
Harris and Chalk Beeson, proprietors of the Long Branch.

Many of these were in recorded action during that year of
1878, and to be in action in Dodge meant trouble was afoot.

That was the year that Bill Tilghman, usually regarded as the most blameless character who fired hot lead on the circuit, found out how the other half lived. If Bill's wife is to be believed, he never drank, swore or thought hard thoughts; but somebody accused him of being an accomplice of Rudabaugh, and into the clink he went.

Five months later the accusation was proved to be an absurdity, but meanwhile Bill had missed a lot of excitement. The chief event of the spring was the slaying of City Marshal Ed Masterson by a cattleman named A. M. Walker and a hand of his called Jack Wagner. Trying to be decent to a couple of tough drunks who were breaking the city ordinance against carrying firearms, Ed got himself shot for his good nature. Whereupon Sheriff Bat Masterson went on the war-path and personally rubbed out the killers.

After finally nailing down Mike Roarke in Fort Worth, Wyatt Earp returned to Dodge in May. The redoubtable Charlie Bassett had been moved up to take Ed Masterson's place. Wyatt was sworn in as his assistant just in time to meet the main influx of trail drivers herding steers up from Texas. The ambition of a good few of these was to hoorah Dodge, just as it was the business of the peace officers to see that they did not. It was while balking such a breach of the peace that Wyatt killed George Hoyt in July, marking the only time prior to his Tombstone days that he found it necessary to do more than wing or buffalo a man.

That the cow-hands sometimes succeeded, in spite of the formidable opposition, is attested by the comedian Eddie Foy, who had come to Dodge in June and was to remain there throughout the summer and early fall. Foy and his partner, Jim Thompson, headed the bill of a variety show, which had to compete with hurdy-gurdy girls, gambling games and liquor for the attention of the audience. To use Foy's own words: "We were going merrily on with the dance when suddenly 'Bang! Bang! Bang!' came a roar of eight or ten big pistols from the outer darkness, the crash of glass from our windows and shrieks from the women.

"Everybody dropped to the floor at once, according to custom. Bat Masterson was just in the act of dealing a game of Spanish monte with Doc Holliday, and I was impressed by the instantaneous manner in which they flattened out like pancakes on the floor. I had thought I was pretty agile myself, but those fellows had me beaten by seconds at that trick."

That Bat and Doc had not vainly taken nose-dives was proved by Foy's subsequent remarks. Eddie had hung up a new jacket on a hook on the wall when entering the place. Going to collect it after the raid, he found several holes in it. Yet riders in from the trail were not the only menace to life in Dodge, as Foy was also to learn. Not long afterwards he nearly got shot by Ben Thompson, mean drunk and looking for someone to bully. Only the timely arrival of Bat Masterson saved Foy for the distinguished career that was later to make him a head-liner on Broadway.

Foy's priceless little anecdote catches Doc at one moment of his stay in Dodge, but what about the rest of them? Wyatt Earp, as he recalls, was busy with his own affairs and only saw Holliday at intervals and by chance, as their paths crossed in the course of their gambling activities. Bat reported of Doc that "he kept out of trouble in Dodge City somehow". This, incidentally, was more than Bat himself was usually able to accomplish. Except during his tenure of office as sheriff, he was seldom long out of hot water while in Dodge. Just the year before, for instance, he had spent a night in the calaboose, for interfering with a marshal who was trying to make a pinch.

Another criticism which could be aimed at Bat's remark was that it was not quite accurate. Doc himself later said that he shared the fate of Bill Tilghman in being accused wrongfully. "In Dodge City," he told a reporter in the course of discussing other crimes he branded as apocryphal, "they accused me of robbing a store, and it turned out that the proprietor had done it himself."

Just how seriously this charge was pressed against Doc is past knowing, but he was in other trouble, albeit not the kind that Bat meant. He had a rowdy, tempestuous slut on his hands, whom he didn't feel he could kick out in the street for which she had a natural affinity. When a man has a nail like that in his shoe, he doesn't need any other type of grief. There are indications that Big Nose Kate liked Doc better when his high rolling was profitable than she did when he ran into those streaks of bad luck to which the best of gamblers are subject. Yet in her own way she must have felt bound to him, too. The normal bar and bedroom fling doesn't last much longer than an attack of hiccoughs. This dragged on for years of intermittent love and warfare. She wanted Doc, and she wanted to live her own life, in the way natural to her profession. The effort to do both probably made her as miserable as it did him.

She cared enough for his opinions, as was proved at a critical time, to get frantic with rage when he told her what he thought of her conduct. On such occasions she would swear not to have anything more to do with him, but his luck didn't hold. When she was ready for a reconciliation, he looked into the past and took her back.

One quarrel has been preserved in tradition because it resulted in Kate's flouncing out of town in the late spring of 1878. In this instance the fight was probably an excuse for answering the call of spring by a vigorous young alley cat. In all likelihood she went to Ogallala or another of Dodge City's cow-town rivals, but her destination isn't in the record. All that is known is that she decamped, leaving word that she would return when, as and if she felt like it.

Doc made use of his liberty to tear off to Colorado, whence was coming music that no Ulysses of the circuit could hear without getting restless. Leadville had been discovered the preceding fall, and now it was the star-shooting wonder of the frontier. The fabulous strikes made by Tabor and a few others had spread word over the country that millions were to be had by the inquiring prospector. The boom was national in scope and rivalled the "Pike's Peak or Bust" madness which had first fairly launched Colorado back in 1859. The wealth of Leadville was in silver not gold, but the quantity available made up for the difference in value. The area was the natural habitat of those who hoped to get rich quick and those who hoped to profit indirectly from this optimism.

Belonging to the latter class, Doc made his way by train and coach to the two-mile-high camp. A couple of years later Leadville was to take its place as one of the ace gambling towns of the circuit. At the time, however, the place had not yet fairly hit its stride. Only a thousand of the thirty-five thousand people that were to be there at its peak period were living in the rambling array of shanties and babbling about silver in the makeshift saloons. But if Leadville was at that time a disappointment as a gambling location, there were other ways of cashing in on the excitement, if a man had the necessary brains and enterprise. Having concluded as much, Doc put his cards away and listened for the fluttering of pigeon wings.

Just what he did is told at some length by Robert M. Wright, author of that classic among Western chronicles, *Dodge City, the Cowboy Capital*. Wright was a notable frontier character in his own proper person. Having fought Indians, hunted buffalo and driven teams all over that section of the plains, he had become one of its leading traders. In Dodge City he was head of the prosperous mercantile firm of Wright and Beverly. At one time he served as mayor of the town, and he was repeatedly elected to represent Ford County in the State legislature.

In 1913 he published his book about Dodge in its palmy days. It does not pretend to be a complete history of the city but is rather an anthology of the events which Wright personally remembered. The people are dealt with in the same way. He recalled Mysterious Dave and Wyatt Earp, for instance, as important town characters, although he wasn't sure of how they pronounced their names after the lapse of years, and he clearly had not had much to do with either. Doc Holliday, notwithstanding the fact that he spelled the surname with only one "l", he remembered very well indeed.

A man of affairs who spent much of his time at the capital of Kansas, Wright did not meet Doc until the summer of 1878, clearly identified by referring to the time as "the first year of the great boom at Leadville". Enjoying the solace of that grand old frontier institution known as "first drink time", Wright made the acquaintance of two men who had just alighted from the west-bound train. What followed is best given in Wright's own words.

"One morning in the early days of Dodge City, two gentlemen, elegantly dressed and groomed, made their appearance at the Long Branch Saloon. One could see at a glance that they were educated and refined, and both men had lovely manners and exceedingly great persuasive powers. They were quiet and unassuming, both were liberal spenders as well as drinkers, but they were never under the influence of liquor. It was only a short time until they had captivated a lot of friends, and I among the number. One we will call Doc Holliday, the other Creek."

Precisely who "Creek" was is something that is difficult to

determine. Wright was always as careful with names as his memory allowed him to be. Every other name or nickname in the book is given in full and most of them can be easily identified with well-known personalities by anybody familiar with the history of the period. It can only be assumed that all that Wright could recall was that his fellow had the word "Creek" in his *nom de guerre*.

That he was a frontier warrior of note is proved by the fact that he was bracketed with Doc himself as being a dead shot with the six-shooter. And when Bob Wright of Dodge City cited a man for skill with the revolver he wasn't talking of palookas. Now there were several gunmen of more than passing skill at arms who had that particular type of stream incorporated in their monikers. Chief among them were Bitter Creek George Newcomb, beloved of Rose of the Cimarron, Bittercrick Jack Gallagher, slain by John Slaughter for his horse-thieving propensities, and Turkey Creek Jack Johnson. The two former flourished later on, but Johnson was coeval with Doc and a few years afterwards fought on Holliday's side in the battles around Tombstone. He is therefore offered here as the most likely companion of Doc upon his return from Colorado and points east.

In any case, to continue with Wright's narrative, they were still having fun when he met them in the Long Branch.

"They had travelled all over Europe, spoke several languages, and the doctor had diplomas from several colleges in Europe, having finished his education in Heidelberg. They and I soon became very intimate. Of course, before our friendship ripened, I took them to be what I thought them, elegant gentlemen; but to my surprise, under a promise from me not to betray them, they told me they were big crooks and gold-brick men."

It seems that while looking the situation over at the new silver camp, Doc and his crony had encountered an Ohio banker who "came to Leadville with scads of ready money hunting soft snaps". Having found this pigeon, the two then cooked up a combination con game and shakedown racket of admirable proportions. Among other things 1878 was the banner year for raids on the stages carrying bullion from the gold mines in the Black Hills to the railhead at Cheyenne. It was these holdups,

F

conducted in chief by the gangs of Sam Bass and Big Nose George Parrot, that the conspirators took as their starting point.

They were, they told the banker, "the last of a gang of mountain bandits who robbed the Deadwood stage". They had succeeded in getting away with a stack of bullion bricks, only to discover that they were marked as United States property. "The government had a record of each brick and the weight of each brick, so they could be identified, which was the reason they were making such a sacrifice, for they themselves could not possibly dispose of the bricks to get anywhere near their value."

In consequence the price they asked for the lot was a mere twenty thousand dollars. The banker was drooling, but he wasn't buying until he had had the opportunity to look the contraband over. Doc and Creek then "brought a brick and had the banker file it at the ends, centre and middle, took the filings to an isolated spot in a fine, white silk handkerchief and applied the acid. The filings stood the test because they had exchanged handkerchiefs, substituting genuine gold filings for the base metal. The banker then demanded to see all the bricks. They had them sunk in a little lake with a gravelly bottom. They drove down and brought up a brick which the banker filed the same way as the other, and took the filings that night after dark, to an old log cabin on the outskirts of town. When they were about to make the acid test again, someone knocked. They blew out the light and made the great change again, and told the banker to take the filings himself to a jeweller, and apply the acid."

Having convinced himself that the bricks were all pure gold, the banker forked over the twenty thousand, but he was still being cagey. To guard against any attempt at hijacking or other shenanigans, he stipulated that one of the stage robbers must go with him as far as Chicago, at which point he could arrange for safe convoy for the treasure to the vaults of his bank. Creek undertook to act as hostage in this manner.

The trip was made without incident until "at some large city east of the Missouri River, an officer came on board, put his hand on the banker's shoulder and said, 'I arrest you as an accomplice in a theft of government gold, which I have reason to believe you have with you!'" Creek, of course, was put under arrest, too, as an accessory.

Well, the arm of the law had an assistant with him who said nothing until his boss had gone to lunch and Creek had been parolled to the gents' room. Then he whispered to the anguished banker, "Why not buy off this United States Marshal?" Thus encouraged, the banker did attempt bribery, when the officer returned from his meal. At first highly indignant, the latter "finally said he would turn the banker loose on the payment of fifteen thousand dollars, and he got the money soon after reaching Chicago. It is needless to say the United States Marshal was no one else but Doc Holliday".

Needless to say, also, the triumphant con men did not stay in Chicago very long. Knowing that detectives would be on their track as soon as the banker discovered the swindle, they made a beeline for Dodge City. The cowboy capital, as Wright remarked, was normally a safe place for criminal fugitives, Jesse James, among others, having found it so.

Doc and Creek hung around for some weeks until they were sure "the hunt for them had been abandoned" and then got on the move again. Flush at the Ohio banker's expense, they travelled in princely style. "The last I saw of the two," Wright concluded his anecdote, "they were starting south, overland, in a buckboard with tent, cooking-utensils, and camp equipage of all kinds. They had along a racehorse, a prize-fighter, a fighting bull-dog and two prize-winning game cocks. They were sports, every inch of them, if they were crooks and both dead shots with the six-shooter."

Other points aside, this story is interesting as an illustration of how Doc impressed contemporaries during periods of gaiety or when he was putting himself out to be entertaining. It is a long whistle from this to the portrait of the congenital sourpuss presented by Bat Masterson and his repeaters.

This is not to assert that Bat was entirely wrong, either. There is ample proof that when Doc did not like people he did not put himself out to be pleasant, and there can be no doubt that his affliction often made him moody and irritable. What should be evident, however, is that his was a highly complex character with a good many sides to it. It would be as absurd to brand him a misanthrope because he was sometimes in a bad humour as it would be to style him hail-fellow-well-met on the strength of Bob Wright's reminiscence.

Just where Doc and Creek were heading when Wright cheered them on their way is unknown. By keeping on south from Dodge they would, of course, be in the Indian Territory and on their way to Texas. If they turned west after crossing the Arkansas, they could have followed the Santa Fe trail into New Mexico. At all events Doc was gone for some while and had parted company with Creek before he turned up in town again.

He was probably absent during Clay Allison's one-man raid on Dodge City, of which so many contradictory versions can be found. According to the pro-Allison faction among historians Clay got tired of hearing about the efficiency of Dodge City's marshals and sent word that he was going to shoot up the town, whereupon everybody crawled into the woodwork. The anti-Allison group holds that the New Mexico outlaw was held in check, and this at least has the support of negative fact. As far as can be discovered Clay did not raise enough Cain in Dodge City to give Abel a crick in the neck.

But if Doc in all likelihood missed Allison's semi-celebrated visit, he was back in Dodge in time to be present when a band of Texans made a much more ambitious effort to capture the city. Inasmuch as an outlaw named Holliday was largely responsible for foiling this assault on the peace, a detailed account of what took place will follow.

CHAPTER VI

I̲ₙ mid-September Dodge had its Indian excitement of the year, staged by Dull Knife, chief of the Cheyennes. The chief knew all there was to know about plains fighting and put several units of the United States Army to school before he was finally cornered. When he passed within a few miles of Front Street he was still going strong, and a contingent of the local citizenry rode forth to help the troops out.

Wyatt Earp was one who had gone along, and on September 24, he returned with a few Indian prisoners, entrusted to him in his capacity as deputy United States Marshal. These he put in the city jail for safe-keeping, pending the time to turn them over to military authorities. Dodge was having supper as this was accomplished. After seeing to it that the braves were fed, Wyatt was making for his favourite beanery when guns started popping right in town.

The shouts which accompanied the firing told Earp that this was no Indian raid. There were trail drivers on the war-path, and a lot of them. The attack could be followed by whoops and explosions as it swept out of the south end of town, across the railroad tracks and the sacred Dodge City deadline—marking the point at which the town's ordinances were supposed to be strictly respected.

Most of the residents were munching their beef at the time, and most of them decided to go on doing so until the Texans got the devilment out of their systems. The few who had remained on duty fore or aft of the bars came to the conclusion that they would knock off for a while after all. About the only exceptions were three inmates of the Long Branch Saloon.

These were (a) an unidentified bartender, (b) a gambler dealing for the house called Cockeyed Frank Loving, and (c) a gambler bucking the bank by the name of Doc Holliday. The bar-keep later reported to Wyatt that neither of these

85

gentlemen bothered to comment when the sounds of pistol
fire started crackling down the street towards them. The house
was losing and couldn't quit, and Doc was riding with luck and
would not.

There was plenty going on, if they had been interested
enough to pay attention. The cowmen were having a good
time on Dodge City's main street, shooting out windows pane
by pane, charging into saloons to help themselves, and to turn
the bars inside out. The people who had taken the precaution
of locking up before leaving were a little worse off than the
others. They had doors to replace, too.

Charlie Bassett and some of the other town marshals were
still chasing Indians, and the rest thought it was a good time
to stand by and wait for orders. That left the task of cooling off
the raiders up to Wyatt Earp, and he, as he told his biographer,
was of no mind to tackle it with just his six-shooters. The situation called for a double-barrelled shot-gun, and he made for his
favourite hangout, where he kept an emergency arsenal. This, as
it chanced, was the Long Branch Saloon.

Approaching it via an alley, he almost got there ahead of
the raiders, but not quite. As he rounded the corner of the
building, he almost ran into a pair of them. Both had their
guns in their hands, while Wyatt's were still in their holsters.

They covered him, and then they whooped with vengeful
joy. The two were Tobe Driskill and Ed Morrison, cattlemen
of some renown and leaders of the present expedition. Earp
knew them both, and they had some reason to remember him.
The last time Driskill had been in Dodge, Wyatt had buffaloed
him by way of persuading him to keep the peace. Some years
earlier, while he was marshal of Wichita, he had had occasion to
treat Morrison in the same fashion.

"By God," Driskill roared, "it's Earp!"

"We've got him," Morrison chortled, after reminding Wyatt
of the old score he had to settle.

If he and Driskill hadn't talked so loud, they might have
done as they wished. As it was, their voices carried inside to
where a pair of top-circuit hands were concentrating on a game
of faro.

Cockeyed Frank had been a trail driver himself, but for the
past few years he had been a gambler. Bob Wright offers the

curious information that he had drowned a man while in Dodge, but he was better known for his prowess with a gun. Wyatt stated that he felt sure Loving would have helped him out; but the latter himself admitted that he was beaten to it by a mile. At mention of Earp's name and the fate planned for him, Frank said that Doc sprang to his feet and ran to the spot where the guns checked in by the house hung on a rack. Snatching his own nickel-plated weapon and another gun that he found beside it, Holliday leaped to the door.

The whole attacking party of some twenty-five cow-hands had by then closed in. Hopped up on whiskey and the excitement of the attack, they stood ready to follow Morrison's injunction, "If he makes a move, boys, let him have it."

The two leaders themselves were engaged in goading Wyatt into reaching for his rod before they shot him down. They knew drawing would be a hopeless gesture on his part, and Earp thought so, too. He was trying to edge towards the saloon door while they were taunting him, but he felt sure that he'd find a hole in Boot Hill before he got there.

"Pray, you son of a bitch," Morrison was urging him. Wyatt meanwhile had decided that drawing was his best move after all. He was aware of the dead man's moment—the second before a man feels the shock of even a bullet through the heart. In the course of that instant he counted on avenging his own murder on at least one of his enemies. He was deciding which one of them to try for when he heard the door of the Long Branch flung open behind him.

"Throw 'em up!" roared a voice. That it wasn't addressing Wyatt was made plain by the tirade of profanity with which it lashed the raiders singly and collectively. "There were times," Earp remarked while later describing the incident, "when Doc swore beautifully."

Wyatt meanwhile had recognized his rescuer by his Georgia accent, but he had not spared Holliday a glance. This was an act he left to the startled cattlemen. When they looked to see who was challenging them, their control of the situation was gone. Earp promptly filled both hands and what had had the look of a reasonably comfortable murder now had the making of a dangerous, if still one-sided gun-fight.

While Driskill and Morrison were trying to adjust their

minds to this new state of affairs, Doc stopped cursing. "What will we do with 'em, Wyatt?" His tone was so matter-of-fact and confident that the nerve of the raiders began to leave them. In the fatal moment of hesitation which followed Doc's query, Wyatt went into action. Lunging forward he laid the barrel of his Colt—an extra long weapon which had been given him by the one and only Ned Buntline—alongside Morrison's skull. Buffaloed, the rancher fell headlong, just as he had done at Wichita four years earlier.

"Throw 'em up!" Earp next echoed Doc's command.

Among the raiders was said to be Pat Garrett, still in his salad days and several years short of the time when he would win Western immortality as the sheriff who slew Billy the Kid. Other gunmen of prowess were there, but the raiding party had lost its impetus, and its individual members their zest for the undertaking. Shedding their six-shooters, they put up their hands, with the exception of one diehard.

"Look out, Wyatt!" Doc yelled, and shot as he did so.

For the second time in two minutes, Holliday saved Earp's life. "Years after," the latter told his biographer, "it was told that Doc Holliday killed that Texan. He didn't, he hit him in the shoulder. The result disappointed Doc, but it was all I needed."

Marching the gang along with their hands in the air, Doc and Wyatt prodded them south across the deadline and the railroad tracks. Their destination was the jail, where the cowmen spent the night, in company with those other raiders who had failed to keep up with Dull Knife. Doc and the man with whom his friendship was now sealed then sauntered back through the empty streets of a town which didn't yet know it had been rescued from invasion. In front of the Long Branch they picked up an almost even fifty revolvers. Put in a sack, these were given to the fined and chastened revellers when they were ordered out of town the next day.

"One thing I've always believed," Wyatt said in concluding his account of the episode. "If it hadn't been for Doc Holliday, I'd have cashed in that night. There was no real call for Doc to make the play he did; everybody else in camp had high-tailed it, including some of my deputies, and why Doc wasn't knocked off is more than I can tell you. He wasn't, and if anyone ever questions the motive of my loyalty to Doc Holliday, there's my answer. In the old days, neither Doc nor I bothered to make explanations; I never was given to such things and in our case they would have been contrary to Doc's sense of decency."

That one shot fired on behalf of law and order changed Doc's status. Thereafter he was only a part-time outlaw for the remainder of his stay in Kansas. Witness Andy Adams in his *Log of a Cowboy*, the gun of Doc Holliday was one that the trail drivers found waiting for them whenever they came to town to get rough. Adams is substantiated in this by contemporary newspaper references and the statement of Dr. A. B. Harbison, who was a physician in Ford County during the period in question.

Writing recently of the place and time, Dr. Harbison remarked: "The Sante Fe Railway was being pushed out through Kansas from Kansas City, following the line of the Old Santa Fe Trail, over which I drove in a wagon in those early years. It was not a continuous building but step by step as the company obtained money and at each step a town was made and became the headquarters for the Texas cattlemen driving their herds over the old Chisholm Trail to the railhead, and these towns of a year or two required the most courageous of men as law officers and none was greater than Wyatt Earp, nor did he have greater assistance than that given by Doc Holliday. . . . I am one of the few living who was there and can tell about it."

Extant, nevertheless, is testimony to prove that Doc did not devote all his time to good works during the fall, winter and spring of 1878–79. In a volume of recollections, which has not so far received the favour it merits, Charles Lowther tells of how he arrived in Dodge City on a freezing early morning in March. He was then a lad in a family headed by his Methodist minister father. The latter led his chilled and weary wife and children to a hotel, only to find that the clerk would give them no accommodations. The best he would do would be to let them sit by the stove in the lobby until the proprietor arose.

When the hotel-keeper appeared, he bawled the clerk out for his ill-treatment of potential guests, for it developed that a couple of rooms actually were available. At the same time the landlord was aware of his employee's dilemma and tried to explain it to the indignant minister.

"Father assured the hotel man that as soon as possible he would look for other accommodations. 'I wouldn't look at it that way,' said the man, 'you see we have got a Doc Holliday in this here town, a gambler and a general all around bad man when he is drunk and the clerk was askeered to give you's the best rooms we had, on account this Holliday party might come in most any time and want the room you-all had, and in that case you would have had to get up and let him have your room.'

"Father exclaimed, 'You certainly don't treat your guests that way here, do you?'

" 'We got to kind of humour a drunk man,' " explained the other.

Joining other guests in the dining-room, the Lowthers heard more of Doc, who had apparently reacted to his domestic unhappiness by treeing the town every now and then. "Nobody crossed him, lest they get him started shooting," the newcomers were informed. "In Dodge City he held dominion. It was because the night clerk had sought to favour him by holding several rooms vacant for Doc Holliday that we had to occupy the parlour from about three o'clock till breakfast time."

But if Doc gave others a bad time, his own troubles were becoming progressively acute. As the trail-driving season had approached its close in 1878, Big Nose Kate had returned to Dodge City. The slack times of winter loomed ahead, and she was in a conciliatory mood. The Holliday *ménage* again functioned without benefit of clergy, or very much blessing from the Devil. Kate belonged to that philosophical wing— not confined to members of her profession; and not confined to women, so far as that's concerned—who would gladly hock a year of quiet bliss to buy two bits worth of stormy melodrama. When it came to amorous explosions Doc was ideal. His hot temper made him sure of giving a satisfactory emotional response, and his sense of obligation made it certain that the row would blow over as soon as Kate was ready.

It was a good thing that it was Dora Hand and not Big Nose Kate whom Jim Kennedy shot by mistake in the fall of 1878. Doc would certainly have been suspected, although a jury might have considered it justifiable 'meretricide'. In the case of Kennedy, after he had been pursued and brought back by a formidable posse which included Bat Masterson, Charlie Bassett,

Bill Tilghman and Wyatt Earp, the decision was to let him go. The grounds were unusual in terms of jurisprudence but made some sense in terms of Western practicality. Kennedy had not succeeded in slaying Mayor Dog Kelley, the true object of his enmity and the intended target of his bullet. Kelley had not even been hit, so there was no reason for him to squawk, and Miss Hand had not been shot on purpose, so it was ridiculous to talk about assaulting with intent to kill. Kennedy was let off with a bullet hole put in him by Bat Masterson and the pangs of regret. Half of these were for missing the mayor and the rest for having killed Dora, whom he, along with everybody else, liked.

The slaying of Dora Hand—remembered as having had a promising stage career under the name of Fannie Keenan before she turned up in the red-light districts of various Western camps —was the last big event on the calendar of Dodge City's banner year. The calm which set in for the winter, and which froze the hearts of the circuit's excitement-loving citizens, was not broken until the spring of 1879.

For the rest of Dodge the big news was that two hundred and fifty thousand longhorns were being rounded up in preparation for a start up the Western Trail. Doc's private worry was that Kate was going to help entertain the trail drivers. It was Doc's turn to get out of town first, if he didn't want to see the so-called Mrs. Holliday soliciting all comers.

Fortunately for his dignity an enterprise was afoot in which he would probably have taken a hand, Kate or no Kate. This was the invasion of Colorado promoted by the Santa Fe Railroad. The purpose of this expeditionary force, entirely recruited from Dodge City, was to call the turn on the Denver and Rio Grande line.

The rival railways wanted control of two strategic Colorado points. One was the Raton Pass, leading from Trinidad down through Las Vegas, New Mexico, and so to the high plains beyond. The other was the Royal Gorge of the Arkansas River. The latter had become of dazzling importance because of the nearby wonder city of Leadville. As yet this had no railroad service, and both the Santa Fe and the Denver and Rio Grande aimed to fill the breach.

The first battle was for the Royal Gorge, and neither railroad fooled around. They fought with everything from revolvers to decisions of the United States Supreme Court, which now favoured one side and now the other.

The Denver and Rio Grande had taken the early tricks through the enterprise of a remarkable engineer named De Remer. Fortifying the heights, he had rammed a line of tracks between the sheer cliffs and the racing river, taking all the toughest risks himself. When he was all through, however, the Supreme Court gave the Santa Fe custody of the Denver and Rio Grande, switch, caboose and ticket office.

Set back on its heels, the local railroad came back fighting under the aegis of an old warrior named General Palmer. While appealing to have the rights of his line recognized by the courts, he organized a railway militia which waged war in all strong-holds of the rival road. As the latter was an out of State concern, while the Denver and Rio Grande was indigenous, the fight took on the aura of a home-rule crusade. Coloradoans cheered, or even joined in the fun free of charge, as minions of the hated national railway were dragged from station and roundhouse, roughed up and kicked out of town.

It was to find an answer to this method of reversing the Supreme Court that the Santa Fe turned to Dodge City and its cadre of famous gunmen. These responded with joy. Here was excitement of a novel order, the pay was good, and there was even some patriotism involved. The Atchison, Topeka and Santa Fe railroad was a Kansas line being oppressed by the citizens of another State. "On to Canyon City"—the town controlling the approach to Leadville—was the battle-cry, as they enlisted.

"They were called to arms," Bob Wright noted, "by the railroad agent, Mr. J. H. Phillips. Twenty of the brave boys promptly responded, among whom might be numbered some of Dodge's most accomplished sluggers and bruisers and dead-shots, headed by the gallant Captain Webb. They put down their names with a firm resolve to get to the joint in creditable style, in case of danger."

Among those joining John Joshua Webb were Ben Thompson and Doc Holliday. In the casual fashion of the region, Bat Masterson took time off from his duties as sheriff to help the rail-road organize a platoon of mercenaries, although there is some question as to whether he accompanied the first echelon. There is also a choice of opinion as to who led the shock troops. Some historians assert that Bat himself did. As noted above, Wright recalled that Webb was the chieftain. Eddie Foy, who had just returned to Dodge after having spent the winter in Leadville, had a still different recollection. According to his published reminiscences, it was Ben Thompson who led the janissaries into Colorado.

Eddie himself was invited to join, and by none other than Doc. The exchange of remarks on the subject which Foy offered is interesting as the only recorded attempt—albeit by a man from the Middle West—to reproduce Doc's Southern drawl.

"That year the Sante Fe and the Denver & Rio Grande railroads were fighting for the right of way up the Grand Canyon of the Arkansas from Canyon City to Leadville, Colorado. Big strikes of silver had occurred at Leadville, the place was beginning to boom, and had as yet no railroad. Both the Sante Fe and the Rio Grande were anxious to reach the new bonanza, the only feasible way was that up the Arkansas Canyon, and there appeared to be room for only one track. So hot did the row become that the Santa Fe asked Dodge City for a corps of gunfighters, which was enthusiastically raised. The Santa Fe being 'our own road', had Dodge's sympathy in the quarrel and, besides, there was promise of good pay for the fighters. Doc Holliday suggested that I join them.

" 'But listen, Mr. Holliday,' said I, 'I'm no fighter. I wouldn't be any help to the gang. I couldn't hit a man if I shot at him.'

" 'Oh, that's all right,' he replied easily. 'The Santy Fee won't know the difference. You kin use a shot-gun if you want to. Dodge wants to make a good showin' in this business. You'll help swell the crowd, and you'll get your pay, anyhow.'

"But," Foy concluded, "I declined to join the expedition much to Doc's disappointment. From time to time reports of the progress of the war came back to us from the front. It was even rumoured along Main Street that our brave lads held the roundhouse at Pueblo for several hours against a large detachment of United States soldiers."

Meanwhile a second detachment had gone out from Dodge. This was definitely led to the scene of battle by Bat, although the rest were not men of particular renown. "Towering like a giant among the smaller men," the *Dodge City Times* reported, "was one of Erin's bravest sons whose name is Kinch Riley. Jerry Converse, a Scotchman, descendant from a warlike clan, joined the ranks of war. There were other braves who joined the ranks but we were unable to get a list of their names. We will bet a ten-cent note they clear the track of every obstruction."

In the meantime, too, General Palmer had got the United States Supreme Court to hand him back the Denver and Rio Grande. For the moment it was only a transfer on paper, as the men from Dodge held the pivotal control point. This was the roundhouse at Pueblo mentioned by Eddie Foy. The evidence indicates that they were bought off at a handsome figure, but not before they had received a tip from the Santa Fe that they were no longer needed.

The great battle at Canyon City never came off, but under cover of all the furore the Atchison, Topeka and Santa Fe had been busy. All the excitement over the Royal Gorge had made everybody else, including the triumphant officials of the Denver and Rio Grande, forget about the right of way through Raton Pass. Each road needed it in order to satisfy transcontinental ambitions, and each had staked tentative claims. While General Palmer and his crew were coaxing Doc, Bat and the rest out of the roundhouse with greenbacks, a group of Santa Fe engineers raced down to Trinidad and secured permanent possession of the pass beyond.

The great battle of the railroads ended with each line scoring a major point. Whether or not they were satisfied with this division of spoils, it was disappointing to the fans back in Kansas. "Finally," to quote Foy again, "the two roads compromised the matter, greatly to the disgust of certain citizens of Dodge, who had been hoping the home boys would be permitted to wipe the D. & R. G. off the map."

As it turned out, several of them ceased to be home boys for Dodge City. The whole circuit was their residence and a number of them went on to the new terminus cities being created by the Santa Fe's progress into New Mexico.

Among them was Doc Holliday. On leaving Dodge he had told Wyatt Earp that he would not return until he learned that Big Nose Kate was plying her trade elsewhere. Pursuant to this plan he began moving from one town to another as his luck with the cards and his skill with a gun prompted. The days of being a guardian of such peace as he felt like keeping were temporarily behind him, and he reclaimed his status as a full-time outlaw.

By all accounts he had killed a couple of men who disagreed with him over points of order before he came to Trinidad. His chief exploit there was recorded in the court records of Las Animas County as well as in the memoirs of several circuit veterans. This was to put a bullet through a gambler named Kid Colton.

The Kid beat the odds by recovering, but by that time Doc had gone on to Otero, New Mexico, which has since yielded such glories as it had to nearby Raton. At least one of the spooks in this ghost town owes his being to Doc, who was arrested on charges of killing an unnamed, and probably unknown, gunman, albeit under circumstances that led the court to exonerate him on the broad Western grounds of "self-defence".

The Santa Fe reached Las Vegas, at the southern end of Raton Pass, on June 1, 1879. Doc arrived soon afterwards. The long-established city called Old Town had been famous as a health resort since before the War between the States. New Town, the terminus settlement set up to the east of it, was anything but that. It was a chaotic development cut to the pattern of Fort Griffin Flat.

Looking Las Vegas over, Doc was pleased with what he found. It was a town with a dual personality, having a prosperous, reasonably respectable business centre as well as its new boom settlement. For a time he made shift to utilize both of these outlets for his tastes and energies.

In Old Town he opened up, for the third and last time in the West, the office of John H. Holliday, Doctor of Dental Surgery. This farewell attempt to retain his status as a professional man did not last long, but it had one important outcome. His office was in the same building as the store of a jeweller named Bill Leonard. He became quite friendly with Leonard, whom he was later to meet in Tombstone, with nearly fatal consequences.

In New Town Doc started rolling with a streak of gambling luck which was to stay with him much of the year. His success as a dealer was hurtful to his attempted come-back as a dentist, however. In the end, as the records of San Miguel County show, he purchased a saloon on Centre Street and forgot about his probes and extractors.

Whether he found old friends, or not, he could not have lacked for old acquaintances, as a subdivision of Las Vegas society was known as "the Dodge City Gang". Then chief among the town's standing cadre of outlaws was Dave Rudabaugh, whose trail Doc had cut for the benefit of Wyatt, when he had first met the latter at Fort Griffin. One of Dave's cronies by then was Captain Josh Webb, leader of the Santa Fe expeditionary force. With a breadth of outlook peculiar to the West, Rudabaugh had ignored the fact that he and Webb had been introduced when Josh was a member of Bat Masterson's posse. When Webb later got thrown into jail for plugging a fellow at the instance of a local justice of the peace named Hoodoo Brown, it was Rudabaugh that sprung the man who had helped to bring about one of his own numerous incarcerations.

But if these were speculative associates, Doc soon had one who can be positively identified. Big Nose Kate had not been pleased by his exodus from Dodge City. It was one thing for her to turn her back on him and quite another for him to act as if he didn't care. The cowboy season at Dodge had not been as much fun as she had counted on, and she had set out to run Doc down.

Just the same she was apparently not in a pacific mood when she succeeded. Presumably her ultimate motive was a reunion, but her immediate aim was to make Doc miserable. According to reports, she was doing well at this when she was interrupted by circumstances beyond her control.

Late in August of 1879, Doc had a falling out with another terminus outlaw named Mike Gordon. Inviting Gordon out into Centre Street, he there shot him dead. This sort of thing had happened so often since the advent of the railroad that the citizens of Old Town had grown restive. Plans were afoot to arrest Doc, and they would have been carried out if he had been slow to move. As it was, he and the horse under him took it on the run along the lower fork of the Santa Fe trail, the one, that is to say, that was not followed by the railroad.

It led to Dodge City, to which Doc was now glad to return. He knew that Kate would no longer be there to embarrass and humiliate him, and he looked forward to seeing Wyatt Earp again.

He arrived in Dodge to find that he was cheated on the second count. Lured by the Tombstone boom, Wyatt had resigned his job on Dodge City's force of marshals and had headed south down the Western Trail, bound for Arizona.

PART III

Wars with the Law
in Southern Arizona

CHAPTER VII

STAYING in Dodge City just long enough to rest up after his posse-inspired trip from Las Vegas, Doc saddled up for Arizona himself. To catch up with Wyatt promised to be no feat, as word had it that his friend was travelling by buckboard, to accommodate his pace to that of James Earp and his wife.

The Earps, it is here timely to remark, were a clannish brotherhood, adding up to five. Jim was the eldest. Virgil, next in line and also married, was then in Prescott, Arizona, and the plan was to pick him up there. Just behind Wyatt, and fourth in the string, was Morgan, who had been urged to break away from Butte, Montana, for a Tombstone reunion. No doubt a similar message had been forwarded to Warren, the youngster of the crew, whose whereabouts at the time are not recorded.

As a service casualty in the War between the States, Jim was limited in his activities. The rest were all gunmen of mark and had served as Dodge City deputies. Virgil had distinguished himself as a peace officer in Prescott before resigning to try his hand at mining. Morgan was holding down the tough job of City Marshal in Butte, when the clan summons arrived to draw him south.

A widower, as has been said, Wyatt rode alone in the buckboard that rolled across the plains in company with that of his brother. Progress was further slowed by the fact that each wagon was tailed by several saddle horses. It took a couple of weeks, as Wyatt recalled, for them to make it south to a crossroads settlement in the Indian Territory called Trail City.

From there it was more or less of a straight shoot westward through New Mexico to the northern pass into Arizona. The southern one was then undesirable, because of the Chiricahua Apaches. The route also had the advantage of offering a fairly level trail, whereas the lower fork of the Sante Fe trail—over which Doc had just travelled in haste—would have entailed driving the wagons up some awkward grades.

Leaving Trail City in the number two rig of the Earp caravan, Wyatt heard hoof-beats in pursuit. "Where are you going, Wyatt?" the rider who caught up with him asked.

"Tombstone," Earp said.

"That's what they told me in Dodge," Doc Holliday allowed. "Guess I'll go with you."

Relieving his mount of his gear, Doc heaved his saddle into the buckboard, added his horse to the led string and climbed on the seat with Earp. It was in this casual fashion that they joined forces for an expedition to the newest and in some ways the most remarkable of the great camps of the circuit.

Nothing could be more typical of that institution than the circumstance which reunited them. At about the same time that Doc had taken it on the lam out of Las Vegas, Wyatt had handed in his marshal's badge. They met in the middle of nowhere and agreed to sample the gambling at a place which hadn't yet earned a place on the map.

The tables at Santa Fe might have tempted them to try the old Spanish colonial city, but they held to the line of march. Wheeling across the uplands to the western edge of the Mogollon Rim, they then dropped down into Prescott.

Virgil Earp agreed to pick up his traps and go on to Tombstone, but Doc decided to write the new silver camp down in his futures book. Thriving on mining itself, in addition to being the Arizona territorial capital, Prescott was no small shakes as a gambling centre. Doc ran into a streak of luck on the town's famous Whiskey Row that topped everything in his previous experience. He refused to commit such gambler's sacrilege as to kick fortune in the face. Telling Wyatt that he would be along by and by, he stayed to buck an unwontedly friendly tiger.

It was getting towards three months later when he decided that his streak had run its course. There had been some bad luck to curdle the good meanwhile. He had added forty thousand leaves to a bank-roll which now resembled a head of cabbage. On the other hand, Big Nose Kate had hit town. The whores of the circuit were flocking to south-eastern Arizona along with the gamblers, outlaws and/or peace officers. Learning that Doc was doing so well, Kate had put away her bad humour.

It was in company that they fared south. Their route led through Phoenix, where irrigation farming was creating a city which Tucson and Prescott had not yet learned to view as a competitor. It ran past Florence, where Charles Poston, first territorial delegate of Arizona, was trying to naturalize the Parsee religion of ancient Iran. It ran through Tucson, anxiously waiting for the Southern Pacific to push its tracks through from the coast. Lastly, the road made easting past the old Butterfield stage station at Benson before it ran south up the San Pedro River valley for twenty-five miles. The travellers were then on the grassy heights, forty-five hundred feet above sea level, where Tombstone sprawled across Goose Flats and sundry adjoining areas.

All the towns of the circuit had histories entertaining to follow for the brief and hectic periods of their respective flowerings. Tombstone differs from the others in that it had a story, whose consecutive events gathered momentum for nearly two and a half years. Of that story Holliday was destined to dominate the curious final episode. He was, as it chanced, one of the last among the major characters to arrive on the scene. Doc and Kate caught their first drink on Allen Street in February 1880. Morgan Earp had ridden down from Montana a few weeks before. Certain other Westerners of mark were also already on deck.

The Tombstone region was the best stamping ground that the outlaws of the Western frontier had ever found. For isolation it was as good as the Big Bend country, and it did not have the drawback offered by the Texas Rangers. The mining bonanza and the connected ore-reducing operations created wealth and drew people to be preyed upon. New towns and the territory's Indian reservations offered markets for all the cows that could be rustled in or out of Mexico. The proximity of the border made smuggling profitable.

There was no territorial police force. The sheriff's office was seventy-five miles away, and so were such nuisances as grand juries and courts. No civic conscience reared its head to speak against license. No vigilantes as yet held secret meetings and plotted against the safety of their erring fellow citizens. In consequence there was no serpent at all in this bandits' paradise until Wyatt Earp and his Buntline special drove up in a buckboard. In passing through Tucson, Earp had accepted a commission as deputy from Sheriff Charles Shibell of Pima County.

Earp is quoted as claiming that he intended to do no more than Shibell asked him to, collecting the fee for the office's civil services and forgetting law enforcement. Granting that was his purpose, he was soon diverted from it. The outlaws of the region—in so far as they were a group and not playing lone hands in the manner of Doc—considered Wyatt's advent a challenge to their supremacy. Knowing the new deputy personally or by reputation, they didn't believe he would wink at their criminal activities. Almost from the first, therefore, they commenced a programme of intimidation designed to drive him out of the country.

When Doc Holliday reached town he found that the feud had already reached a fairly advanced stage. The outlaws had stolen the deputy sheriff's favourite horse and were having great fun over his inability to recover it. Wyatt had added to the enmity they felt for him by riding shot-gun on the bullion stages they had previously made a practice of looting. Before doing so he had interviewed some of the suspected stage robbers, explaining just what would happen to them if they tried to hold up a coach he was guarding. They had answered him with threats of their own; and they were men who usually meant business when they talked of killing.

As Doc became embroiled in this quarrel, because of his friendship for Earp, and for other reasons, a brief account of the opposing gang is in order. The leader of the rustlers at that stage of affairs was an old wolf named N. H. Clanton. Texas had considered itself too small to have room for him and California had felt the same way. He had been run out of the latter State just as Arizona's infant cattle industry began to develop. As soon as the influx of prospectors had made ranching comparatively safe from Apache raids in the lush grasslands around Tombstone, he had moved into the south-east corner of the territory.

Aiding him in the formation of an international rustling combine there, were Joseph Isaac, or Ike, and Phineas, known as Phin, Clanton. The family had apparently run out of Biblical names when William, called Billy, arrived. When it came to war Ike's chief talent was shooting enemies in the back. Phin was a determined, if unsensational clansman. Billy was a tough kid with an extra ration of boldness and gun-shooting skill. All three were accomplished rustlers, fences and hijackers.

Old Man Clanton had something of a genius for organization. His men played watch-dog over almost every water-hole in a region covering several thousand square miles of range. Every rancher who wished to continue in business had to join him, buy stolen cattle from him, or otherwise play ball. The only allowed exceptions were a few big operatives like Colonel Henry C. Hooker and John Slaughter, who could afford to hire enough gunmen to hold the rustlers somewhat in abeyance.

On the Clanton side the owners of the largest spread were a couple of brothers named Frank and Tom McLowry. Coming from Mississippi by way of Texas, they had manœuvred their way into what was tantamount to partnership with the rustler leader. Having the status of big ranches, they were very useful. Cattle stolen in Mexico could conveniently be fattened on their extensive holdings before being sold to neighbouring cowmen or delivered for slaughter.

Rustled cattle was the bread-and-butter of the outlaws, but they had other sources of income. The occasional stage hold-ups, aimed at getting the silver bullion entrusted to Wells, Fargo Express guards, supplied them with a considerable amount of treasure, supplemented when possible by the indiscriminate robbery of all insufficiently-armed travellers. More profitable was the hijacking of smugglers plying back and forth over the international boundary. Potentially most lucrative of all were a wide variety of shakedown rackets.

The region where the Clantons and their henchmen operated was bounded on the west by the Whetstone and the Huachuca Mountains. From these two-mile heights the land swept down to form the San Pedro and the even lusher and broader Sulphur Springs Valley. Separating them were the Dragoons, once the stronghold of the Chiricahua Apaches and still used by them as their great chief Victorio flitted in and out of Mexico in the course of his war on two nations. He was also much in the Chiricahua range which bounds the Sulphur Springs Valley on the east. Beyond it was the San Simon Valley, hard against New Mexico.

Tombstone was the capital and metropolis of the area. Tributary to it were Charleston, Fairbank and Contention City, communities along the San Pedro which had grown up around the stamping mills which crushed the ore in preparation for removing the silver. Charleston in particular, which was located not far from the Clanton ranch, was an outlaw hangout. So also was Galeyville, east away on the slopes of the Chiricahuas. Farther to the north San Simon and the old settlement of Fort Thomas were also rustler outposts.

Although he was eventually in it up to his chin, and almost above his head, there is no positive evidence that Doc was active in the Tombstone feud during his first months in southern Arizona. Something of how he did occupy himself sticks to the record, nonetheless. For one thing he operated a saloon bought with his Prescott winnings.

He did not name the establishment in the newspaper statement which included this information. He did say, though, that he found himself obliged to assert the rights of management in the matter of preserving order. Speaking of Tombstone, Doc told a reporter: "I thought I saw a chance to make a little money, and so I opened a gambling house. Things went along all right for a time, but at length some of the boys got an idea that they were not winning often enough, and they put up a job to kill me. I heard of it, and the next night, when they came in, I made them a speech, told them what I had heard, said that sort of thing couldn't go on in any well-regulated community, and then, just to restore order, I gave it to a couple of them."

The correspondent of the *New York Sun*—who obtained this quote from Holliday—learned from another citizen that Doc was guilty of interfering with the freedom of the press. Perhaps referring to the dual killing cited above, this fellow said: "I remember one time in Tombstone he killed two men in one night, and the next day he called on the editor of the paper and said that, as he was opposed to sensational literature, he hoped there would be no undue prominence given to the occurrences of the evening before. When the paper came out in the afternoon it had a three-line item, saying that it was understood that two men had been found dead on the streets, but that the reporter had not learned their names. The same issue had a long editorial article on the advantages of Arizona as a health resort."

Then well before Boot Hill was shined up and its population artificially increased by over-zealous custodians, it contained a

WARS WITH THE LAW

grave marker which commemorated one other quarrel and its outcome. "Conly shot by Doc Holliday", so runs this terse and definitive bit of reporting. Neither history nor tradition casts light on who Conly was or what he had done to earn Holliday's displeasure.

A few of Doc's comings and goings during 1880 have also found recorders. He was in Tucson on and off to sample the gambling, although the tale of the wholesale slaughter he wrought there is doubtless as mythical as he himself asserted it to be. So, too, is that other story he laughed off, to the effect that he spent some months as chieftain of a sheriff-chasing gang of desperadoes in the Calico Range of southern California.

On the other hand he was his own warrant for the fact that he took a look at the northern fringes of Mexico. "Down on the border," to use his offhand wording, "I had two or three little scrapes but they didn't amount to much. A party of drunken greasers came climbing over us one night, and I had to fix one or two, and at another time I had a fight with a room full of them, and started a grave-yard there, but it had to be done in the interest of peace."

One more thing that is established is that he went back to Las Vegas to dispose of the Centre Street saloon which he had been forced to abandon, following the slaying of Mike Gordon. In the way of the West, that crime was now as buried in the past as the killing of Cock Robin. Certainly Doc made no effort to be self-effacing, for his first act was to seek out a man and aim a gun at him.

The incident is recounted in the reminiscences of Miguel Antonio Otero, later governor of New Mexico. "During the year 1880 Doc Holliday arrived in Las Vegas." He had hardly left the train when he learned of an opportunity to wind up some unfinished business. "Holliday had had some serious difficulty with Charlie White back in Dodge City, which was the immediate cause of White's departure from that place."

Perhaps White was the man Doc mentioned as having wrongfully accused him of theft while in Dodge. At all events Holliday learned that Charlie was then tending bar in New Town. He went to call on his foe without delay.

"White was in the act of serving some thirsty customers," Otero proceeded, "but recognizing his old enemy from Dodge

City, White quickly emerged with a gun and the duel began in earnest." After several exchanges of shots Charlie collapsed behind the bar he had used as a barricade and Doc thought he had done for him. It turned out that Charlie had merely been stunned by a bullet which grazed his skull, but by the time Doc found that out it was too late to do anything about it. "White had evidently tired of frontier life, for he left for his home in Boston on the very next train going East."

Otero then went on to define the attitude of Western law towards inconsequential shootings as well as to give his personal impression of Doc. "No arrests were made. It was simply allowed to pass, as no one was interested in either Holliday or White, and the peace officers in Las Vegas were much too busy looking after their own games. . . . Doc Holliday remained a few days in Las Vegas before taking his departure for Arizona, and I met him quite frequently and found him to be a very likeable fellow."

While all this was going on, Tombstone had been undergoing significant changes. People were still pouring into town, which began to count on supplanting Tucson as the territorial metropolis. Capital on a major scale had been invested in the silver mines, and these were putting increasing numbers of men on steadily growing pay-rolls. The Southern Pacific Railway stretched through Benson on its way to make connections with the Santa Fe in New Mexico. This not only stepped up the immigration rate but facilitated the flow of merchandise and offered handy shipping points for the region's booming—if largely illegal—cattle industry.

All these economic factors combined to boost the quality of Tombstone as a gambling town. That in turn served to bring in several prominent circuit citizens whose presence, steady or temporary, helped to strengthen the position of the Earps. Among the new arrivals were Bat Masterson (no longer sheriff of Ford County, Kansas), Sherman McMasters, Texas Jack Vermillion and Turkey Creek Jack Johnson.

But the outlaws were also gaining recruits, and some among them were likewise known wherever *aficionados* of the circuit gathered to talk shop. One was William Brocius Graham, usually called Curly Bill. After serving his apprenticeship as an outlaw in his native Missouri, he had first attained professional eminence in Texas. Kansas had likewise heard the bark of his gun and the clink of his glass. Dark and burly, he was a cheerful, personally popular thief with a natural talent for leadership.

John Ringgold, more commonly called Johnny Ringo, had had a more or less similar career. He, too, had left Missouri for other parts, including a series of railhead cattle towns. In Texas, according to some authorities, he had taken part in the Mason County war, among other things, before coming to Arizona.

It was in their social rather than their geographical backgrounds that Curly Bill and Johnny differed. The latter had attended college in a day when only young men of good background normally did so. Nobody has yet lifted Ringo out of his setting of myth to allow a good look at him, so legend will have to go unchallenged. According to this he was Byronic in mood, appearance and past. Wavy auburn hair surrounded a handsome but unhappy patrician face. He was subject to alternate fits of noble generosity and savage cruelty. He drank, not out of good joy in the liquor, but to forget other and better days. He packed the classics in his duffle and read them in the original Greek and Latin during breaks in his rustling and hijacking expeditions. He even received letters in a graceful feminine hand, and each one cast him adrift in despond for days thereafter.

Ringo's reputation with a gun was like everything else about him, awe-inspiring but hard to nail down. The only corpse in and around Tombstone which can definitely be assigned to him is that of one Louis Hancock. While in one of his black moods Johnny encountered this fellow in an Allen Street saloon. Offended because Hancock ordered beer after he had invited him to drink whiskey, Ringo shot him while the unsuspecting Louis had his beak in the suds.

Frank Stilwell was another prominent figure who joined the rustler ranks. His brother was Jack Stilwell, a famous plainsman and scout, who later became a successful attorney; but Frank himself was a man of no mean talents. It was later said of him that he held up the bullion stages so often that the horses knew and responded to his voice better than they did to any of the drivers. Still another who cast dubious repute on a renowned name was Hank Swilling. Pima on the distaff side, he is said to have been one of the illegitimate get of Jack Swilling, patron saint of Arizona's irrigation economy and the triumphant leader of its one Civil War battle.

Among a host of lesser outlaws some are worthy of notice on the ground that Doc encountered them at one time or another. The list includes Pete Spence, Johnny Barnes, Luther King, Frank Patterson, Rattlesnake Bill, Harry Head, Pony Deal, Jim Crane and Joe Hill. Included also was Bill Leonard, whom Doc had known at Las Vegas and with whom he now renewed his friendship. On reaching the Tombstone area, Leonard had thrown in with the bullion thieves, who found his professional ability as a jeweller useful to them. It made no difference to Doc. When he liked somebody, that was all there was to it. A man's standing with the community was of no interest to him.

To return to the gang as a group, its growth and ambition kept pace with the growth and increasing wealth of Tombstone. It was inevitable that the rustlers would not for long overlook a prize which was at once valuable in itself and the key to dominance of the entire area. Yet to attain this goal it was necessary to force the acquiescence of certain gentry, late of Dodge City.

Wyatt Earp was on the rustlers' list of major nuisances for two principal reasons. In addition to being a deputy sheriff he had been rewarded—as much for his Republicanism as for his prowess—by being appointed deputy United States Marshal for the district. That combination, plus the fact that he was secretly in the employ of the Wells, Fargo Express Company, kept him in contact with the outlaws on a number of fronts. How much his enemies guessed about his connections with Wells, Fargo it is hard to say, but he flashed his two peace officer badges at them with irritating frequency. Moreover, he had the backing of mighty gunmen whenever he stood in need of it. Chief among these was Doc.

It has often been said that Doc was the real leader of the Earp faction, but that was probably not so, any more than it is true that he was a follower of Wyatt's. He was a partisan who would go the limit in backing a friend up, but all that can be learned about him adds up to prove that he was a lone walker, to whom giving orders was as foreign as to receive them. Earp himself repeatedly testified that Doc wasn't called upon to help in the tough spots. He simply showed up at the right time with his gun ready.

There had no doubt been previous incidents, but Doc's active involvement in the feud cannot be traced to earlier than the late summer of 1880. At this time Sherman McMasters—not to be confused, though he sometimes is, with a Clanton follower of the same last name—informed Wyatt that he had spotted the latter's missing horse in Charleston. Wyatt went down to the river town to see about it, but his own statement, made in court, shows that this was not the solo expedition described in certain accounts.

"Myself and Doc Holliday happened to go to Charleston," this testimony affirms. "We went there for the purpose of getting a horse that had been stolen a few days after I got to Tombstone." He then went on to say that Billy Clanton had tried to ride the horse out of town but was intercepted and forced to give it up.

Inevitably Doc himself was put on the list of those not wanted by the region's organized outlaws. Inevitably, too, the result was to doghouse him where the politicians who throve by protecting those gangsters were concerned.

John C. Frémont, a wonderful explorer and a wretched territorial governor, was then head man in Prescott, where he spent as little time as possible. Not venal himself but criminally negligent, he had allowed his authority to be taken over by anybody who cared to. On the spot was a fine group of high-binders who welcomed the opportunity Frémont handed them. They had connections with county and local governments throughout Arizona, and where an adequate representative was lacking, they sent one. Having already proved his reliability as the territorial representative of two different counties and as sheriff of one of them, John Behan was entrusted with organizing the newly developed eastern half of Pima, for which larger plans were already afoot.

Wyatt Earp made it easy for the man he was later to recognize as his arch-enemy by paving the way for him. There was dissatisfaction with Sheriff Shibell's *laissez-faire* policy towards criminal activities, and Deputy Sheriff Earp shared it. When an opposing faction announced plans to run a man called Robert Paul on a let's-get-action ticket, Wyatt declared that he would back Paul, and handed in his resignation. Glad to be rid of a deputy with finicky notions about the importance of enforcing the law, Sheriff Shibell restored the *status quo* by appointing tried and true John Behan in his place.

What the boys on the inside knew, that Wyatt in all likelihood did not, was that a new county would be formed the
next year. Whether Shibell was re-elected or not was therefore of small moment to Tombstone, though the outlaws and
their political protectors fought for him, as they wanted the
continuance in office of a collaborating Pima County sheriff. It
was in an effort to intimidate the opposition that Curly Bill
organized a raid on Tombstone in the fag end of October
1880.

The town at this period had only a provisional government,
whose officers were largely engaged in the pursuit of personal
profit. Mayor Randall and his collaborators had sold half the
town-site to his cronies. They were preparing to dispose of the
rest when the citizens awoke to what was going on. As diarist
George Parsons was one of these, the struggle to take back
Tombstone from the mayor can be followed in detail; but only
one phase of it is pertinent here. Those who banded to cope with
Randall and his associates formed the nucleus of the vigilante
group which later backed the Earps in their struggle against the
Clantons.

In the meantime, only one of Tombstone's public servants
seemed to feel the responsibilities of municipal office. That was
Town Marshal Fred White.

When Curly Bill led his crew into town, with intent to
hoorah it, White did not hold back, as he could have been
pardoned for doing in the absence of backing from his superiors.
Having no deputies, he appealed to the Earps—including Doc—
for help in rounding up the raiders.

In the course of the fracas that followed Fred White was
slain by Curly, and it was Doc—as he himself remarked to an
interviewing newspaperman—who incurred the wrath of the
outlaw leader by putting him under arrest. For some decades
Western chroniclers have differed as to whether the exploit of
jailing Bill should be credited to Virgil Earp or Wyatt. It was not
Doc's practice to deny anything, including his own life, to one,
in particular, of this pair of brothers, but at the same time he could
hardly have foreseen that their partisans—writing decades later—
would stake out claims for them to this undertaking. Doc's
personal claim dated from 1882, and he plainly saw nothing to
get excited about. Far from trying to dramatize it or play it up

into a major feat of arms, he treated the matter with casual brevity.

"Trouble first arose with them," he said in the course of describing his difficulties with the cowboys of southern Arizona to a Denver reporter, "by the killing of Marshal White by Curly Bill. Marshal White fell into my arms when he was shot and I arrested Curly Bill."

Trouble with the same men broke out the following week, when the outlaws came into town to stand with guns beside the sundry polling places. On this occasion they were anticipated, and the forces backing Bob Paul for sheriff of Pima County stymied the invasion by posting two armed men to watch each one sent by the Clantons.

In spite of thus being defeated in Tombstone, Shibell was declared to have carried the county. The decision was challenged and reversed, largely through the enterprise of Wyatt. That took some months to bring about, however. While waiting for the court to unravel the case, Paul took Earp's old place as Wells, Fargo shot-gun guard on the bullion stages.

One thing which gave the Earp forces a boost also occurred at this time. Presumably at the insistence of the nascent law-and-order party, White was replaced by another officer who meant business. The new Town Marshal was Virgil Earp. That gave the clan a new peace officer's badge to replace the one Wyatt had forfeited by supporting Paul. Wyatt, it will be recalled, still retained his post as deputy United States Marshal.

For reasons not given, Virgil was not on the ticket at Tombstone's first regular election in January 1881, which was marked by other personnel changes. Mayor Randall had recently decamped because, as Parsons delicately put it, he "didn't like the smell of hemp". Voted into office was John P. Clum. Formerly an Indian agent, wise enough to win the confidence of most Apaches and tough enough to throttle Geronimo's early efforts at rebellion, Clum was a first-rate newspaperman, too. In May of 1880 he had started the *Tombstone Epitaph*, making it the organ of citizens opposed to rule by violence and skulduggery.

The turn of the year brought an event of even greater significance. On January 8, the act creating Cochise County out of the eastern half of Pima County was duly signed by Governor Frémont, who took no further interest in proceedings. His

H

indifference, and the resulting choice of officers for the infant county, form an important contribution to Tombstone's central tale.

What is still true of most Western States was even more the case seventy-odd years ago. The sheriff was by long odds the most significant county officer, not to mention the one best nourished on fees and patronage. Under Arizona's territorial charter he was even the tax collector, and he got a cut from property transactions as well as from about everything else that went on. In a rich mining county like Cochise the potential take was big.

The logical candidates for sheriff were Behan and Earp. As a Republican, Wyatt might have been considered a cinch as an appointee of a G. O. P. administration which had few constituents to choose from. Frémont's tendency to leave everything to his subordinates made the matter a toss-up. The latter belonged to the territorial Democratic organization which controlled the bestowal of all patronage which Frémont did not claim.

Behan was their man, and the odds established by precedent favoured him; still nobody was sure of what Frémont would do. Behan, therefore, took steps to get Wyatt out of the picture. Approaching him, he promised the post of chief deputy and a sizeable percentage of the expected revenue if he withdrew his candidacy for sheriff. Feeling he was getting a good bargain, in view of Frémont's undependability, Wyatt made a deal with him.

When the appointment was duly awarded to the sole applicant, Behan did not put Earp on his staff. In the first place he could not afford to outrage his colleagues by appointing a Republican. In the second place he had no more use than Shibell did for an operative who might try to enforce the law on people who could otherwise be depended on to pay off

Among those that Behan did appoint as deputies were Frank Stilwell, the region's champion stage robber, and a horse-thief named Gates, who seems to have been the one that borrowed Wyatt's nag. Others were Dave Neagle and William Breakenridge. The latter did not play a leading part in the Tombstone feud but was important as a man who lived to publish a lively and cheerful account of his own knavery in the role of Behan's henchman.

It is a curious fact that Breakenridge left a host of admirers who chose—and the survivors still elect to do so—to deny the rascality in which he so obviously rejoiced. But it is all in *Helldorado* for anybody without personal feelings in the matter to read and chuckle over with him. He must have been a likeable old high binder, just as in his younger days he was a clever and uninhibited scamp.

It was he who got Curly Bill to help him shake down taxpayers who were loath to pay to a sheriff's office which was offering them no protection against outlaw depredations. It was he also who set down in words of one syllable just how Behan and his deputies protected the rustlers from the consequences of their law-breaking. This friendly co-operation included tipping the rustlers off that the heat was on, seeing to it that they were heeled after they had been disarmed, and even springing them from jail, once they had been arrested. If what Breakenridge flatly stated Behan did is not to be interpreted as downright and deliberate collusion with known criminals, acts have no meaning and words no significance.

The political organization of which Behan was the local king-pin was a tightly knit one. The treasurer of Cochise County was John Dunbar, partner of Behan in a livery stable, and former member of the territorial legislature which had voted Cochise County into being. The man who had taken the floor lead in putting this measure across was a Solon named H. M. Woods. He followed up his success by turning up in Tombstone as one of Behan's deputies.

He also became publisher of the *Tombstone Nugget*, which was the official organ of the county political ring and the defender of the rustlers in all their works. This newspaper was owned by a Prescott string-puller named Hugo Richards, credited with being the man responsible for getting the territorial capital moved from its natural locus at Tucson to Prescott. He was also largely responsible for the move to break up Pima County. This at once dealt Tucson another blow and furnished elegant patronage for such faithful party-liners as Messrs. Behan, Dunbar and Woods.

Speaking with reference to Tombstone, the protection line ran directly from the inner council of the dominant clique at the territorial capital down through an efficient and dependable county organization, and so to an outlaw band astraddle

an international boundary. This band, moreover, was growing
in strength and enterprise as the new leadership offered by Curly
Bill and Ringo gradually wrested the control away from the
more conservative hands of Old Man Clanton.

Now here was an ointment that shouldn't have had any flies
in it. There turned out to be at least four, of whom three were
named Earp and the other Holliday. It gradually became apparent
that nothing would work as it should while they remained on
deck. Controlling Tombstone, they prevented the politico-
gangster ring from developing all the lucrative shakedown rackets
which would otherwise have been feasible. In forays out of town,
they carried the war to highway robbers who would otherwise
have met with small interference.

Personal antagonisms added to the general fury created by
this blocking. These have been dealt with in some measure in
other accounts, but none has previously traced Doc's private
differences with certain king-pins of the opposition.

Chief among these, of course, was the sheriff. "A word
further about this man Behan," Doc told a reporter. "I have
known him a long time. He first ran against me when I was
running a faro bank, when he started a quarrel in my house,
and I stopped him and refused to let him play any more. We
were enemies after that. In the quarrel I told him in the presence
of a crowd that he was gambling with money which I had given
his woman. This story got out and caused him trouble. He always
hated me after that, and would spend money to have me killed."

There are a couple of versions of what started Frank
McLowry's enmity towards Doc. One runs to the effect that the
quarrel, as was the case with Behan, took place over gambling.
The other asserts that the disagreement occurred at Nellie
Cashman's Russ House, where Doc's gun forced Frank to quit
beefing about the food served by the admired and respected land-
lady. Whatever the true reason, bad blood certainly existed, and
it may have gone into action of which the record is now lost.
McLowry's last words implied that he had tried to kill Doc at
least once before their final encounter.

Presumably it was Under-Sheriff H. M. Woods of the
Nugget whom Doc called upon to express his distaste for sensational journalism. If that is mere guesswork, it is established
that he helped foil an effort to ruin the biggest gambling joint in

town, which was taking the play away from one owned by the political ring.

W. H. Harris, late of the Long Branch at Dodge City, had been lured to Tombstone by the amounts being tossed on the boards there. So had a big-time operative from San Francisco called Lou Rickabaugh. The two had gone in partnership to buy out the Oriental Saloon, situated on the north-east corner of Allen and Fifth.

Rickabaugh was no lily. Eddie Foy asserted that when he played in Tombstone he saw Lou shoot a trouble-maker and order the corpse to be tossed out in the gutter, without losing either his temper or track of the cards. Nevertheless, he was not able to cope with the band of toughs which began to heckle the customers nightly under the leadership of a gunman called Johnny Tyler. Faced with this dilemma, the owners of the Oriental took Wyatt into partnership.

In consequence Earp was there to observe when Tyler and his warriors started cutting up the night after the new partnership was established. He carried the fight to Johnny himself, but it was Doc, by Wyatt's own statement, who kept the gangster's twelve followers from interfering. They were all lined up in front of Holliday's nickel-plated forty-five, when Wyatt gave Tyler the bounce.

In between innings Doc's life took other courses. There was Kate to be alternately liked for old times' sake and endured with what patience a choleric man could muster. The mistake at Dodge City had not been repeated, however. There was no nonsense about calling her Mrs. Holliday in Tombstone. She was Big Nose Kate Elder, a whore he lived with when she felt like it. There was thus no strain on his pride, whenever she flounced off to try some other brand of cat-nip. By the same token there were no strings on him while she was away. Witness his declaration of war on Behan, he was betimes having dealings with other women.

His informal *ménage* made him an object of criticism for Tombstone's better element, but its members might as well have tried to bring a rhinoceros down with spit balls. Doc was oblivious to the normal social pressures of community life. At Dodge City he had been vulnerable because of his fondness for Kate and because his personal pride was under assault. Here where he was subject to nothing more than adverse public opinion, he was utterly unconcerned.

In spite of many explosions, the feud with Kate remained a stalemate until March of 1881. Then an event took place which motivated and channelled all the hot action of the ensuing fourteen months. This was an attempted hold-up of the Benson stage.

A Benson correspondent of the *Phoenix Herald* told what happened in a dispatch dated March 15, which was the day of the occurrence. "On the arrival of the coach Grand Central of the Kinnear & Co. Line, this evening, it had sad freight of one man in his death-shoes, from the assassins bullet. The stage changed horses as usual at Drew's station, half-way between Tombstone and Benson, and as it was crossing a large arroyo about three hundred yards after leaving the station the highwaymen ordered it to halt at which the driver 'Bud' said to them 'hold up', but as they spoke they also shot, and it is supposed killed the driver as he fell between the wheel-horses. In an instant R. H. Paul, Wells, Fargo & Co.'s messenger, brought his gun to bear, and at his first shot one was seen to reel as if hit. The result of the second shot was not known. The robbers continued firing, striking Peter Roerig in the left side, of which he died at 9 p.m., soon after arrival here. Paul and Renshaw, the station agents, have gone to the scene of the fight. There were four men supposed to be white men who made the attack. The driver's name was Eli Philpot, commonly known as Bud. The passenger's name who was killed was Peter Roerig, a native of Kenosha, Wisconsin."

If this unsigned letter didn't respect certain grammatical nuances, it was pretty good reporting. He got all the facts in except the provenance of Philpot, a deficit made up by a more literary-minded correspondent a few days later. "Bud Philpot, the stage-driver who was killed on the San Pedro below Contention City, night before last, was strictly a frontier man. He was born in an emigrant wagon on the Platte on a cold, blustery day in April 1859. It may be said of him, like Victor Hugo, that he was born on the march."

It could also be said of him that he died in March, leaving a great deal of excitement behind him. Frightened by the shots fired, both by the would-be robbers and the guard, the horses had run away. This had forced Paul to give up the fight in favour of recovering the trailing reins. By the time he had succeeded in getting the panic-stricken animals under control the stage had reached Benson.

Bob Paul was the man who had run against Charlie Shibell for sheriff of Pima County. He was thus the man Wyatt Earp had resigned to support, and the one the rustler gang had worked so hard to defeat. With help from Wyatt, Paul had proved on a recount that he had actually won the election he was declared to have lost. Shibell promptly appealed the matter in court and kept the star while judgment was pending. Sweating out the decision, which was ultimately handed down in his favour, sheriff-elect Paul put in his time guarding stages—as heretofore noted.

Ordinarily it was the sheriff of Cochise County that would have been first notified, but Paul knew too much of Behan's alliance with the rustlers to consider such a course useful. Instead he sent a wire to Wyatt Earp. The latter had no jurisdiction where ordinary robbery or theft was concerned, but the stage had also carried mail. As a deputy United States Marshal, Earp had grounds for taking up the case, and he therefore made for Drew's station.

What Wyatt discovered and found out from Paul was reported in part by still another letter from Benson to the *Phoenix Herald*, dated March 16. Referring to the robbers, this missive stated that "they were four in number, had wigs and beards of rope yarn and their trail led east as if starting for San Simon. It is not known whether either of them was hit. The driver was killed instantly. Fifteen shells, Winchester model of 1879, were found at the scene of the shooting."

The nature of the false beards was ascertainable because they had been left behind along with the cartridge shells. Returning to Tombstone, Wyatt paid no heed to Sheriff Behan's efforts to discourage pursuit. Instead he deputized Virgil and Morgan Earp; Marshal Williams, the local Wells, Fargo agent; Bat Masterson and Bob Paul. They rode forth at dawn.

Wyatt did not deputize Doc Holliday, although Doc had been standing by ever since the news from Benson had reached town, for a quite sufficient reason. What Earp had learned from Bob Paul convinced him that one of the robbers was Doc's old pal, Bill Leonard, formerly of Las Vegas.

Seeing Earp go into action, Behan trailed along, taking Breakenridge with him. Observers merely, they took no part until the deputy United States Marshal's posse finally caught one of the four bandits, an outlaw named Luther King. Behan then claimed the prisoner on the ground that the actual crime of murder would take precedence over the attempted one of interfering with the mail. Against this point Wyatt could scarcely argue. He led his men in pursuit of the remaining three, leaving the sheriff to take King back to jail.

Behan did take the bandit as far as Tombstone, though Jim Hume, a Wells, Fargo trouble-shooter who had been sent out from San Francisco, asserted that King was never brought as far as the sheriff's office. But whether the event took place in the courthouse, or in a private residence as per Hume's contention, this much is agreed upon by several observers of the current scene: entrusted to the custody of Under-Sheriff Woods, the rustler was allowed to postpone his incarceration while he sold his horse to County Treasurer John Dunbar, partner of Behan in the ownership of a livery stable. While Dunbar was busy drawing up the bill of sale, and while the trusting Under-Sheriff was paying attention to this fascinating operation rather than to his prisoner, that scoundrel sneaked out of a side door, never to darken it or any other Tombstone entry or exit again.

Up to this time the average Tombstone citizen had not known much about Behan, then only two months in office. The feeling which the potential vigilantes came to have for him probably started with this incident. "King, the stage robber, escaped tonight early from H. Woods who had been previously notified of an attempt at release to be made," Parsons confided to his journal. "Some of our officials should be hanged. They are a bad lot."

Catching this undertone, the county politicos realized that some explanation had to be made. Going to work on the problem, they came up with a counter-attack which was executed in the columns of the *Tombstone Nugget*, of which Woods himself was the publisher.

The posse pursuing Leonard, Crane and Head meanwhile had a rough time of it. Following the rustlers through country where the outlaws could always get hospitality and fresh mounts —both of which were denied to the peace officers—they had been utterly worn down. Finally Leonard *et al* had slipped over the border and the posse had returned to Tombstone.

There they learned that they themselves were accused of planning the robbery. The word was that Wyatt Earp and Marshal Williams had cooked it up. Bob Paul was in on it and had not really tried to return the outlaws' fire. As for the hold-up men, one of them was Doc Holliday; indeed it was he and none other who had fired the shot which killed Bud Philpot. Bat Masterson seems to have been left out of the reckoning, but the other two Earps were implicated. Somehow, operating by remote control, they had managed to arrange for King's escape. "It was a well-planned job by an outsider," the *Nugget* commented darkly, "to get him away. He was an important witness against Holliday."

The case against Paul was that he was in the driver's seat when the stage reached Benson, in place of the defunct Philpot. Wood's minions of the *Nugget* tried to popularize the notion that Paul had been there all along, having talked the driver into swapping places with him. This was no sale because of its absurdity, as a robber would never have armed Philpot, a man who was not in on the game. Moreover, if Paul, acting as an accomplice, had been at the reins, he could have halted the team and made the robbery an easy success instead of a messy failure.

The case against Marshal Williams was that nobody would have been aware that bullion was being transported on the stage in question unless somebody in the know had sent word. John Clum, writing in the *Epitaph*, made short work of that contention. "Whenever treasure is shipped, a messenger is sent on that stage; when there is no treasure, there is no guard," Clum asserted. "Under these circumstances any intelligent person can deduce whether the coach is *en bonanza* or *en borusca*."

The case against the Earps was that they were known associates of the others. No further circumstances were adduced to support the charges against them, although the *Nugget* was full of suspicions which it did not withhold from the public.

The case against Doc Holliday was built on a couple of facts hitched to at least one untruth and a string of assumptions. "On the afternoon of the attempted robbery he engaged a horse at a Tombstone livery, stating that he might be gone for seven or eight days, or might return that night. He left town about four o'clock armed with a Henry rifle and a six-shooter. He started for Charleston, and about a mile below Tombstone cut across to

Contention. When next seen, it was between ten and one o'clock at night, riding back into the livery at Tombstone, his horse fagged out. He at once called for another horse which he hitched in the street for some hours, but he did not again leave town."

The facts were that Doc had ridden forth from Tombstone and that he ordered a second horse some hours after he returned. The falsehood was that he had not come back until about ten o'clock, for when the show-down eventually came, there was ample court testimony to prove that he had returned several hours earlier. The rest consisted of speculation. This can be confidently claimed, inasmuch as the man who shadowed him—far enough to see him "cut across to Contention" from a point "a mile below Tombstone", for instance—was never named.

The only circumstance the *Nugget* omitted was the one they could count on everybody knowing. Doc, as he himself would be the last to deny, was a friend of Leonard's. What's more he had advertised the fact by riding down river to visit the outlaw in his roost near Drew's station from time to time.

But it was up river that he had headed on March 15. "As for riding out of town with my six-gun and rifle, I did go over to Charleston that afternoon, and as it's the hang-out of certain persons who dislike me intensely, I went prepared for any attentions they might offer." He had gone there, Doc went on to say, because he had heard of a lively poker game. It had broken up by the time he arrived, hence his early return. He had ordered the second horse after hearing of the robbery, in case Wyatt asked him to join a posse. As this had not happened he had spent the night dealing cards as usual.

In itself the accusation did not feaze Doc at all, nor did it make any difference to him whether people believed it or not. The only thing that disturbed him was the thought that his name was connected with a bungled crime. "If I had pulled that job," he protested, "I'd have got the eighty thousand. Whoever shot Philpot was a rank amateur. If he had downed a horse, he'd have got the bullion."

For the time being, the hurt to Doc's vanity was the most dangerous injury caused by the *Nugget's* charges. Meanwhile the story of Tombstone was enriched by another episode.

CHAPTER VIII

ALTHOUGH pushed somewhat into the background by the strangely balanced combination of Curly Bill and Johnny Ringo, Old Man Clanton remained titular head of the rustlers. This was so much the case that the gang still bore his name for months after he was fertilizing scrub cactus in Tombstone's Boot Hill.

He was not yet so engaged in early summer of 1881, however. Knowing more of the international smuggling trade than the newcomers, he it was who led a picked group of gunmen through one of the secret passes, used by upholders of the principle of free trade from both sides of the border. In addition to Ringo and Brocius the expedition included Ike and Billy Clanton, Frank McLowry, Joe Hill and Rattlesnake Bill Johnson.

In a gash in the Chiricahuas fittingly called Skeleton Canyon, the Clantons ambushed a crew of Mexicans and hijacked seventy-five thousand dollars' worth of silver bullion. Some nineteen smugglers died of dry gulching; and international goodwill found a new low a short time afterwards. Curly Bill and Johnny led a cattle raid into Sonora, killed fourteen Mexican ranch hands and had themselves some fun torturing a few that they caught alive.

Old Man Clanton wasn't in on that particular deal, but he contracted to handle the stock which the raiders drove north. That turned out to be a mistake. Riding on the trail of the stolen herd, a bunch of Mexicans ambushed him, settling, among other things, all dispute as to the leadership of the Cochise County outlaws. Curly Bill furnished the executive and organizing energy thereafter. Ringo supplied plans and inspiration when he felt like it. There were times when he didn't, and then it was not necessary for him to hang out a "Please Do Not Disturb" sign. No doubt there had been others beside Louis Hancock who had died to punctuate one of Johnny's black days. In any case it is on record that when his associates saw the storm clouds piling on that intellectual brow, they tip-toed away and left him to his Latin.

A by-product of Old Man Clanton's demise was that Jim Crane—one of the would-be robbers of the Benson stage as well as one of the certified murderers of Philpot and Roerig—was shot down along with him. At about the same time Bill Leonard and Harry Head got killed while attempting to hold up a store belonging to the brothers Haslett in Huachita, New Mexico.

As Luther King showed no intention of riding that range again, and Doc's friend Leonard lived long enough to confess the whole business before cashing in his last chip, the case would seem to have been pretty well wound up and disposed of. As far as results were concerned, it had a long way to run. Meanwhile there had been a development that nearly did for Doc.

What really caught up with him was a law of nature. The man who once attempts to make a wedding veil out of a night-gown must eventually pay for his folly. He will also incur the hatred of the party of the second part when he finds out his mistake. Such a liaison as that shared by Doc and Kate should have been cut with a knife when it became a nuisance to him, and it undoubtedly would have been except for his dogged insistence on paying his debt. If the result had certain comic aspects, Doc himself was in no position to enjoy the fun.

As far as Kate was concerned, the situation might have been considered highly satisfactory, in view of her limited domestic ideals. She had an arrangement which allowed her to do as she wished, while furnishing as much in the way of a permanent alliance as she desired. But rugged individualist though she was, there was enough femininity in her make-up to lead her to covet something that was not in the cards as she dealt them. When she was in the mood for Doc's company she wanted his admiration and affection.

In consequence Doc still retained the power to hurt her feelings. This is a known fact and not guesswork, because when Doc expressed his opinion of her in the privacy of their boudoir, she would go on a toot and air her wrongs in public. Alluded to in the memoirs of various contemporaries, these threnodies for outraged love were not quoted. They can, however, be easily imagined by anyone who has ever observed a lusty tart saturated with booze and self-pity. Whoever wanted to listen could hear about everything from the lynch mob at Fort Griffin to Doc's latest ungrateful remark, and anybody who didn't want to hear had better get at least a block away.

Among those who did wish to give ear was the indefatigable John Behan. When Doc thus drove Kate to drink and the recitation of her woes early in July of 1881, the sheriff did not show boredom at an old tale, already many times told. Instead he and County Supervisor Mike Joyce decided they wanted to comfort this tortured soul. Inviting Kate to join them, they bought her all the liquor she wanted, agreed with her that Doc was a villainous ingrate, and cheered her up by throwing in some criticism of their own.

When they emerged from this conference Kate was blind drunk, and the two county officials were in possession of a document. Although they had drawn it up, she had affixed her signature below. This deposition was to the effect that John H. Holliday had indeed been one of the men who tried to hold up the Benson stage.

On the strength of this accusation Behan arrested Doc for complicity in the above-mentioned crime. To quote the *Phoenix Herald* of July 12, 1881, which in turn quoted the *Tombstone Nugget* of July 8: "A warrant has been sworn out before Justice Spicer for the arrest of Doc Holliday, a well-known character here, charging him with complicity in the murder of Bud Philpot and the attempted stage robbery near Contention some four months ago. The warrant was issued upon the affidavit of Kate Elder, with whom Holliday has been living for some time past. Holliday was taken before Judge Spicer in the afternoon, who released him upon bail being furnished in the amount of $5,000, W. Earp, J. Meagher and J. L. Melgren becoming sureties. The examination will take place before Judge Spicer."

In addition to ponying up the money to free Doc, Wyatt got his brother, City Marshal Virgil Earp, to put Big Nose Kate in jail and out of touch with liquor. Sobered up, she testified at the trial that she had signed some sort of paper while tossing drinks with Behan and Joyce, but she said she could not remember what was on it.

That was not all the testimony which favoured Doc. A man named Fuller, usually called Old Man to distinguish him from his son Wes, stated that Doc had not returned to town late on the night of March 15, as charged by the *Nugget*. He knew this to be a fact, because when he was heading towards Tombstone in the wagon with which he hauled water for that city, Doc had caught up with him at about four in the afternoon of the day in question. Holliday had, moreover, hitched his horse at the tail of the water-wagon and climbed into the seat with Fuller. Riding in this manner, they had reached Tombstone something after 6 p.m. The hour was of some importance, as by that time the Benson stage had left for the haul down the valley to Benson.

Wes Fuller was an apprentice gangster whose testimony was later used in an effort to hang Doc. His father might have been expected to take the Clanton side, if any, but Old Man Fuller was not gaited that way. Nor was he the only one who was sure Doc had not stirred out of town on the evening in question. In addition to Wyatt himself, who had talked to Doc just after receiving the wire from Bob Paul, a number of men testified that they had seen Doc dealing faro at the Alhambra on the night of all the excitement about the stage robbery.

There were other repercussions, but for Doc the one of the most immediate importance was that it marked the end of an obligation. Accounts had finally been squared with Big Nose Kate. She had saved his life, putting him in a durance that was at first pleasurable and next a lasting pain in the neck. Now she had come within an ace of being his bane. Everything was nicely balanced, and they were through. He closed the books by giving her a thousand dollars and telling her that she had to get out of town.

For once Kate didn't argue. She knew Doc well enough to realize that, even leaving the jeopardy in which she had placed him out of account, she had done the one thing he could not forgive. Other infidelities he might stomach, but not that of turning up in the enemy camp in time of war. She left Tombstone forthwith and never again attempted, so far as can be determined, to communicate with the man who had meant so much and so little to her.

Notwithstanding those developments, the accusations tossed by the *Nugget* were believed by many. If they did not bother Doc, they did cause embarrassment to Wyatt. As the field general of Tombstone's law and order party he had a hard time explaining why his chief associate was a man known to have been an outlaw in the past and accused of being one still.

Even before the blow-up resulting from Big Nose Kate's furious spree, Earp had felt the pressure and had been working hard to relieve it. Seeing that the only way to remove suspicion from Doc was to bring Leonard, Head and Crane to trial, he had talked Wells, Fargo into offering a substantial reward for their apprehension. He had then gone to Ike Clanton, whom he had figured as a double-crosser, and offered him the entire sum in exchange for his co-operation.

Ike had run true to estimated form by agreeing, but he had surprised Earp by bringing in Frank McLowry. The latter's willingness to play ball may in part have been due to factional undercurrents among the outlaws. Both he and Clanton belonged to the original cadre of rustlers which was being superseded by the Curly Bill-Ringo combine.

Whatever the motivating forces, though, McLowry and Ike Clanton agreed to arrange a trap for the stage robbers. Their one provision, not counting acceptance of all the reward money, was that no word of their duplicity must reach their gangster colleagues. In Cochise County then, just as in Chicago or Kansas City now, stool pigeons were promptly rubbed out.

As related above, the stage robbers got themselves involved in fatal trouble, Crane dying with Old Man Clanton and the other two in New Mexico. This at once spoiled Earp's plan and made it kick back on him.

Deprived of the reward money, Ike Clanton and Frank McLowry still saw themselves faced with the danger that winning it would have entailed. Johnny Ringo and Bill might find out that they had *planned* to sell out three members of the gang. The two worried outlaws increased the frequency of their visits to Tombstone in order to check on bar-room gossip.

Wyatt Earp had not talked. He had not told Doc, because the latter would not have liked to know about a plot to ensnare his friend, Bill Leonard. He had not even talked to Marshal Williams, the Wells, Fargo agent. Tombstone's telegraph station was in the express company's office, however, and Williams had thus been able to read the exchange of messages between Earp and Wells, Fargo headquarters in San Francisco.

Making his own deductions, the agent had had sense enough

to keep them to himself for several months. An extra cargo of hooch had finally opened the flood-gates of speech then. Proud of his shrewdness in figuring out the plot, he babbled of what Clanton and McLowry had been up to.

Even before that the rustlers had been working up steam. In the middle of October 1881, they and several associates had caught Morgan Earp walking along a street unarmed and alone. To him they gave the warning that the Earps and Doc Holliday would be killed if they didn't pull out of town. That was only one threat of many issued directly and broadcast generally. The peril to City Marshal Virgil Earp and his small corps of allies had even become a matter of common knowledge. It was well known as far away as Tucson, where the *Star* reported that if the Earps had not been men of more than ordinary spunk they would have recognized the odds against them by throwing in the towel.

The indiscretion of Williams had piled wood on this fire by making Frank McLowry jittery and Ike Clanton panic-stricken. Doc returned from a gambling expedition to Tucson to find that Ike was in Tombstone engaged in contradictory activities. With one side of his mouth he was denying everything and ascribing the rumours spread by Williams to an Earp plot to ruin him. With the other side he was charging Earp with having betrayed details of the conspiracy to Doc Holliday.

Dubbing that a lie, Doc went forth to interview Ike. He was incensed on more ground than one. He did not blame Wyatt for trying to trap the stage robbers, even though they included his friend, Bill Leonard. Earp himself owed no loyalty to Leonard and his efforts to arrest the bandits came within the legitimate bounds of his duties. The case of Ike Clanton was filed in a different cabinet. As a fellow gangster, Ike was bound in blood not to betray Leonard and the rest, let alone compound the treachery by attempting to profit in cash.

It was in bitter anger, therefore, that Doc sought Clanton out and read the riot act to him in tones that could be heard for a couple of blocks in any direction. In retaliation Ike sketched plans for killing Holliday and the Earp brotherhood in the near future. For the present, however, he elected to leave Tombstone and talk things over with Frank McLowry, east away in the Sulphur Springs valley.

Apparently Ike also took counsel with his brother, Billy, and with Tom McLowry, for it was in their company that he and Frank rode into Charleston a couple of days later. In the mill town on the San Pedro they added Billy Claiborne to their party by springing him from jail. Young Claiborne had been in hokey for killing one of several men he had shot in an effort to earn his chosen name of Billy the Kid. This he could safely do in as much as the original owner of that soubriquet had recently forfeited his claim to it, Sheriff Pat Garrett officiating.

There was, according to the gangster law of all ages, and places, but one way in which Ike and Frank could disprove the charge that they had been guilty of trying to co-operate with the law. They had to attack the peace officers they were supposed to have conspired with. This is what they now planned to do, and they reported as much to their associates. Pleased, Curly Bill and Johnny Ringo spread the news. They even headed a pub-crawl of gangsters which let the patrons of every saloon on Allen Street know just what was in store for Doc, Wyatt, Virgil and Morgan.

The law-and-order party had likewise concluded that the time for action had arrived. Reluctant to take the step at first, they formed a vigilante unit which sided with the city administration and opposed the Cochise County regime. "The situation in Tombstone," as Mayor John P. Clum later said, "was aggravated by the general feeling among the citizens that the peace officers of the county under Sheriff John Behan were in sympathy with the lawless element which roamed south-eastern Arizona and it was deemed wise to guard against every possible depredation of these outlaws. Our plans for law enforcement and protection of our lives and property were fully and freely discussed with Wyatt Earp and his brother Virgil. This fact establishes beyond any question the high esteem and confidence which the leading citizens of Tombstone entertained towards both Wyatt and Virgil."

That feeling of confidence did not, it should be emphasized, extend as far as Doc Holliday. Clum himself once grumbled that—except when it came to his proficiency with weapons—Doc was an unfortunate choice as a representative of the better element. It must be allowed that he had a point there. From his open alliance with Big Nose Kate to his equally frank friendship for Bill Leonard, Doc's local record was not of the sort that the

I

disciples of law and order could properly endorse. As for his past record—familiar in lurid detail to all except rank greenhorns—it gave the sheriff and his allies too many pegs to hang their hats on.

But Doc stayed on as a titular member of the better element, because Wyatt had to have him. Some friends had been shot or had gone on to other camps. Bat Masterson left in order to answer the hurry call of a surviving brother, up against gun-play, as Ed had been, in Dodge City. The ready guns with which to stand off the growing strength of the outlaws were all too few.

Doc, meanwhile, had just as soon have gone elsewhere as not. If the worthy citizens looked with a fishy eye upon him, he didn't give a belch in a brewery what happened to them. Nor was he concerned, as they were, to promote the welfare of the town and protect the source of their income. He had no issue except his friendship for a man, and nothing to gain but a fight that might be his ending.

How real that danger was is easy to demonstrate. It is estab-lished that in the course of the Earp-Clanton feud Doc Holliday came within a skinny cat's whisker of losing his life at least nine different times. Of these, four involved efforts to have him swing, while the remaining five entailed gun-play or ambush.

One such occasion had followed close upon his release on the charge of complicity in Bud Philpot's murder. Doc celebrated this court victory plus the exit from his life of Big Nose Kate, with earnest thoroughness. How much a man whose standard ballast was a couple of quarts thought he needed when tossing a spree is something that is difficult to compute. But whatever it took to do the job, Doc had it under his belt when he ran into County Supervisor Mike Joyce in company with an unnamed side-kick.

This was the only known occasion in Doc's history when he was past handling an emergency with finesse. But if he was not up to par when it came to action, his memory remained sound. Mike Joyce had sat in with Behan when the latter per-suaded Kate to sign the document intended as Holliday's death warrant.

While Doc was giving the supervisor his views on the matter, his enemies got near enough to make him the meat in their sandwich. Trying to make sure he wouldn't get a chance to draw, they suddenly jumped him from two directions.

Frail as Doc was, this rough and tumble was no contest; yet his attackers hardly had things their own way. Joyce was getting ready to shoot the man whom he and his partner had borne to the floor, but by the time other inmates of the saloon had hastened to break it up, Doc Holliday had already shot. Somehow, as he went down, he had managed to draw, pull trigger and score twice. For souvenir of the engagement Joyce had a hole in his left hand, while the other fellow got a bullet through one foot.

Behan and Wyatt, acting for once in unison, later saved Joyce's life. Aggrieved about his sore fist, the supervisor accosted Earp and Holliday, when the latter was in shape to handle himself. The sheriff dragged Mike away and Wyatt talked Doc into staying put. This was in all likelihood one of the occasions which led Bat Masterson—who had not yet left Tombstone then —to make one of his dicta about John Henry Holliday. Remarking on his affection for Wyatt Earp, Bat went on: "The depth of this sentiment was shown not only by Doc's demonstrated willingness to stake his life for Wyatt without second thought; it was even more clearly established by the fact that, despite his almost uncontrollable temper and his maniacal love of a fight, Doc Holliday could avoid trouble when there was a possibility that some encounter might prove embarrassing to Wyatt. On more than one occasion Doc actually backed down before men whom he easily could have killed, simply because gun-play at the time would have reacted unfavourably against Wyatt. To appreciate that fully, you had to know Doc."

Earp and Behan both had good reasons for wanting to avoid anything that would make headlines at this time. The sheriff had been caught out in an attempted frame-up and wished no further airing of the subject. At the same time his move had been successful to the extent that suspicion still clung to Doc in the minds of many. Wyatt accordingly was anxious for Doc to hold still until the affair had more or less blown over. He turned down, as he later stated, an offer of Doc's to blow town. Leaving the ties of friendship out of the question, that was something he could hardly afford. At the same time he was more aware than ever that his alliance with Holliday was dubious public relations. This, of course, was what the astute county politicos had long realized and capitalized upon.

It was on the basis of Doc Holliday—his outlaw record

padded with certain fabrications of their own—that they were able to create the myth of the Earp gang. It was one of their best strokes, for if it did not win the battle of Tombstone at the time, it nearly killed Doc by remote control, after he had left Arizona; and it dogged Wyatt Earp, to embitter the remainder of his long life. That life ended a quarter of a century ago, yet the tradition of the dark and mysterious gang is still strong enough to win belief in the teeth of evidence which gives it the lie.

Aside from fighting a crew whose thieveries and murders are a matter of record, what did the Earp gang do? Nobody can say, unless they point to the *Nugget* story designed to cover up the fact that the publisher of that paper let one of the real robbers leave his custody. This canard, that was left a dead duck when it was brought into court, is all that research can find which remotely hints at underworld activities on the part of the Earps.

The case of Doc was something else again. In addition to the fast gun-play which had made him an outlaw in two States and territories before he came to Arizona, he was a con man when occasion offered, and a very competent one. It is probable that he broke about every commandment in the decalogue, plus a few that Moses—who had not been to Fort Griffin Flat—had never dreamed of. Yet in spite of divers accusations there is nothing to show that he was ever involved in robbery, accomplished or intended. More than that, there is not the slightest proof that he was engaged in any gang activities. Only when he happened to be on the side of the law did he act in collusion with any group. Whatever he did lawlessly he did by himself or with a picked confederate.

That confederate, it can confidently be stated, was not one of the Earps. Wyatt was a cool, canny operative who knew how to turn opportunity to his advantage. He had, indeed, the instincts and competitive temperament which were later to turn him into a successful businessman. The accusation that he was crooked, above and beyond the canons of gambling or mercantile trading, has no foundations but hatred. The charge against his brothers can also be ranked as an absurdity.

Yet the tales told against them helped to divide the town's residents, as the struggle to decide who would control Tombstone built up to its first climax. The Earps were under pressure from all sides, and the fact that they felt this was responsible for delaying the show-down until it was almost past due.

Ike's visit and the subsequent gathering of Clanton forces at Charleston was the first warning that the time had finally come. Clanton's return on the night of October 25, made it an inevitability. What followed can be traced from court testimony and other reports of eye-witnesses.

Ike rode into Tombstone with Tom McLowry and spread boasts of vengeance in a succession of Allen Street saloons. Eventually these threats reached the ears of Doc Holliday, who decided to look Ike up. Finding him with a group of friends in the Occidental, Holliday braced him with characteristic directness. "Ike," he said, "I hear you're going to kill me. Get out your gun and commence."

When Ike answered that he was unarmed, Doc glared first at him and then at McLowry and told them that if they came to Tombstone making war-talk again, they had better go heeled. At this juncture Morgan Earp arrived to call Doc off. As Doc was acceding to his friend's request, Clanton and Tom McLowry took occasion to remark that they would not only take Doc's advice but would shoot him on sight.

Wyatt Earp, who was also drawn to the scene of the disturbance, persuaded Doc to call it a night. "A gun-fight now, with you in it, would ruin my chance to round up this bunch," he insisted.

Nevertheless, he had trouble keeping the peace himself when he met Ike a little later in the evening. Clanton announced that he was armed and full of fight. He was indubitably full of liquor, as Wyatt reminded Ike when the latter announced that he was now ready to get Holliday. "Go sleep it off," Wyatt advised him. "Doc will kill you." Ike, meanwhile, had changed the subject from Doc to that of the Earps. "You had the best of it tonight, but I'll have my friends tomorrow. You be ready for a show-down."

The next development was reported by John Clum. On the way to the office of the *Epitaph* on the morning of October 26, the mayor saw Ike standing on the corner of Fifth and Allen, armed with both a rifle and a revolver. Thinking he was being funny, Clum asked the rustler where the war was. When he reached his office, however, he found it abuzz with accounts

of Ike's activities of the night before. This was shortly supplemented with tidings wired from Charleston to the effect that
Frank McLowry, Billy Clanton and Claiborne had left for Tombstone. Before the morning was well advanced they had put in
their appearance.

It is manifest that up to this point, at least, Wyatt had hoped
to avoid an open engagement of the sort Ike claimed he was
planning. This was implicit in his decision to let Doc sleep to his
customary late hour. With Doc alerted, as he well knew, it would
be difficult to avoid picking up the challenges which his enemies
were again broadcasting.

At all events Doc was not called upon to participate when
the Earp brethren set out to round up the rustlers. Virgil caught
Ike, and Wyatt had an encounter with Tom McLowry. Both
rustlers were fined and deprived of their weapons by the magistrate's court to which they were hauled. As they were not jailed,
however, they promptly went forth and secured new arms.

That was known, because they were observed by many who
later testified to that effect. Their actions were being carefully
observed, not by officers or newspaper reporters but by excited
Tombstone citizens, anticipating the blow-off. The whole town
had heard the threats of the Clantons and the whole town knew
the choice facing the two factions.

There was apparently but one person in all of Tombstone
who was not aware that gunfire, blood and sudden death were
imminent unless one crew or the other begged off and quit.
That person was Dr. John Holliday, knocking it off in his room,
while the pot of big trouble was being brought to a boil.

CHAPTER IX

THE brothers Earp had made their headquarters in Hafford's Saloon, on the corner of Fourth and Allen. This was not a lucky accident. The owner, like Wyatt himself, was an undercover operative for Wells, Fargo.

As it turned out there was no need for his special information bulletins that day. Citizens of all sorts—the friendly, the hostile, and the merely curious—took it upon themselves to look the Earps up and keep them posted as to what the Clantons were doing. The rustlers were not leaving town. They were not checking their weapons while remaining in Tombstone. On the contrary, they were repeating their threats against the lives of the Earps and Doc, alternating them with assertions that the town's peace officers wouldn't dare to come and get them.

Among these who called at Hafford's was Sheriff John Behan. By the charter which made Tombstone a county seat the sheriff could be deputized to keep the peace in town, whenever the City Marshal saw that to be necessary. Behan, nevertheless, rejected Virgil Earp's request that the sheriff should go with him to disarm the Clantons, as the law demanded. He not only refused but when Virgil expressed his intention of throwing the outlaws in jail, Johnny said, "You try that, and they'll kill you." After making this statement, the sheriff went back to the O. K. Corral to report to the rustlers, for whom he was acting as lookout and liaison runner.

The fuse had burned that short on an explosive set of circumstances when Doc bestirred himself. The day was one on which his disease was felt as more of burden than usual. Wherefore, as was customary with him on such occasions, he leaned on a cane as he made his way to a restaurant. While eating breakfast he first learned of what was afoot.

Heading for Hafford's as soon as he'd gulped down his meal, he arrived just as the three Earps had come to a decision.

Whatever the outcome, the rustlers had to be faced. If they were not arrested and disarmed, Virgil would have to forfeit his post as City Marshal and all three of them would have to get out of that part of the country before the triumphant outlaws or a jeering citizenry hazed them out. More than the law of the land was involved here. There was the law of the West, decreeing that a personal issue could not be walked away from.

The odds against them had now increased. A vigilante who went to the O. K. Corral to case developments reported that the original five had been joined by Wes Fuller, outlaw son of the man whose testimony had saved Doc a few months before. The vigilante also reported that he had been stopped by the Clantons and given a message to deliver. This was to the effect that if the Earps didn't come to the O. K. Corral to fight it out they would have bullets in them before the day was over, anyhow.

That did it. Exchanging glances, the three brothers made for the street. They had just reached it when they were hailed by Doc, making it down Allen as fast as his cane could help him. Upon learning that the Earps had decided to have it out with the rustlers, he nodded his approval. "It's about time. I'll go along."

When Wyatt observed that there was no sense in Doc's getting mixed up in a fight that was essentially aimed at himself as an individual and at Virgil as the upholder of law and order in Tombstone, Doc was outraged. "That's a hell of a thing for you to say to me," he remarked.

The fact that Doc was then incorporated in the expedition represented a complete change in the attitude of the Earps. Starting out by trying to avoid a street fight—which they were clear-sighted enough to see as dangerous politically, in addition to the personal peril involved—they were now reconciled to the probability of its occurrence.

They did make one final effort to achieve a peaceable end, though. There was to be no show of arms as they approached the corral, where they would make a formal demand of the outlaws' weapons before taking further action. In conformance with this plan, Virgil gave his sawed-off shot-gun to Doc, who wore a long top-coat, taking Holliday's cane in exchange. Withdrawing an arm from one sleeve, Doc put the weapon out of sight, and the expedition was ready for its advance north one square up Fourth Street and west half a block on Fremont.

As half of Tombstone had been watching for just such a development, there are ample accounts of their progress to supplement the one left by Wyatt. The three Earps, all six-footers, wore the black affected by professional gamblers. They also wore set, grim expressions to match the business of the moment. Doc was nattily clad in light grey and was whistling to himself.

At the start of their march they saw John Behan standing with Frank McLowry at the corner of Fourth and Fremont. Hearing an onlooker's cry of "Here they come," the sheriff and the outlaw withdrew towards the O. K. Corral.

In common parlance this establishment was a livery stable, with open-air pens for nags at the rear. That much of it extended only to an alley which bisected the block from east to west. North of the alley property consisted of an open yard. Fencing it on the Fourth Street end was the studio of Arizona's pioneer photographer, C. S. Fly. The office of a mineral assayer furnished a wall on the Third Street side. It was against this adobe bulwark that the two Clantons, the two McLowrys and Claiborne had taken their stand. The sixth man, Wes Fuller, was posted in the alley, where he could both observe the progress of the enemy and guard against any surprise attack down this approach.

Noticing Fuller running back down the alley to announce their coming, Doc growled, "You ought to have cut him down."

He made this remark to Virgil, in the best position to have shot at Fuller, as the Marshal was in the lead and on the outside of Fourth Street's eastern walk. Behind him walked Morgan while Doc was tailing Wyatt. Arriving at Fremont, however, they broke column of twos to deploy. They then advanced west with Virgil on the inside. Wyatt was next, then came Morgan, with Doc on the north end of the line.

They were just short of Fly's studio when Behan ran up to them. Sheriff John has not received his due in a number of books about Tombstone, where he is portrayed as a bush leaguer in the big time. He was anything but that. He was a bold, clever man who did not baulk at harrying some of the most capable gun-slingers that the world has known. He accomplished that, not through any frontal attacks but by a succession of stratagems which kept them in hot water with the courts and the very people that the Earps—Doc need not be included here—were trying to defend.

Yet in this one sequence, Behan miscued several times in a row. There are explanations for his bungling, though. A situation he thought he had under control had got out of it, and his position was bad. He was a peace officer who had been seen openly hobnobbing with armed outlaws while these were challenging the duly appointed authorities of the town.

Behan had evidently counted on having a choice of two good things. If the Earps dodged fighting with the rustlers whom the sheriff had helped to egg on, they were finished right there. But if the Earps did pick up the challenge, Behan counted on his influence with the outlaws to enable him to steal their thunder. He would disarm the Clantons to become the hero of the day, making a fool of the Earps on a much-ado-about-nothing basis.

Only when Doc and the Earps were on their way did he find out that he had miscalculated all around. The Clantons refused to surrender their weapons to him, and what had looked like a beautiful situation had suddenly become a very ugly one for any sheriff of a county to be in.

For once he lost his head and did something silly. It should be borne in mind, however, that there were no easy outs from the box in which he had put himself. Finding that his allies would not play ball, he could see nothing for it but to try to hold off his enemies. He, therefore, ran to intercept the group of marshals and made an appeal to the very officer with whom he had laughingly refused to co-operate a short while before.

"It's all right," he told Virgil, "I've disarmed them."

A question brought out the fact that the outlaws had not been put under arrest, though Behan claimed he would correct that oversight immediately. "All right," City Marshal Earp took him up. "Come on."

But Behan had already discovered the fruitlessness of such an attempt. He made one effort to pull the rank he didn't have—for when it came to keeping the peace in Tombstone, the town's chief of police was in charge, not the county sheriff—and then ducked into Fly's studio. Safety in this case was only one motive. Windows from the photographer's shop overlooked the O. K. Corral, allowing any inmate to keep tabs on what transpired there.

After their brief pause to parley with Behan, the three men in black and the one in grey swept on to where their challengers waited. When they got as far as the corral yard, the Earps turned left from the street and slanted into it. Doc Holliday carried on for a few paces and then stopped. From where he took his stand he could prevent any move on the part of the rustlers to take advantage of their superior numbers by executing an enveloping or flanking manœuvre.

From where Doc stood, too, he could see everything that went on. Wes Fuller had already decided that he was a non-combatant, but the other five outlaws were strung out along the adobe wall at the west end of the lot. Ranging from Billy Clanton at nineteen up to Frank McLowry, thirty, they were a rangy crew of huskies, dressed in the fashion of cowboy dandies. The tradition is that they were a handsome squad of hellions, but it can be assumed that Doc took less note of that than he did of their armament. Unlike the guns belonging to the Marshal's party they were all on display.

South towards the corral proper was Billy Claiborne, sporting two guns slung from his belt in holsters. Billy Clanton, Ike, and Frank McLowry each had one holstered six-shooter. Tom McLowry, who was nearest to Doc, had a six-gun shoved in the waist-band of his pants. There were also a couple of rifles, one each in the saddle-boots of the two horses hitched at Tom's left. These were strategically placed so as to keep the outlaws secure from anything but a frontal attack. The animals were, in fact, effective in offsetting Doc's flanking position. He held the string of the bag, but he was more or less shut out of the action until the situation changed.

Meanwhile, he watched his friends stalk into the corral, keeping going until Virgil was confronting Claiborne and Ike Clanton, while Wyatt faced Billy Clanton and Frank McLowry, and Morgan was opposite Tom. Virgil, who still carried Doc's cane, now used it as a truncheon of office. "You men are under arrest," he told them, raising the cane on high for emphasis. "Throw up your hands."

Never was a police officer more swiftly obeyed. Hands snapped up, right enough, and there were guns in them when they did so. As this was not unanticipated, guns also leaped from where the Earps had them in various hiding-places. Six men therewith began firing. The number does not include Doc. He had a shot-gun in his hands, but no target that he could use a scatter-charge on without running the risk of hitting someone on his own side.

Meanwhile, he could see nearly everybody else in action. On the left wing Virgil had let go of the cane and was reaching for his own revolver. As he was so engaged, he was under fire from Billy Claiborne, who loosed three wild shots at him before he dashed to join Behan in Fly's studio. In the centre Wyatt was exchanging bullets with Billy Clanton and Frank McLowry, who doubled up in agony over a slug in the belly. Close at hand Morgan was handicapped in his duel with Tom McLowry, because the latter was shooting from behind one of the horses.

Only one man had not armed himself. That was Ike Clanton, whose double-crossing and subsequent loud talk had initiated proceedings. He just stood where he was until the sight of Claiborne's flight and Frank McLowry's gasp of agony combined to show him what he wanted to do. He dashed for Wyatt, shrieking his peaceful intentions.

First blood for the outlaws, in the meantime, went to Tom McLowry, who shot Morgan Earp. Ripping across the base of the neck just outside the aorta, it ploughed through his right shoulder. "I've got it!" he groaned.

Wyatt had just time to tell his brother to drop flat, out of the line of fire, when Ike was upon him. It is the most remarkable circumstance of this engagement—and one incidentally which enraged Doc—that Earp had the restraint to keep from firing at a man who charged him in the middle of such an affray. All he did, though, as Ike grabbed him and pleaded not to be killed, was to shake him off. "This fight's commenced," he growled. "Get to fighting or get out!"

Ike chose the second course, leaping for the door which Behan opened for him. Behind him his younger brother was showing that he was of the stuff of Old Man Clanton. Billy stood his ground, although he had been nicked by Wyatt and seriously wounded by Virgil. The Town Marshal's bullet broke Billy's gun-arm, but young Clanton proved both his gameness and experience by making "the border shift". This was a toss and a catch, from the stricken right hand to the hale left.

Doc was still frozen out of the action, but there was plenty

for everybody else except Frank, seemingly finished as he
staggered about in a state of shock. Billy and Virgil exchanged a
couple more shots with the result of evening the score between
them. Left hand and all, young Clanton gave Marshal Earp a bad
leg wound, high up on the thigh. Billy did not have time to
thumb the hammer again, though, before Morgan, who had not
seen fit to lie doggo, shot him through the chest. At about the
same instant Wyatt found himself under fire from Tom
McLowry, who still made a small target where he crouched
behind one of the horses. Determined to smoke him out, Wyatt
creased one of the already terrified and plunging broncos. Both
animals then snapped their reins and dashed away.

Here at last was Doc's chance to pull trigger. Tom McLowry
had made a jump for the rifle in the saddle-boot of the nearest
horse. That would have saved him the time and trouble of
reloading, but he still had two shots left in his revolver. When he
failed to reach the Winchester, he levelled one more shot at
Wyatt which never left the chamber. Doc gave him both charges
from the shot-gun, tearing him open amidships.

Doc was not aware of his success, as Tom leaped for the
corner of the corral and started to make off down Fremont. It
was the headless chicken lunge of a dying man, for Tom fell
within a few paces, never to go on. But Doc, who had never
liked the shot-gun as a weapon, thought it had failed him.
He threw it from him in disgust and drew his nickel-plated
Colt .45.

At this juncture the garrison of Fly's studio went into action,
taking the Earps from the rear. Whirling to meet this new threat,
the wounded Morgan fell headlong. Doc aimed two shots at the
studio window from which the attack had come. When his
bullets zinged into the building, the sniping stopped, but that
wasn't all that happened. The rear door of the studio popped
open and Ike Clanton made a break for it. Doc tried for him
twice, but the distance was too great and Ike disappeared into the
livery stable of the O. K. Corral.

Although a six-shooter, the revolver of the frontier was
normally loaded with only five cartridges. Experienced gunmen
always left the hammer on an empty chamber, as the weapon had
no other safety device. Doc thus had but one shot left in his gun,
when he faced around again.

Still dangerous, Billy Clanton was sidling along the wall towards the comparative shelter of the corner. Frank McLowry, who had pulled himself together with amazing courage and fortitude, was executing the same manœuvre, firing as he went. Wyatt's bullet went through Billy's hips, pinning him in place, but Frank still retreated towards Fremont Street. When Doc turned from firing at the drygulchers in the studio, he found McLowry looking down his throat and grinning like a stuffed wolf.

As later reported by several who heard it, Frank's remark is interesting but baffling. Unmistakably he referred to some passage at arms between Holliday and himself of which the details have been lost.

"I've got you this time," he announced.

"You're a good one if you have," Doc is reported as answering. At the same time he swung into the classic dueller's stance, offering as target only the right side of his skinny body.

Three shots were fired at almost the same instant. Doc's went through Frank's heart. Morgan, firing from where he was stretched on the ground, put a bullet through Frank's forehead. McLowry's own slug hit Doc's holster, which he wore high on his right hip, and cut a swathe along his back.

Billy Clanton, who had slid down into a sitting position, was still trying to make a fight of it. Mumbling prayers to be allowed to get off one more shot, he kept struggling to lift his gun, while Wyatt and Virgil watched him in case he succeeded. Doc aimed his revolver at Billy Claiborne, who fled out of the studio's rear door in the wake of Ike Clanton, but there were no bullets left. The hammer fell harmlessly. So, too, did Billy Clanton, who now sprawled in the dust.

Seldom has so much action been crowded into so little time. Witnesses disagreed as to just how many seconds elapsed between the moment that Virgil raised Doc's cane and that other one when the gun slipped from Billy's helpless hand, but the most conservative estimates did not go above a minute. In that brief period the action had been wound up and the actors disposed of in a manner to excite the envy of an Elizabethan dramatist.

Of the nine men involved, Ike Clanton and Claiborne had fled, both McLowrys were dead, Billy Clanton was breathing his last, and Virgil, Morgan and Doc were wounded. Of those who had stood their ground only Doc and Wyatt, who was unscathed, remained in any condition to carry on.

They had reason to be glad they were in shape to fend for themselves. Wyatt was getting ready to take care of his brothers when the door of Fly's studio again opened, this time to let out John Behan. The sheriff tried to put the Marshal's party under arrest for murder committed in the streets of Tombstone.

He was not the only one to rush upon the scene. As previously indicated, the fight had been anticipated by most of the residents and businessmen of down-town Tombstone. Scores had been watching for it, and scores now hurried to look the carnage over. There were, therefore, plenty of witnesses when Behan made his move and Wyatt repulsed him. "I won't be arrested but I'll answer for what I've done," Earp declared. "You threw us, Johnny. You told us they were unarmed."

The sheriff could go no further at the moment, as the vigilantes arrived to take over. Asserting that the City Marshal and his deputies had their support, they carried Virgil and Morgan to the former's home. They also posted a twenty-four hour guard to fend off any reprisal attempted against the wounded men.

Why they thought this necessary is made clear by Parsons, who was on a prospecting trip the day of the battle but arrived back in Tombstone the following day. "A raid is feared upon the town by the cowboys," he confided to his journal, "and measures have been taken to protect life and property. The 'stranglers' were out in force and showed sand."

But if peace was thus fitfully maintained, Tombstone was from that moment on as bitterly divided as any mediaeval Italian city, torn apart by the feuds of the Guelfs and the Ghibellines. For the two parties the town's two leading newspapers can be cited as spokesmen.

"The feeling of the better class of citizens," Mayor Clum's *Epitaph* declared, "is that the marshal and his posse acted solely in the right in attempting to disarm the cowboys, and that it was a case of kill or get killed."

Chief Deputy Sheriff Wood's *Nugget* had no such kind words for the city's police chief and his assistants. Whether the guiding genius of this journal was Woods himself or John Behan—as half seems likely—the paper had a longer story to tell, and it did a good job of it. For the second time that year it wove a propaganda web designed to finish Doc. And this time the web was not flimsy in the part reserved for the Earps. The story was good enough to push them to the wall and put them on the defensive in more than a legal sense. In place of being peace officers, arraigned to answer a routine charge of homicide committed in the line of duty, they found themselves forced to show cause why they should not be indicted for deliberate and unprovoked murder.

For all that has been written about the hearing that followed, little or nothing has been said about a curious aspect of it, and one of great concern to Doc. Taken at its face value, the charge was basically the misuse of police power for private ends. The principal defendant should have been Virgil Earp, the city's duly constituted police sachem. The others had the status of only temporary deputies.

As the hearing developed, though, attention was centred on Doc and Wyatt. Virgil, along with Morgan, was excused from appearing because of an incapacitating wound. The result weakened the official appearance of the case, shifting the emphasis to bear upon the personal issues involved. That in turn made all ears more receptive to the notes being beaten out by the *Nugget's* war-drums.

These were capable of soft, even pathetic measures. And it was the appeal to popular sympathy which proved most damaging. To begin with, so the tale of pity and terror ran, hard-working cowboys had come to Tombstone, where they had been rubbed out by a ruthless police force, spurred on by who knew what malicious motives. Oh, these young range riders might have been a little obstreperous in their talk, but they hadn't meant a thing by it. Point one, then, was that the attack was utterly unprovoked.

These local cowboys were in so amenable a frame of mind that they had already agreed to get out of town. Heeding Sheriff John Behan's fatherly advice, they had seen that to remain in Tombstone was to court trouble. This was so far from their real desires that they had given Behan their word to leave and let things cool down. Point two, therefore, was that they were practically paroled to the sheriff at the time they were attacked.

These honest cow-chasers were so little expectant of trouble that they had not been prepared for it. This took more fadoodling than the other two, but a little juggling of facts accomplished wonders. Billy Claiborne's two guns were disposed of by omitting Claiborne from all discussion of the incident and concentrating on the Clantons and McLowrys. Ike had not drawn his gun—at least until he fled into Fly's studio. He might as well not have had one up to that point, so the *Nugget* took it away from him. That left three to be accounted for. The gossip of the town showed that Frank McLowry and Billy Clanton had been seen firing by a number of people; but inquiry showed that Tom had been hidden from view by the two horses behind which he took shelter, so most were not sure about him. Promptly the *Nugget* became sure about him. Poor Tom had no gun nearer to his hand than the rifle he had vainly tried to snatch from a saddle-boot. Point three, accordingly, was that Tombstone's marshals, those dismounted Cossacks, had cut down all but unarmed men.

In fabricating their tale the county politicos did not scruple to lace it well with corn of the stickiest consistency. They began with Billy Clanton. At nineteen, Billy was of the age that young men are now considered ripe to meet everything from burp guns to tanks and shrapnel, but the *Nugget* wept to think that this rosy-cheeked youth—who had already proved himself an expert at murder from ambush—should have been shot at by six-gun slingers. To squeeze a few more drops of pathos out of the story, his age had been shaved down to seventeen—or that of Billy the Kid at the time of the Lincoln County war. Then it seems that young Clanton had a mother who was a woman of tender piety.

Taking advantage of some respite between rustling raids and hijacking expeditions, Billy had promised her that he would not die with his boots on. Yea, and to this filial promise he had been true. With his dying breath he had asked those around him to take his boots off, because his mother would have it so.

Not content with that blob of treacle the *Nugget* had under-taken to ennoble Ike. It was not for his own life that he had been concerned when he braved the fire of Wyatt's murderous guns, all unarmed though he himself was. Far from it. His only thought had been for his younger brother, whom he knew to be his mother's darling. It was for Billy that he had pleaded, and when he rushed on into Fly's studio after finding that his prayers were made to deaf ears, he carried a broken heart with him.

K

What Behan and his associates knew is what Marc Antony knew when he harried Brutus to his death with false sentimentality about that self-seeking enemy of all liberty but his own, Julius Caesar. They knew that they could arouse popular fury on behalf of dead men in the breasts of people who hated and feared those same men when alive. Mass sentiment was against the Earps, as it had always been against Doc, from that time on.

One thing must be said in preparation for a discussion of the hearing to decide whether or not Doc and his friends should be tried for first-degree murder. The numbers of people who had flocked to the scene had destroyed all the evidence that a modern crime investigator would use in reconstructing what happened. Either deliberate allies or souvenir collectors had removed guns and empty shells. The bodies of the dead McLowrys had been moved from spots that had not been previously charted, and the footprints of the antagonists had been obliterated by the tracks of many noncombatants.

The defence, in consequence, started with the handicap of having to prove what took place by the logic of secondary evidence. Fortunately for Doc and Wyatt they had the services of a top-flight lawyer, Tom Fitch, who had had an editorial career in San Francisco and a political one in Utah before coming to Arizona, and was one of the most accomplished legal lights west of the Mississippi.

His strategy was to let the prosecution's witnesses pile it as high as their imaginations would allow. On cross-examination he did not seek to demolish their stories but merely to clarify their statements concerning certain points. It was only when this had run its full course of several weeks that he showed what use he meant to make of these accusations.

Meanwhile, the accretion of testimony was building up a hostility to which even the judge, Wells Spicer, felt it necessary to heed. He had begun by admitting Doc and Wyatt to bail but had reversed his decision. A court document shows that midway through the trial the defendants were suddenly calaboosed. Fitch obtained their release by habeas corpus proceedings, backed by the specific complaint that his clients were imprisoned in spite of the fact that bail had been granted and paid.

Even some of the vigilantes were getting worried and perhaps cooling off in their support. George Parsons, himself a "strangler", jotted in his journal that it looked bad for the Earps midway in proceedings.

In general the prosecution testimony followed the lines laid down by the *Nugget*, but certain things had been added. Billy Clanton and the McLowrys had not been hit while fighting but rather while their hands were up in the air in proof of their peaceful intentions. While so conducting themselves they had been shot from guns jammed against their bodies.

The motive for this unheard-of savagery was presented by Ike Clanton. Doc and the Earp brethren, he told the court, had been desperately afraid that Crane, Head and Leonard would reveal their part in the Benson stage hold-up. They had therefore each sought Ike out separately, begging him to use his influence to obtain a guarantee of silence from the bandits. Then after the three robbers had had their testimony quashed for ever by death, the Earps had turned on Ike himself. Now it was *he* who knew too much, and the battle of the O. K. Corral had been arranged for the sole purpose of making sure that he would keep quiet.

Ike's statement, which required several court sessions to deliver in its entirety, was the prosecution's clincher, and one which the majority thought good enough to hold. At that point, however, Tom Fitch was at last free to present the defence's case. He began by calling up a formidable list of witnesses, who had seen and heard what the cowboys wished they hadn't. In sum, these witnesses served to dispose of the *Nugget's* three cardinal points.

The contention that the attack was unprovoked was answered by the word of reputable Tombstone citizens to the effect that they had heard the slain men, as well as Ike Clanton, uttering threats against the life of Doc and the Earps. The witnesses had, moreover, seen the rustlers defying city ordinances by going armed in town.

The second contention—that Behan had the situation under control—was sufficiently answered by a deputy county attorney, named W. S. Williams, whom Fitch had subpoenaed. This gentleman had gone to see Virgil Earp as the marshal lay in bed the evening after the fight. While he was there, they had been joined by the sheriff, who was worried about his equivocal position. To clear himself of a possible charge of conspiring with the outlaws, Behan had explained that in the excitement of the moment he

hadn't made himself plain. What had happened was that he had
tried his best to disarm the outlaws, but they had defied him.
Anxious to stop the fight at all costs, he had appealed to the
Earps, although not with the intent of deceiving them.

The third contention, featuring the points that the Clantons
had been taken unawares and unarmed, was also refuted by
numerous witnesses. They had seen the outlaws—Tom McLowry
and Ike Clanton included—packing guns in preparation for an
encounter which had been the talk of the town hours before it
occurred.

Medical testimony was adduced to show that the rustlers
had not been shot at close range, as the prosecution maintained.
Coroner H. M. Matthews and Dr. George Goodfellow demonstrated that wounds on the arms of Billy Clanton and Tom
McLowry proved they were not shot with their hands in the air,
but rather while their arms were in the position normal to men
firing six-guns.

Wyatt testified for the defence and Virgil made a deposition,
but for reasons that aren't at all clear Doc was not called to the
stand. It is understandable that Fitch would want to bury him if
he could. His established outlaw record, amplified by the things he
had been accused of doing in and around Tombstone, would make
him a defence counsel's nightmare. But why the prosecution did
not pounce upon him is something that stumps the imagination.
The best guess seems to be that its attorneys did not want
to evoke any more support for Wyatt's testimony, which
already had the backing of Virgil's deposition, not to mention
logic.

In any case, there were no further witnesses after Wyatt had
spoken and Virgil had written. The case was then in the hands of
Judge Spicer, who had the task of going through a mass of
conflicting evidence before ordering John H. Holliday and the
brothers Earp to be either freed or tried for murder under a legal
code which made death by hanging mandatory.

CHAPTER X

Judge SPICER was deliberate but thorough. His lengthy report, presenting his decision and the reasons for it, showed that he had considered all phases of the testimony, weighing every statement against both the moral and physical probabilities.

In his own way, which was the ponderous but searching way of the law, he took up the *Nugget's* three general points, plus the special ones raised by the witnesses for the prosecution. As his word settled the legal issues—even if they failed to quash the arguments which have raged over the case ever since—they are worth presenting in some detail.

In the nature of his position, and probably of his mind as well, he ignored some of the features of most importance to frontiersmen, including all those who participated. These were the personal matters of individual pride and the maintenance of prestige. Thus Doc and the Earps could look for no help to the code of the West with its warm allowance for emotional drives.

Dealing with the *Nugget's* first point, the one which declared that the Earps had wantonly started bullets flying in the streets of the city, the judge posed some queries. "Was it for Virgil Earp, as Chief of Police, to abandon his clear duty as an officer because his performance was likely to be fraught with danger? Or was it not his duty that as such officer, he owed it to the peaceable and law-abiding citizens of the city, who looked to him to preserve peace and order, and their protection and security, to at once call to his aid sufficient assistance and proceed to arrest and disarm these men? There can be but one answer to these questions, and that answer is such as will divert the subsequent approach of the defendants towards the deceased of all presumption of malice or illegality. When, therefore, the defendants, regularly or specially appointed officers, marched down Fremont Street to the scene of the subsequent homicide, they were armed as it was their right and duty to be armed when approaching men whom they believed to be armed and contemplating resistance."

The contention that the Clantons and McLowrys had not expected an encounter was also dealt with by the judge, who disposed of it in discussing the testimony of numerous non-combatants. These had concurred in declaring that the so-called cowboys had been broadcasting threats to kill the Earps and Doc if they did not get out of town. Defence witnesses had further-more made it plain that the tension built up by the war-like activities of the outlaws had kept the town in a state of growing excitement which fully prepared it for the final explosion. When the marshals had emerged to march up Fourth Street, for instance, many had raised a cry of "Here they come." What was public knowledge, in a word, was least of all secret from the principals.

Treated in due course was the charge that Tombstone's chief of police and his deputies had fired upon unarmed men. It was obvious, Spicer commented in substance, that some of the out-laws not only had been equipped with weapons but had shown both a readiness and aptitude for using them. Marshal Virgil Earp and Deputy Morgan Earp had been seriously wounded and might have been killed. What His Honour could have added but did not was that if the bullet which hit Deputy John Holliday had swerved an inch to the right, it would have smashed his spinal column.

What the judge did say was that Billy Clanton and Frank McLowry were undoubtedly armed and that the testimony of witnesses, not to mention the logic of circumstances, justified the assumption that they all were. Albert Bilicke, owner of the Cosmopolitan Hotel in Tombstone and later to run the biggest hostelry in Los Angeles, had seen Tom McLowry carrying a gun as he emerged from a shop and sped to rejoin his associates at the O. K. Corral. Some had testified that they had observed Ike and Billy Claiborne to be armed, while a couple of others had watched the whole crowd buying cartridges at Spangenberg's gun-shop.

So much for the *Nugget's* three articles of condemnation. Next to be dealt with were the two additional charges brought by the prosecution. One was to the effect that the Earps had opened fire without warning, while the outlaws had held their hands high in surrender until they had found themselves actually

wounded. Noncombatant witnesses supported the medical testimony of Coroner H. M. Matthews and Dr. George Goodfellow
—shortly to become one of the leading surgeons of San Francisco
—in proving this could not have been so. According to their
findings the wounds cited by the prosecution must have been
incurred while the arms of Frank McLowry and Billy Clanton
were in the position normal for men firing revolvers. Then
Probate Judge Lucas and one or two others were sure they had
seen Billy and Frank with guns in their hands before they were
observed to be hit. Acceptance of the foregoing evidence auto-
matically brushed away the accusation that the Clantons had
been shot by guns jammed against their bodies.

The prosecution had rested its case mainly on the testimony
of surviving participants in the action. Included were Behan,
Wes Fuller, Claiborne and Ike Clanton. Although each had
spent most of the critical battle moments in flight or in hiding,
all professed to have a consecutive knowledge of everything that
went on. Unfortunately for the prosecution they contradicted
each other, and, in their eagerness for vengeance on Doc and the
others, they had thrown in details which showed no respect for
logic.

John Behan, who might ordinarily have been expected to
make a good witness, was a bad one, because he found no way of
getting off the hook of his own making. The friendliest inter-
pretation of his actions could not get around two points: he had
not disarmed the outlaws himself, and he had tried to interfere
with the peace officers who had undertaken to do so. The best he
could manage in the face of the circumstances was to say, "I
considered those men under arrest, but I don't know whether
they considered they were."

If he was forced on the defensive, witnesses undertaking the
attack hadn't done much better. Banking on Doc's bad reputation, they had decided that he was a good man on whom to pin
the responsibility of firing not only the first shot but several
others that followed it in rapid succession. To make this feasible
they had to take his shot-gun away from him. Some dispensed
with it altogether, making it a matter of mystery as to how Tom
McLowry turned up, with two buckshot charges in his midriff.
Others gave the shot-gun to Virgil at the other end of the battle
line, whence he could not possibly have blasted Tom before the

buckshot had spread far beyond the neat lethal clusters located by the autopsy.

Weighing these and other inconsistencies, the judge declared that the contradictions found in some of the testimonies made it difficult to believe that some of the witnesses had observed the action with the careful attention to details to which they pretended. He next proceeded to come to grips with truth as he saw it.

Although the prosecution had appeared in the wrong on all provable matters, Spicer took note of the fact that the evidence was not conclusive on a couple of points. The answer to these, in his opinion, could be found in the matter of the motive alleged against the Earps. This was Ike's charge that the fight had been cooked up by the defendants as an excuse for killing him, because he knew too much about the Benson stage hold-up.

It was then that Doc had reason to be glad of something for which he had bawled Wyatt out at the time. "What the Hell did you let Ike get away for?" he had indignantly asked his friend right after the O. K. Corral engagement.

"He wouldn't draw," Wyatt had excused himself.

As it turned out, it was the sparing of Ike which completely destroyed the prosecution's case, as Judge Spicer made clear when he finally reached the end of his decision. "The testimony of Isaac Clanton that this tragedy was a result of a scheme on the part of the Earps to assassinate him, and therefore bury in oblivion the confessions the Earps had made to him about piping away the shipment of coins by Wells, Fargo & Co., falls short of being a sound theory because of the great fact most prominent in the matter, to wit: that Isaac Clanton was not injured at all, and could have been killed first and easiest."

Observing that the grand jury of Cochise County was then in session and was at liberty to take action if its members found fault with his decision, Spicer freed Doc and the others. As it happened, the grand jury took the same view as the judge, but that had no effect on Tombstone's citizenry, the vigilantes excepted. The funny-bone of sentimentality had been properly worked on by the *Nugget*, and the case won in the light of judicial reasoning was lost in the emotional tribunal of popular opinion.

Building on that public support, the outlaws and the county political ring declared war on Tombstone's city government. In this nutcracker play the function of the rustlers was to harry, intimidate and kill, while that of Behan and his cronies was to see to it that no harm came to them therefore.

The first move was to distribute notice that certain men would be subject to assassination if they did not leave town. That Doc and the Earp brothers were on the list of those marked for bushwhacking need hardly be said. Tom Fitch was on it for having successfully defended them, Judge Spicer for having handed down the decision which cleared them, and Albert Bilicke and Dr. Goodfellow for having offered testimony damaging to the prosecution. John Clum made the list on two counts. One was that, as mayor of Tombstone, he had given the Earps, if not Doc, his official support and personal approval. The other was that, as editor of the *Epitaph*, he continued his attacks on the brigands of Cochise County.

Clum very nearly got rubbed out as he left by stage for a business trip back East, but the details are not pertinent to this narrative. What is of moment is the record of a couple of attempts to ambuscade Doc Holliday. As to one of these efforts, no more is to be found in the record than that the disappointed hopefuls were Ike Clanton and Frank Stilwell. The other is described in some detail in the reminiscences of Deputy Sheriff William Breakenridge.

"One dark night . . . I ran up against a gun barrel which was placed against my breast. Looking up, I saw it was Frank Stilwell.

"I asked him what he was trying to do, and he said that a certain party had boasted that he was going to get him that night, and that he would not do it if he saw him first. I told him that it was too late for him to kill anyone that night, and that he was in enough trouble already, and to put up his gun and go home. He did as I told him, and went down the street, and I turned back wondering whom he was after, but about the middle of the block I met Doc Holliday who roomed a short distance up the street on his way home. It flashed through my mind that I had inadvertently saved Holliday's life that night."

The foregoing anecdote is interesting as a vivid illustration of the relationship of Cochise County outlaws and the sheriff's office. It is not certain whether Frank was still an employee of that office as well as a prominent gangster, but it seems probable from the tone of Bill Breakenridge's remarks that he was not.

Yet in either case a deputy sheriff caught a man whom he exactly understood to be in ambush in the streets of a city with intent to murder. Beyond giving the would-be assassin a few words of fatherly advice, Breakenridge did not interfere with him. Nor did this peace officer think that it came within his province to warn the victim—exposed to further assaults by his *laissez-faire* policy—after he had identified him.

It would be unfair to one of Breakenridge's cheerfully amoral tendencies to say that he ever felt the need of justifying his conduct. He did, however, define his attitude when he and several other Cochise County officials illegally furnished Johnny Ringo with bail.

"There was a law and order committee formed in Tombstone that stood in with the gang opposed to the sheriff's office and it was reported that they had gone to Charleston to arrest Curly Bill and a lot of cowboys and bring them to Tombstone. Ringo was anxious to get down there and be with his friends."

It was unquestionably the protection and comfort offered by the Cochise County politicos which enabled the cowboys, as the *Nugget* insisted on calling them, to move into Tombstone after the trial of Doc and the Earp brothers. Allen Street became the crucial line of a stalemated battlefield. For three months the rustlers periodically patrolled this avenue under arms. They did not go farther than that, because the Citizens Safety Committee, spearheaded by Doc and the Earps, were there to check them.

Writing at the time, Parsons gives vivid pictures of the city in a state of potential explosion. Writing in reminiscence, Clum later told why nothing came of it. The rustlers always quit just short of a show-down, he declared, primarily because of Virgil and Wyatt Earp. Clum, it will be remembered, looked askance at Doc, whose championship of law and order he referred to as infrequently as possible.

So the truce was somehow kept by day, even though dry-gulchers were ready for action by night. The nearest thing to an open blow-off was a meeting between Doc and Johnny Ringo. There may, indeed, have been two such encounters, for the accounts differ enough to allow for that. One, however, there unquestionably was, and just what took place is not a matter of doubt. Parsons passed within a couple of feet of Doc and Johnny, as both stood ready to draw, and put it on the record while the picture was still sharp in his mind. "Bad time expected with the cowboy leader and D. H. I passed them both not knowing blood was up. One with hand in breast pocket and the other probably ready. Earps just beyond. Crowded street and looked like another battle. Police vigilant for once and both disarmed."

Frank King, who later worked under Behan when the latter was in charge of the territorial prison at Yuma, has a Holliday-Ringo story he presumably got from the former sheriff. Furthermore, it checks with a version offered by Walter Noble Burns, who got much of his material from Wyatt Earp or sources friendly to him. According to this twice-blessed tale, Ringo took his stand in the middle of Allen Street, challenging Holliday to bite on the other end of Johnny's neckerchief and shoot it out at that intimate nearness. Liking the notion, Doc was blithely striding out to accommodate Johnny when the law intervened. In terms of its own obligations the law would have been acting with propriety, but in stopping such an engagement between the two most interesting characters on the circuit it was committing a sin of its own against frontier history.

The law—or as much of it as was represented by the sheriff's office—took further action following one of these encounters. What, if anything, was done in the case of Doc is not in the record; but Ringo, as Breakenridge recalls in an anecdote which names Johnny as the aggressor, was brought before Sheriff Behan. After disarming but not otherwise inconveniencing a man who was trying to promote a pistol-fight on the main street of a city, the sheriff found business elsewhere. After ostentatiously putting Ringo's two six-guns in the unlocked drawer of a desk, Breakenridge also sauntered out, leaving the outlaw alone in the office. When the deputy returned a little later, the weapons and their owner were gone.

But if the guns for one reason or another never went off by day, they finally did by night. Emerging from a saloon not long before midnight of December 29, 1881, Virgil Earp was dry-gulched. Parsons, who was being treated for a broken nose by Dr. Goodfellow, was once again on the scene at the right time. "Tonight about 11.30," so runs the entry under the date in question, "Doc G. had just left and I tho't couldn't have crossed the street—when four shots were fired in quick succession by heavily charged guns, making a terrible noise and I tho't were fired under my window under which I quickly dropped, keeping the adobe wall between me and the outside till the fusilade was over. I immediately tho't Doc had been shot and fired in return, remembering the late episode and knowing how pronounced he was on the Earp-Cowboy question. He had crossed though and passed Virgil Earp who crossed to the west side of Fifth and was fired upon when in range of my windows by men—two or three concealed in the timbers of the new two-story adobe going up for the Huachuca Water Co. He did not fall, but recrossed to the Oriental and was taken from there to the Cosmopolitan being hit with buck-shot and badly wounded in left arm with flesh wound above left thigh."

The identity of the would-be murderers was never successfully established. Wyatt told his biographer that he believed that those in ambush were Ike Clanton, Frank Stilwell and Hank Swilling. Parsons agreed with Wyatt where Ike was concerned, but his other nominees were Curly Bill and Jack McLowry. The latter was a brother of Frank and Tom, who had come vengeance-bent from Texas on hearing that they had been slain.

With his left arm shattered and his whole system suffering from shock and loss of blood, Virgil was out of action for the duration. He was furthermore missed, because the Earps no longer had the advantage of having the city's police chief on their side.

Mayor Clum, whose nearly disastrous journey has already been cited, was still in the East when early January brought the end of his one-year term. Elected for 1882 was a fence-straddling character named Carr, whose running mate for the post of City Marshal was former Deputy Sheriff Dave Neagle. In spite of the latter's association with Behan, even Wyatt Earp seems to have liked him. He does not appear to have been a man of much force, however, and he was certainly in a difficult position. The vigilantes ignored a shilly-shallying administration, to fight the battle for law and order on their own. Neither they nor the county outlaw faction were willing to be schooled or ready to quit. Somewhat unhappy about it but not knowing quite what else to do, Neagle continued to take orders from his old boss, the sheriff.

Behan was thus much more strongly entrenched than he had been at the time of the battle of the O. K. Corral. His weakness then was that he had been opposed by the Town Marshal, backed by the weight of Tombstone's entire city administration.

Now, however, he was sheriff bearing down on none but private citizens.

Reviewing the new line-up, Behan thought he saw a way to crack the nut. He therefore got a justice of peace in Contention City to issue warrants for Doc and Wyatt on the old charge of murdering Billy Clanton and the two McLowry brothers.

Wyatt later contended that if they had entrusted themselves to the sheriff, they would have been waylaid and murdered before they reached the mill town on the river. Beyond peradventure he had every reason for this suspicion, which was one that the vigilantes shared. When the prisoners put in their appearance, therefore, they were neither unarmed nor unaccompanied. A vigilante escort followed the unhappy sheriff and his deputies all the way to Contention. There the magistrate decided he didn't want any part of the business and hastily agreed with defence attorneys that —inasmuch as there had been no new evidence to justify a second hearing—the principle of double jeopardy should throw the case out of court.

Habeas corpus proceedings, as an extant document demonstrates, then pried the sheriff's grip loose entirely. Doc and Wyatt were accordingly free to return to the Cosmopolitan Hotel, to which Virgil had been moved for his protection. From this field headquarters they could keep close watch upon leaders of the rustler faction, holding forth under arms in another Allen Street hostelry.

But siding with Earp and, quite incidentally, helping to save Tombstone from lawless predators were avocations only for John H. Holliday. Even in time of war the business of making a living must somehow be attended to, and for Doc that meant gambling. What happened to his own establishment is nowhere set down, but it was probably destroyed in the great fire of June 1881, which ate up most of the other saloons in down-town Tombstone.

Doc continued to flourish as a high roller throughout his stay at the big silver camp, however. Herbert Asbury, whose survey of American gambling is perhaps the most comprehensive yet published on the subject, devotes a passage to Doc, whom he cites as one of the two really top-hand gamblers of the Southwest. John Dougherty, also in Arizona at the time, was the only other regional free-lance of the cards whom Asbury considered in the same class with Doc. All fields considered, Dougherty

seems to have been held the better of the two, but the tradition of
Doc's peculiar wizardry at poker remained a handsome tradition
long after Holliday was pushing up such scant weeds as grow on
untended Western graves.

Thus the gambling went on, and so did the vigilance. There
was also aggressive action in the making. Going over the head
of Sheriff Behan, the Citizens Safety Committee made a direct
appeal to the territorial administration for aid in fighting criminal
oppression.

Frémont, who had never liked the idea of governing a wilderness province, had by then resigned. John Gosper, who pinch-
hit for him, pending the appointment of Frémont's successor,
had the interests of the territory genuinely at heart. As he showed
in his report to the United States Secretary of the Interior, covering the year 1881, he also had a reasonably clear idea of what was
going on in Cochise County.

In view of the fact that Arizona had no militia or territorial
police force up to that time, Gosper was powerless to handle
the situation by force of arms. He therefore took the advice of
United States Marshal Crawley P. Dake, which was probably
planted in that officer's brain by Wells, Fargo & Company. In
any case, what Dake recommended was that his deputy (and
Wells, Fargo undercover operative) Wyatt Earp, should be
placed in charge of a special United States Marshal's posse
empowered to clean up the Cochise County gang of outlaws.
This having been agreed upon, warrants of arrest for Curly Bill,
Ringo and the rest were duly forwarded to Wyatt.

Men who had been only vaguely on the fringes of the story
were at this juncture certified as featured figures. One that
Wyatt deputized was Turkey Creek Jack Johnson, whom Earp
had known in Deadwood, and who may have been Doc's partner
in the beautiful gold-brick game at Leadville. A second was
Sherman McMasters, who had been the one to tip Wyatt off
when Earp's stolen horse turned up in Charleston. A third special
deputy was Texas Jack Vermillion, of whom nothing is known
except that he had presumably been in the Lone-Star States before
coming to Arizona. Whatever else any of them may or may not
have been, however, they were all expert pistoleers and accomplished plainsmen.

Doc and Morgan completed the posse, along with Warren

Earp. Youngest of the Earp clan, the latter had earlier played no publicized part in the Tombstone wars. Now he either volunteered or was drafted to step into the vacancy created by the wounding of Virgil.

But before the special posse could get into action, Deputy United States Marshal Earp was called upon to perform a duty which had become routine around Tombstone. A stage had been robbed and Wyatt and Morgan sallied forth to investigate it, inasmuch as it carried mail.

Evidence led to the conclusion that the hold-up had been executed by that veteran highway robber Frank Stilwell and a fellow named Pete Spence, also prominent in Cochise County rustling circles. Stilwell had become so bold through long immunity that he had made small effort to cover his trail. Nor was he greatly concerned when the Earps arrested him. He made the boast that Behan would spring him as soon as he was brought into the office. The sheriff did, indeed, give Stilwell and Spence their liberty as soon as they were put in his custody, but he could not afford to ignore the Federal charge entirely. Before letting the bandits out on bail, he bound them over to appear before a Federal grand jury convening at Tucson on March 21, 1882.

A few days before that scheduled appearance, Frank and Pete rode into Tombstone, with the avowed purpose of getting legal counsel. They and divers other gangsters were thus in town the night Morgan Earp was slain, while he and Wyatt were taking their ease in an Allen Street bar and billiard room.

Parsons's entry for March 19 tells the story. "Another assassination last night about eleven o'clock. I heard the shots, two in number. . . . Poor Morgan Earp was shot through by an unknown party. Probably 2 or 3 in number in Campell and Hatch's while playing pool with Hatch. The shots, 2, came through the ground window leading into alley running to Fremont Street. . . . Geo. Berry received the spent ball in his thigh, sustaining a flesh wound. The second shot was fired apparently at Wyatt Earp. Murderers got away, of course, but it was and is quite evident who committed the deed. The man was Stilwell in all probability."

After holding an inquest, Coroner Matthews came to the same conclusion that Parsons did and added several names. "The finding of said jury," he reported, "was that his (Morgan's) death was caused, as they believe, from the effect of a gun-shot or pistol wound on the night of March 18, 1882, by Pete Spence, Frank Stilwell, one John Dee Freeze and an Indian called Charlie and another Indian, name unknown."

Holding a council, Doc and Wyatt came to several conclusions of their own. The first was that if they remained in Tombstone it would be just a question of time before they, too, were bush-whacked. The second was to take the war-path themselves. The third was to relieve themselves of the necessity of guarding the wounded Virgil. The best solution to this problem, as Virgil himself agreed, was for the latter and his wife to entrain for Colton, California, where the senior Earps were then living.

Wyatt travelled with his brothers—one dead and one an invalid—as far as Tucson. To help ensure against any attempt to finish Virgil off, the entire posse of deputy United States Marshals went along. Previous accounts name only Doc as Wyatt's ally on this occasion, but the Pima County Grand Jury, which subsequently issued warrants for the whole crew, can be accepted as authority for the presence in Tucson of the others as well.

Before they left Tombstone, Wyatt had received information to the effect that several of the rustlers had preceded them to Tucson. That news was confirmed when Joe Evans, a fellow United States Deputy Marshal, boarded the train a station short of the old city on the Santa Cruz.

"Frank Stilwell, Pete Spence, Ike Clanton, and a breed I don't know are in town," he warned. "They've been getting telegrams all day from Tombstone and know you're on the train." Before taking leave of the Earp party, as the train pulled into Tucson, he also reminded them that they would be on their own, as Bob Paul was out of town.

Now established in office as sheriff of Pima County, Bob Paul was the man who had been riding shot-gun on the Benson stage when Bud Philpot and Pete Roerig had been killed, almost a year ago to the day. For timely support he was under debt to Wyatt. Furthermore, he knew all about the rustlers and their political allies, as he had reason to do. In addition to trying to frame him for a highway robbery rap, they had nearly cheated him out of the election he had won and they had come even closer to slaying him.

There was thus every reason to believe that he would have acted to control the visiting gangsters had he been present. As things stood, Doc and Wyatt found the situation in Tucson to be much what it was in Tombstone. That is as much as to say that they were in danger of being ambushed wherever they turned.

They had an hour or so of vigilance to maintain before they caught the train back to Benson. Something prior to that time the west-bound coaches would carry Virgil on towards California. Once clear of the Tucson yards, the wounded man and his wife could be figured as reasonably safe from assassin attack.

In view of subsequent developments it is important to note what Doc Holliday did, or rather did not do, while handling his share of this bodyguard assignment. As far as can be made out, the rest of the deputy marshals were detailed to scout Tucson generally, while Wyatt and Doc stood watch over the Virgil Earps. This involved watching them while they ate in the station restaurant. Thereafter, according to Wyatt, Holliday remained in the dining-room to order a snack for both of them, while Earp went to the train to see his brother and sister-in-law off. For this reason Doc was not with Wyatt when the latter finally spotted Frank Stilwell and Ike Clanton.

"I came on them across the railroad track as it was getting dusk," Wyatt told a reporter of the *Republican* while on a visit to Denver in 1895. "Each of them began to shoot at me. I had a shot-gun.

"I ran straight for Stilwell. It was he who had killed my brother. What a coward he was! He couldn't shoot when I came near him. He stood there helpless and trembling for his life. As I rushed upon him he put out his hands and clutched at my shot-gun. I let go both barrels and he tumbled down dead at my feet."

While this was happening, Doc was doing nothing more nocuous than waiting for a hash slinger to bring two orders. He didn't often miss a chance to be in on a shooting scrape, but he had nothing to do with the killing of Stilwell, not even in the way of being *particeps criminis*.

At the time, however, small attention was paid to who had done what. The main point was that Wyatt's action had laid him and Doc open to renewed attack by the law, in addition to the constant threat of gangster assault. John Behan, as they realized fully, was not the man to let this opportunity pass.

L

The fact of outlawry never bothered Doc, as he was accustomed to having that status six days out of every seven. For Wyatt it was new, but fury at Morgan's murder was driving him so that he did not care. Passing up the first train back to Benson, he and Doc prowled all over Tucson in hopes of finding one of the other rustlers before they picked up the rest of the posse and returned east.

Arriving in Tombstone, they found that Behan had run true to form. The news was that he had been in touch with Tucson by wire, asking for notification of any charges against Earp and Holliday. Johnson, McMasters, Vermillion and Warren Earp were not mentioned, these being secondary targets for the sheriff's malice.

Meanwhile the vigilantes had not changed sides. None was indelicate enough to ask for details, but blanket approval was given to the result. The nearest thing to a direct reference to the incident seems to have been offered by Albert Bilicke, who welcomed them back to the Cosmopolitan Hotel. "Frank Stilwell'll never rob any more stages," he cheerily reflected.

Rising after a much needed rest the next day, Doc and Wyatt learned that Behan was beginning to get results. Paul had returned to Tucson, and though he had not yet telegraphed a warrant, Ike Clanton had sworn to a murder charge, offering himself as a witness.

It so happened that the telegraph operator was a vigilante, who took thought to bring this message to Wyatt before showing it to the sheriff. Earp asked and obtained one hour of grace, which was used to alert the posse and hold council over a farewell meal.

About the time they had finished eating, word was brought that Behan and Town Marshal Dave Neagle were in the lobby, while eight deputies stood ready to back any play that was made. Unimpressed with that information, the deputy marshals descended the stairs on their way to take the field against the rustlers. Using Neagle as a catspaw, the sheriff suggested that they submit to arrest, but when this motion was vetoed with a show of arms, Behan chose to let the matter drop.

There were no further delays, except for one incident which served to illustrate Holliday's consistent dislike of the double-barrelled shot-gun as a weapon of war. When the Marshal's posse lined up to depart from the hotel, each had a rifle waiting in the saddle-boot of his mount. On his person each wore two guns, holstered at the hip. Wyatt and Warren Earp, Texas Jack Vermillion, Sherman McMasters and Turkey Creek Jack Johnson all carried double-barrelled shot-guns. Doc, however, was without this piece of armament as they brushed past the sheriff's deputies and swung down Allen Street towards the corral where their horses chewed the bit. As they passed the bank of H. Solomon, the owner, like everybody else in Tombstone who could conveniently do so, was watching their progress. Noticing that Holliday was without a shot-gun, he took one from the bank's defensive arsenal and hurried to catch up.

"Take it, Doc," he urged and, albeit unwillingly, Doc obeyed. In part this was doubtless due to recognition of a well-intentioned act. It probably had more to do with the fact that Doc had not forgotten Solomon's part in helping to raise bail for him and Wyatt, following a previous march to a corral.

This one was completed without trouble. The six men secured their mounts and walked them back down an aisle of spectators. Sheriff Behan and his men were still on deck, but they let the horsemen pass and forebore to follow.

"The sheriff," as the Tombstone correspondent of the *Tucson Star* noted in describing the whole episode, "made a weak attempt to arrest the Earp party, but Wyatt Earp told him he didn't want to see him. The Earp party then got their horses and rode slowly out of town. There is an uneasy feeling among the outlaw element, as Wyatt Earp is known to be on the trail of those who attempted to assassinate Virgil and who murdered Morgan in cold blood."

There was ample reason for this uneasiness. Wyatt wanted lives for a life, and he had men with him who understood and approved such a method of balancing the books. That first evening, however, the deputy United States Marshals only went far enough to be entirely free of the city. At that point they camped for the night, waiting to learn of developments in their rear before pushing forward.

While they were making breakfast the next morning, a vigilante arrived to tell them what they wanted to know. "Johnny Behan's raising a posse to arrest you." This in itself caused no surprise. What did so was learning the names of the deputies. Behan had finally taken off the gloves to show his hand, complete with brass knuckles. Sworn in to keep the peace in Cochise County were the very gangsters who had long been terrorizing it. Johnny Ringo, as well as Ike and Phin Clanton, were among those riding with the sheriff. Curly Bill had been put in charge of a subdivision of the posse which would manœuvre independently.

Another piece of information took the form of a supplementary report of the coroner's jury which had investigated the killing of Morgan. This added to the names of Frank Stilwell and Pete Spence those of Hank Swilling and Florentino Cruz.

Now when Wyatt had been granted the authority to recruit special deputies, he had been given warrants for every man on Behan's newly-formed posse, save for the sheriff himself, and a couple of his regular staff members. Earp had also been given warrants for about all the men who were subsequently accused of killing his brother. Included was Frank Stilwell, upon whom the ultimate warrant had already been served. Excluded was Cruz, of whom Wyatt had previously had only hearsay knowledge.

The first move was to head for Pete Spence's ranch, where Florentino Cruz—sometimes known as Indian Charlie—was reported to be hanging his hat. Pete was absent; but Indian Charlie was caught when he tried to slip away, Sherman McMasters creasing his thigh with a rifle bullet to halt the retreat. Cruz then withdrew into Spanish, but here again McMasters was too much for him. Cross-examined in his own tongue, Florentino not only confessed his identity but put the finger on other outlaws.

Confirming what Breakenridge had guessed, the half-breed said that Frank Stilwell and Ike Clanton had twice tried to bushwhack Doc in Tombstone. The partially successful attack on Virgil had been undertaken by Johnny Ringo, Ike Clanton, Stilwell, Swilling and a fifth man whose name he said he could not remember.

"He's a liar," Doc insisted, when this was translated, but Wyatt told McMasters to pass the point up for the time being. Indian Charlie then went on. Although all of the gang's high command had been in on the plot which resulted in the slaying of Morgan, he said that only three men had stolen down the alley behind Hatch's Saloon to do the actual shooting. These were Curly Bill, Stilwell and Hank Swilling. The function of Ringo and Spence had been to stand guard at one end of the alley and hold the horses. Others, unknown or at least unidentified by Cruz, had been on duty at the alley's opposite end.

When Florentino had told that much, Sherman tried to pin him down as to his own part in the assassination. Evidently feeling that he had passed the major share of the blame on to where it would stick without hurting him, Cruz finally admitted that he had waited with Ringo and Spence, having been paid to help gun down any possible pursuers of the trigger men.

On learning of this participation in Morgan's slaying, Wyatt asked McMasters to translate one more time. Indian Charlie was told that he would be allowed to go free if he could shoot Wyatt down, and that he would be given the advantage of the draw. He could start going for his gun when "one" was said in Spanish, while Earp would make no move until the count of "tres".

As it was his best hope for both survival and freedom, Cruz took the chance Wyatt offered him. He lost and was left where he was, for a warning to his fellow rustlers—and a weapon for Sheriff John Behan. Here was a killing which had been committed in John's own bailiwick. He need not apply to the reluctant Bob Paul to get on the trail, nor could the culprits, if caught, be claimed by Pima County.

Behan did swear out warrants for murder as soon as he learned of the corpse at Pete Spence's ranch. As his action almost succeeded in ending Holliday's career, it is important to consider Doc's relationship to this second killing in revenge for the death of Morgan. He himself never talked, even when his neck was in chancery because of the episode. The only man to pass down an account of what happened was Wyatt, who took the full responsibility upon himself. Doc was implicated as an accessory, but no more so than most of the other members of the posse, and not as much as Sherman McMasters, whose rifle had made Indian Charlie pause in flight.

This was a legal point which gave him small concern as he and his associates went on with their man-hunt, though. They themselves, meanwhile, were being hunted in their turn—warily, if relentlessly, by John Behan and more boldly by the squad of special deputy sheriffs led by Curly Bill.

If these gangsters were useful to Behan's purpose, they also in some sense defeated it. It was the nature of the posse enlisted by the sheriff of Cochise County which gave Bob Paul of Pima an excuse for not using the warrants in his possession. "Whenever Pima County desires the arrest of Wyatt Earp," Paul is quoted as declaring, "I'll let Wyatt know I want him, and he'll come in . . . If he is in Cochise County when I am ordered to serve a warrant, I'll ask Sheriff Behan to go with me, but he must go alone. I have told him, but he persists in cloaking the most notorious outlaws and murderers in Arizona with the authority of law. I'll have nothing to do with such a gang."

The situation was unusual, even in the annals of the West. If the deputy United States Marshal was legally empowered to arrest most members of the sheriff's two flying columns, so also was his nibs of Cochise County entitled to lay the Federal officers by the heels. The three-cornered horse chase cut trails all up and down the wide valley of the San Pedro, on both sides of that stream. The hope of the sheriff was that his two forces would catch the deputy marshals in a squeeze. The strategy of the latter was to spar for a chance to engage one detachment at a time.

Eventually an encounter did take place, with fatal results to Curly Bill Graham. This engagement has been described in a number of chronicles, but Doc's own brief summation has been generally ignored.

"We were out one day after a party of outlaws," Holliday told a reporter not long after the event, "and about three o'clock on a warm day, after a long and dry ride from the San Pedro River, we approached a spring which was situated in a hollow. As we did so, eight rustlers rose up from behind the bank and poured from thirty-five to forty shots at us. Our escape was miraculous. The shots cut our clothes and saddles and killed one horse, but did not hit us. . . . Wyatt Earp turned loose with a shotgun and killed Curly Bill."

What Doc omitted to give was a circumstance later described by Wyatt. The horse Holliday referred to had been killed under Texas Jack Vermillion while the deputy marshals were retreating from their exposed position, and it was Doc who rode back under fire to take Vermillion up behind him.

After the slaying of Bill there was further manœuvring for position but no decisive action. In the upshot, however, the outlawed deputy marshals held the field, while Behan rode home to hand the county his expense account.

The grumbling of the citizenry over the nature of his activities and their cost was only one of the factors which induced the sheriff to disband his posse. While he was away, Governor F. A. Tritle, who had finally been appointed to succeed Frémont as chief executive of Arizona Territory, had arrived in Tombstone, just in time to learn of several new outrages committed by Cochise County gangsters. His comments and threats of future action were such as to make Behan pull in his horns.

It is probable that the sheriff suggested to surviving rustler leaders that they would do well to lie low. At all events they did so, retiring from the Tombstone area to wait for better times. Ringo and Ike Clanton reputedly dropped below the border, while others sought outlaw hide-outs in the San Simon valley.

To these strongholds over against New Mexico they were followed by the posse of marshals, but that is about all that the excited and contradictory Arizona newspaper reports make clear. Doc and Wyatt were reported killed at least once—a handicap which didn't prevent them from slaughtering enemies in the next edition. And so it went, to the tune of more drama than information.

One clue as to what actually happened is to be found in the general outcome. Some few of Cochise County's professional malefactors were never seen in those parts again. It is reasonable to suppose that some of them got lonesome—what with the passing of Curly Bill and the withdrawal of John Behan's public support— and left for other parts. It is also reasonable to suppose that others gave rumour a basis, by standing their ground and getting shot.

As to Doc's part in all this, the record is no more clear than it is when dealing with the episode as a whole. Somehow he stood the weeks in the saddle and the many hundreds of miles of riding over rugged country. This was an endurance test to wear down hardened cavalrymen in top condition, but he coughed and kept on going. For the rest, the tales which circulated—to be picked up by papers scattered over the West—attest that he did not go along for the ride. The gaudier accounts put five new cadavers in his private Boot Hill. The conservative ones dangled but two or three new scalps from his belt.

As was usual with him, Doc made no personal claims. A reporter later quoted him to the effect that thirteen rustlers had been killed all told, although he identified none as his own victims. This total probably reached back to include Billy

Clanton and the McLowrys, as well as Stilwell, Florentino Cruz and Curly Bill. The owners of the other seven pair of boots are as unknown as the details of their slaying.

Arizona officialdom, in the meantime, had turned a blind eye towards the sounds of firing from the San Simon valley. After Behan thought it wise to dissolve his posse, the one composed of deputy United States Marshals had encountered no legal opposition. It was only when the war was over and won that they were in difficulties. All were on the wanted list in both Cochise and Pima Counties.

To surrender in either one would have been, in the light of their knowledge of the form book, to commit suicide. While they trusted Paul as an individual, they did not believe he could protect them from assassination—in or out of the cheese-box Tucson used for a jail—if Johnny Ringo and Ike Clanton should ride back over the border to find them helpless. As for Behan, of course, they believed in nothing but his enmity.

They could not remain in Arizona and avoid arrest, yet they foresaw that Behan's hatred might create a problem wherever they went. In place of being able to avoid the law by simply moving elsewhere, in the way normal to the West, they might find themselves hounded by extradition proceedings. Following an exchange of wires with various people, however, they received an indirect invitation from Governor F. W. Pitkin to come to Colorado.

As men wanted for murder do not customarily find a welcome from the administration of any State, extraordinary influence must have been exerted on their behalf. That adds up to more drag with the governor of a State than the governor of a mere territory could be expected to have, but Arizona's Governor Tritle was the messenger boy if not the man who pulled the strings. According to Earp, it was Tritle who advised him to go to Colorado after due consultation with its chief executive. As the latter had reputedly agreed not to honour any writ of extradition without a court hearing on the case, Wyatt—reasoning that he could convince any unprejudiced judge that he was justified in his actions—thought himself safe.

Earp was safe, but it turned out that Holliday decidedly was not. Instead, Doc stepped into a bear trap from which he once more barely emerged with his skin.

PART IV

The Living Legend
and the Dead Man in Colorado

CHAPTER XI

RIDING out of Arizona, the posse of wanted men disposed of their mounts in Silver City, New Mexico, and entrained for Pueblo, Colorado. There Doc separated from the others, who went on to the new boom town of Gunnison in the western part of the State.

Why the parting took place is a matter of guesswork, but it is reasonable to assume that Doc and Earp had disagreed as to the best course of procedure. The record supports such a conjecture, too. Contrary to much that has been written on the subject, Earp did not stand by to face extradition proceedings, but rather elected to lie low in a hide-out distant from Denver. Doc, on the other hand, took his chances in the capital, which he reached on May 15. It is furthermore evident that he checked in at the sheriff's office upon his arrival. Charles T. Linton, who was a deputy sheriff of Arapahoe County at the time, made it plain that he knew just where to find Doc, when a man claiming to be an officer from Arizona asked help in locating Holliday. That likewise took place on May 15.

Accompanying the newcomer, who gave his name as Perry M. Mallen, Linton found Doc in short order. Whereupon Mallen pulled a dramatic two-gun act and announced that he was making an arrest. Unarmed himself, Doc submitted to Perry's custody.

So much for the beginning. What followed was the most remarkable sequence of events in even John Holliday's storm-ridden existence. All in all, it was something that could not have taken place anywhere but in the West, and it only happened there once.

Denver was greatly excited by Mallen's feat. Its citizens might be somewhat confused as to exactly what had taken place down Tombstone way, but they had all heard of the feud in Cochise County. They had also heard of Doc, whose surname

newspapers usually spelled "Holladay" to match the Denver
street called after the famous stage-coach tycoon.

"A highly important arrest was made in Denver last night,"
the *Rocky Mountain News* told its readers on May 16, "in the
person of the notorious Doc Holladay, leader of the famous Earp
gang of thugs, murderers and desperadoes, who have made their
headquarters in Arizona and who have committed murders by
the dozen. The arrest was made by Sheriff Perry Mallen, who has
been on the track of Doc since the desperate fight had with the
gang by the Sheriff's force of Tucson, Arizona, six weeks ago in
which Sheriff Stilwell was killed in an attempt of the gang to
murder Charley, a brother of Deputy Sheriff Clintry, murdered by
one of the Earps in a billiard hall at Tombstone a few weeks ago."

There was no reason for Denverites to question what read
like a straightforward summary of the facts. The scrambling,
however, is so complete as to seem artful. Behan's former deputy,
Frank Stilwell, was promoted to take Paul's place as sheriff of
Pima County. Sheriff Stilwell died in the defence of a brother of
Deputy Sheriff Clintry—representing, no doubt, a hazy recollection of Ike Clanton. As to Clintry's brother Charlie, this was a
shadow presumably cast by Indian Charlie, a nickname of
Florentino Cruz. Unlike the latter, this Charlie survived, while
unlike Ike Clanton, good old Clintry himself had been killed. For
a crowning touch, moreover, he had been foully murdered in a
Tombstone billiard hall.

This transfer to the fictitious Clintry of the actual fate of
Morgan Earp serves to underscore the most significant feature of
the story. That is the shift of every point which might have
served to win sympathy for the Earps to bear down with its full
weight on behalf of the other side.

Just who Mallen himself was and in just what county he
functioned as sheriff were questions the *Rocky Mountain News*
evidently had not paused to inquire. The paper was much too
happy with Perry's success to go into such unimportant details,
and it went on to make this clear. "Sheriff Mallen deserves great
credit for the persistence with which he followed up the man. He
met him in Pueblo but did not dare undertake the arrest there and
waited until he came here. Holladay, while in Pueblo, went
armed to the teeth, but here put on the ways of civilization, laying
aside the firearms with which he had been accoutred. The total

amount of reward for the capture of Holladay is in the neighbour-
hood of $5,000. He will be taken back to Tombstone, but it is
feared that he will be hanged if he reaches there."

There were a few more facts in the tail of the story than in its
beginning. Doc, himself, as shall shortly be seen, substantiated the
statement that he had met Mallen in Pueblo. John Behan had run
true to expected form by broadcasting promises of a rich reward
for the capture of Doc and Wyatt. The danger to Doc, if he
should be taken back to Arizona, was no part of an exaggeration.
Certainly Doc himself did not think it was.

The *Denver Republican* was equally impressed with Mallen's
exploit, although it identified him as a police officer from Los
Angeles rather than as a sheriff of an Arizona county. What a
California cop was doing on the trail of a fugitive from Arizona,
the journal did not stop to explain. It was too full of its enthralling
discoveries about the captive outlaw.

"Who was the prisoner? was soon on the lips of everyone,"
the *Republican's* reporter wrote as he hit his full stride. "The
question is soon answered. Doc Holladay, the prisoner, is one of
the most noted desperadoes of the West. In comparison Billy the
Kid or any other of the many Western desperadoes who have
recently met their fate, fade into insignificance. The murders
committed by him are counted by the scores and his other crimes
are legion. For years he has roamed the West, gaining his living
by gambling, robbery and murder. In the South-west his name
is a terror. In fact, he is no other a personage than the leader of the
murderous gang of cowboys who have been lately operating in
the vicinity of Tombstone, Arizona, and the head of the lawless
element of Tucson, Arizona."

In this account Doc was not only saddled with whatever
crimes could be laid to the account of the Earps, he was also
given Curly Bill's place as head of the "cowboys", which is to say
the rustlers of south-eastern Arizona. Between the two papers cited
he had thus been made personally reponsible for every act of law-
lessness which had given national notoriety to Cochise County.
Denver's other daily, the *Tribune*, also took up the chorus.

In tune with this music Mallen was the city's social lion and
Doc its caged one. To the opinions of most of Denver's citizens
Doc was no doubt as indifferent as he had been at all times and
places, but there were eyes from which he would have wished

these accounts hidden. He and the others had come to Colorado in the belief that they would there get a hearing before courts unaffected by the influences of excited public opinion and sensational reports. As Doc examined his Denver press notices, he saw this hope fly out a window from which iron bars prohibited his own exit.

Yet Doc turned out to be not without friends, and the identity of at least one of them is cause for astonishment. On May 17, the *Rocky Mountain News* gave Holliday's side of the story, which it did in the form of indirect reporting rather than of an interview containing any direct questions. In substance this was a brief summary of the feud between Wyatt and Behan, concluding with the remark that Wyatt and the others "are now somewhere in the Gunnison [country]."

But the article containing this information went on to say, "Holladay is well known by General D. J. Cook and others of the Rocky Mountain detectives, and has also many other acquaintances in Denver who put a good deal of faith in his story."

Now Dave Cook was Colorado's crime buster extraordinary. He was the man most responsible for the fact that the Wild West was not nearly as wild in Colorado during the late seventies and early eighties as it was in any of the surrounding States and territories. Most of the famous peace officers of the region were sheriffs or town marshals, whose jurisdiction was limited to a comparatively small area. Cook's power extended not only through Colorado but beyond its borders. This he had achieved by forming an inter-State peace officers' league, whose members had mutual-aid responsibilities.

There is not the least doubt that Doc should have been as "well known by General D. J. Cook" as the *News* declared he was, but that he should be known favourably is passing strange. Doc was one of the notorious killers of the circuit, and a good part of his reputation had been earned in Colorado.

Why should Cook have chosen to go to bat for Doc, or indeed why should the whole administration of Colorado have taken its extraordinary course with regard to this case? The answer offered here is admittedly no more than a supposition. It is furthermore a guess that will remain without vindicating proof, in as much as the records of Wells, Fargo & Company were destroyed in the great San Francisco fire of 1906.

Yet the only thing that fits the case is that the long arms of this powerful organization reached out to protect one of its useful operatives. This was not Doc, himself, but Wyatt Earp, who had been in the express company's employ throughout his two and a half years in Tombstone, and seemingly before that.

Consider the circumstances. A great figure in the society peculiar to the circuit, Wyatt had done nothing to rate much standing elsewhere. Even the circuit trails he had followed had not taken him to Colorado, so there was no popular feeling in his favour which could be viewed as a favourable influence. On the contrary, the Denver papers showed that the chief things known about him were the reports of a hostile Tombstone press. As of May 1, this had been augmented by the once friendly *Tombstone Epitaph*, for Clum and his partners had been bought out by the politicos of Cochise County.

These facts notwithstanding, a politically ambitious governor, counting on re-election as a stepping-stone towards the United States Senate seat he hoped for, stuck his electoral neck out on Earp's and Doc's behalf. Though known to be in Colorado, Wyatt remained untroubled. Though known to be in Denver, Doc was not arrested until the arrival of Mallen forced action.

Doc, himself, may be thought of both as the beneficiary and the fall guy of the measures taken to protect Wyatt Earp. Left to himself, he would probably have simply skipped out of Arizona and thumbed his nose at the law, just as he had done following his various other killings. Once arrested, though, he had help of a sort never before given him. Those striving to cover Earp could not sacrifice Holliday without paving the way for the arrest of the man they really wanted to protect.

It seems manifest that the original script called for doing nothing and hoping the newspapers never got wind of what was going on. Sheriff Paul couldn't ask for extradition until Earp was in custody somewhere. Governor Tritle of Arizona couldn't sign the writ until he got the request. Sheriff Michael Spangler of Arapahoe County would have no reason to hold anybody until somebody from Arizona should bring charges. As for Governor Pitkin it could not be proved that he so much as knew that Holliday and Earp were in Colorado until their arrest called it to his attention.

There is every reason to believe that this game of knowledgeable silence would have worked, except for one factor which
couldn't have been figured on in advance. This was the eagerness
of Sheriff-Police Officer Perry Mallen of Arizona or Los Angeles
to pick up five grand in blood money. His avaricious intrusion
caused acute discomfort to all the worthies mentioned above and
a general scurrying to cover up.

Deputy Sheriff Linton, who had known of Doc's presence as
soon as he came to Denver, had to go into his act as a hustling
peace officer and help to arrest the criminal. Sheriff Spangler had
to get on the job and query Governor Tritle as to whether
Arizona wanted Doc. By-passing the outraged Behan, Tritle
passed the buck to Bob Paul. The latter knew better than anybody in this group that Holliday had not killed Stilwell, but Doc
was the bird in hand. Reluctantly, but not as reluctantly as if the
arrested suspect had been Wyatt Earp, he initiated extradition
proceedings.

As an amusing disclosure was to prove, Marshal Byers of
Gunnison was not in on the game, but then he was in no position
to railroad Wyatt out of the State unless Governor Pitkin should
give the word. The latter did not do so, preferring to ignore
Earp's existence, as long as Holliday was the newspaper topic of
the moment. He said nothing directly, but from His Excellency's
office issued rumblings to the effect that the governor would
have to be sure that Arizona Territory was prepared to protect
any prisoner turned over to it by Colorado.

Pitkin was in a spot he could not have enjoyed, but he can be
left to stew in his political juice, pending the arrival of the
extradition papers from Arizona. Before that could happen Bat
Masterson charged on the scene. As always, he was ready to
break his neck to help a friend; but in this instance the friend and
the man he was helping were not one and the same. Unable to
come himself, without making matters worse, Wyatt had wired
Bat at Trinidad and asked him to go to work on Holliday's behalf.

At that time Bat was a deputy sheriff of Las Animas County,
Colorado, but he aimed at making a monkey of the law rather
than at upholding it. The plan he adopted was said to have been
suggested by Doc's legal counsel, who probably got the idea from
Holliday himself. However that may be, the scheme was to use the
prisoner's reputation as a con man to save him from a murder rap.

Going to Pueblo, where Doc had helped him hold the
Denver and Rio Grande roundhouse three years earlier, Bat per-
suaded City Marshal Jamieson to issue a warrant for Holliday's
arrest. It has later been claimed that this dummy charge was for a
stage hold-up, but that was not what the Denver papers reported
at the time. "The warrant," the *News* stated in its issue of May 19,
"charges Holladay with being an operator in a confidence game
at the place above named, by which a 'sucker' was relieved of the
sum of $150. While Marshal Jamieson was sitting in the Sheriff's
office Deputy Sheriff Charles Linton brought in 'Doc' Holladay.
It is said that the Marshal showed his warrant and asked to
immediately take Holladay along with him, when Sheriff
Spangler refused to let him do so, saying that Holladay was
already held on one charge and that he could not be taken to
Pueblo unless a writ of habeas corpus was granted by Judge
Elliott."

Although a scheme to hoodwink the law, it was itself based
on a legal point. By filing a Colorado claim to him Bat could
ease Doc off the gallows. At the same time the crime of which
Holliday was accused did not involve a large enough sum to
seem in any way extraordinary. A rat was smelled, none the
less. "Sheriff Spangler," the article continued, "says the arrest
by the Pueblo parties is a put-up job to secure Holladay's release.
He says that . . . he shall hold Holladay till the arrival of officers
from Arizona, but that he shall not deliver him to them unless
they show they have proper authority."

In addition to trying to pry Doc loose with a ruse. Bat spoke
up manfully in his defence. However dourly he was to write of
Holliday's character in 1907, it was not thus that he referred to it
in 1882. "I tell you," he insisted to a reporter of the *Republican*,
"that all this talk is wrong about Holliday. I know him well. He
is a dentist and a good one. He . . . was with me in Dodge, where
he was known as an enemy of the lawless element."

"Such in substance," the reporter went on, as he ceased to
quote Bat and spoke in his own person, "is Masterson's story.
He claims that Mallen is a fraud and a friend of the cowboys,
whose only object is to get Holladay back in order that he might
be killed."

Bat also took it upon himself to make his accusations against
Mallen in person. This was done, according to the *Denver*

M

Republican of May 20, in the presence of Bob Paul. The latter had by then arrived from Arizona, but the warrant authorizing him to take custody of Doc had not yet been forwarded from Prescott.

"Holladay's friends," this newspaper item observed, "say that Paul is a friend of the prisoner. . . . He, however, will take Holladay back safely, as it is his duty to do, the prisoner having been indicted for murder by the last Grand Jury for the murder of Frank Stilwell. Part of the conversation between the officers last evening was in relation to Mallen's claim that Holladay was the man he had hunted for seven years for killing a man back in Utah. Masterson asserted positively that Holladay had never been in Utah, and Mallen finally acknowledged that he might have been mistaken."

But if friends turned up to speak their piece in Denver, so did enemies. One was a man not otherwise identified than as "a gentleman, recently from Arizona". Operating on the "guilt by association" principle, he proceeded to damn Doc on the strength of a bunco game featuring Virgil Earp. His conclusion that Doc was guilty of murder in Tucson because his friend Virgil had skinned a sucker in Tombstone was played up to the extent of almost a full column in the *Rocky Mountain News* of May 21.

Still the net result of the conflicting testimony was some betterment of Doc's standing in the scale of popular opinion. This was reflected by a growing difference between the attitudes of Denver's daily papers. As was to be expected, Doc found steadfast enmity in the *News*. Its owner, W. H. Byers, was a crusader whose hatred of outlaws in any form dated back to the early days of the city, when Charles Harris was its gangster over-lord. For speaking out at that period Byers had been kidnapped and generally given a rough time, and the doughty editor had gone around looking for criminals he might devour ever since. The *Tribune* and the *Republican*, on the other hand, had cooled off in their early enthusiasm for the increasingly mysterious Mallen, even if they had not yet gone so far as to champion Doc.

What the *Republican* did do was what all the Denver papers might have done earlier, if they hadn't been so bent on building Doc up into the arch-monster of American history. In the lull before the extradition papers arrived from Arizona, Holliday was finally given a chance to tell his side of the story in his own words. As this is the only full-fledged interview to be found in the record it is doubly interesting. Here, for once, Doc was dealt with by a man who was neither friend nor enemy.

"His features are well formed," the *Republican's* representative noted, "and there is nothing remarkable in them save a well defined look of determination from his eyes which the veriest amateur in physiognomy could hardly mistake. . . . The first thing noticeable about him in opening the conversation was his soft voice and modest manners. He explained the case as follows: 'The men known as cowboys are not really cowboys. In the early days the real cowboys who were wild and reckless, gained a great deal of notoriety. After they passed out their places were taken by a gang of murderers, stage robbers and thieves, who were refugees from justice from the Eastern States. The proper name for them is rustlers. They ran the country down there and so terrorized it that no man dared say anything against them.'"

Asked if he anticipated a bad time when brought back to Arizona, "Holladay paused for a minute and gazed earnestly out of Jailer Lambert's room into the rain outside and then said slowly, 'If I am taken back to Arizona, that is the last of Holladay'. After a pause he explained by saying: 'We hunted the rustlers and they all hate us. John Behan, Sheriff of Cochise County, is one of the gang, and a deadly enemy of mine, who would give any amount of money to have me killed. It is almost certain that he instigated the assassination of Morgan Earp. Should he get me into his power my life would not be worth much.'"

The foregoing paragraph is significant as assigning a definite and dominant place to Behan in the councils of the Cochise County outlaws which has not usually been allowed him. That he protected them with dexterity and success has previously been demonstrated. That he profited by their activities is too obvious for further comment. But what about Doc's accusation that the sheriff used the rustlers as hatchet men?

The picture of Behan as the half-comic bungler is owing to Earp, speaking in contempt of a man who avoided Wyatt's own direct methods of dealing with enemies. But, however circuitously he may have operated, Behan earned a draw in the war between them. It is true that Doc, Wyatt and their helpers smashed the power of the politico-gangster combine in Cochise County, but the squeeze Behan put upon the Earps—who found themselves gunned from ambush, and then in peril of the law when they sought to carry the fight to the assassins—drove them out of Arizona. In the comfort of prosperous later years Wyatt could afford to belittle the sheriff. But Doc was in prison with a noose hanging over him, and he knew that it was John Behan's malignant energy which had reached out to jail him and tie the hangman's knot. Situated as he was, it is hardly to be doubted that he said what he did in sober earnest. It also seems reasonable to hold that he was speaking from knowledge.

Repeating the assertion that Behan had instigated the murder of Morgan Earp, Doc mentioned a personal enmity between Morgan and Behan not to be found in later accounts. These tend to give the impression that there was a feud between Behan and Wyatt which the other two Earps took up purely on their brother's account. That is not what Doc had to say on the subject. According to him, Behan "was afraid of and hated Morgan Earpp, who had quarrelled with and insulted him several times. He feared Earpp and had every inducement to kill him".

The interview next took a turn to cover the man regarded as the Colorado instrument of Behan's vengeance. Doc could not say whether Mallen was or was not put onto him by the sheriff, but he did describe some of the curiosities of the fellow's conduct. "The first time I met him was in Pueblo just before I came to Denver. He approached me in a variety theatre and introducing himself said he wanted to do me a favour in return for saving his life in Santa Fe once. I told him I would be very thankful for any favour he wanted to show, but he must be mistaken about my saving his life in Santa Fe, as I had never been there. He did not reply to this, but told me that he had just come up on the train with Josh Stillwell, a brother of Frank Stillwell whom I was supposed to have killed, and that he had threatened to shoot me on sight. . . . I met him in a saloon a few days afterwards and asked the bar-keeper who he was. He told me that Mallen represented that he was a ranchman who had sold out on the lower country and was looking for a location, upon the strength of which he borrowed eight dollars at one time and two dollars at another. . . . The next time I saw him was in Denver when he cropped his guns on me and caused my arrest. Paul does not know him, and I believe he is a crank. He acted like one in Pueblo, when he took down his clothes and showed me a mark which he said was a bullet wound but which was the mark of disease. I laughed in his face, the thing being so funny I couldn't help it."

With his next question the reporter asked the whereabouts of Wyatt and the rest. To this Doc's answer was, "In Colorado, over in the Gunnison, I believe."

"Didn't you have a quarrel with them in Pueblo a few weeks ago?"

"We had a little misunderstanding," Doc admitted, "but it didn't amount to much."

"Would they help you now?"

"Yes, all they could; but they are wanted themselves, and of course, couldn't go back with me without putting themselves in danger, without doing me any good."

What Doc knew but naturally did not add was that Wyatt was helping him as he could not have done, if he himself were behind bars. The newspaper accounts contained numerous references to the activities in Doc's behalf of a faction described only as "Holladay's friends". Some of these were no doubt Doc's own acquaintances, met in Denver in the course of previous visits, or picked up in the course of his far-flung circuit peregrinations. But it was Wyatt, working through Masterson, who kept this propaganda group active and vocal. And it was Wyatt, or such forces as he could set in motion, who induced the Governors of a State and a Territory to go to astounding lengths to save the neck of one of the South-west's most notorious killers.

At the time, however, it did not look as if any of these efforts would be successful. "Holliday's hope," as the *Rocky Mountain News* gleefully announced in an article published the same day as the *Republican's* interview, "is vanishing into very thin air."

Yet even under this extreme pressure, when it looked as if he would have to pay the ultimate penalty for a crime he never so much as witnessed, John Henry Holliday did not crack. Inevitably the *Republican's* reporter had asked him the crucial question. "You are charged with killing Frank Stillwell. What do you know about the affair?"

To this Doc replied only, "I know that Stillwell was a stage robber and one of Morgan Earp's assassins and that he was killed near Tucson, but I do not know that I am in any way responsible for his death."

Just before he thus brushed aside an effort to make him talk, the article explained why his hope was vanishing. Bob Paul had arrived in Denver, there to wait the forwarding from Prescott of the extradition writ which would authorize him to bring Doc back to Arizona.

"But Sheriff Paul of Tucson," the reporter said, "will take you to that place, will he not?"

"Yes," Doc had replied, "and therein lies my only chance for safety. I would never go to Tombstone. I'd make an attempt to escape right outside this jail and get killed by a decent man. I would rather do that than be hung by those robbers there."

"Cannot Paul protect you?"

"I am afraid not. He is a good man, but I am afraid he cannot protect me. The jail is a little tumbledown affair which a few men can push over, and a few cans of oil thrown upon it would cause it to burn up in a flash, and either burn a prisoner to death or drive him out to be shot down. That will be my fate."

If Doc had spoken well of Sheriff Paul, the latter—who was interviewed by the *Rocky Mountain News* on the same day that the *Republican* sent a man to quiz Holliday—did handsomely by Doc.

The *News*, it should be noted, had by this time finally managed to spell Doc's name correctly. "Was Holliday regarded as a desperate character?" the paper's representative asked of Paul.

"Not by any means," Paul scoffed at the suggestion. "He was always decently peaceable, though his powers when engaged in following his ostensible calling, furthering the ends of justice, made him a terror to the criminal classes of Arizona."

After dealing with the circumstantial evidence that had induced the Pima County Grand Jury to indict Doc, Paul went on to say, "I also hold warrants for the arrest of Wyatt and Warren Earp, Sherman McMasters and John Johnson, who accompanied Holliday, guarding Virgil Earp on the night of the murder." Though omitted from the list, Texas Jack Vermillion had without doubt also been indicted.

What should be distinctly borne in mind was the difference between having warrants for arrest at the behest of the Pima County Grand Jury, and a writ of extradition from the Territory of Arizona. Bob Paul had, or rather was expecting to have, such a writ for Doc Holliday only. Meanwhile, what was being doing to protect Wyatt was manifest in some passages from the *Tombstone*

Epitaph which were tacked on to the *Republican's* interview of
May 22.

The *Epitaph*, by this time speaking for Behan and his cronies,
who now owned it, was puzzled and plaintive—as it had reason
to be. Its editor was aware that some sort of monkeyshines were
afoot, though he couldn't yet fathom the play. Noting discrep-
ancies in the reports from Colorado he chose to place the blame
for causing confusion on Town Marshal Sid Byers of Gunnison.

"We have half an idea that S. Byers of Gunnison is a fraud
and a delusion," the *Epitaph* muttered, "from the fact that he
telegraphed yesterday to Chief of Police Neagle, making inquiries
as to the character of the Earps. Gunnison is two hundred and
seventy-five miles from Denver and the Earps, according to a
telegram received late yesterday, are still in jail in Denver."

The Tombstone paper was justified in its error, as Sheriff
Spangler had been something less than frank in his communi-
cations, which the *Epitaph* proceeded to quote. "Mr. Behan
received a dispatch from Mr. Spangler, Sheriff of Arapahoe
county, stating that he had the culprits. The following is a copy
of the dispatch:

"'Denver—Have your men in jail. Let me know what to do. M.
Spangler.'

"Mr. Behan immediately telegraphed to hold the prisoners
securely, and as soon as he could secure requisition papers he
would start for them. Later in the day the following dispatch was
received:

"'Denver—Have arrested Doc Holladay. The Earps are here. As
soon as you come will take them. Answer.'"

That second telegram, though still misleading, confessed that
Wyatt and the others had not been taken into custody. What
Spangler neglected to say was that "here" referred vaguely to
Colorado at large—an area where the sheriff's jurisdiction was
severely limited—and not specifically to Denver.

Originally Behan had been notified of Doc's arrest at the
insistence of Mallen, whose position as an accredited representative of Arizona law was then not a matter of any doubt.
But while making an official show of doing business with Behan,
the administrations of Colorado and Arizona promptly began to
second-deal him.

What made fast work necessary was that Behan had pushed

matters, while Paul had adopted a policy of not bothering the
Earps until his hand should be forced. "We learn by the *Tucson
Star*," the *Epitaph* complained, "that Sheriff Paul of Pima was
astonished at finding that Sheriff Behan of Cochise had applied
for a requisition from the Governor to take the Earps. As the
arrest of the latter was due to Behan's exertions entirely there is
no merit in Paul's surprise except that he is sorry for the Earps.
Did Paul offer any reward for their capture? Did he do anything,
in fact? It is something singular, also, that it never struck the
Sheriff of Pima County to apply for a requisition until the Sheriff
of Cochise County had telegraphed for one."

John Behan got the run-around from the Governor of
Arizona, exactly as he had from the Sheriff of Arapahoe County.
*Cannot have requisition until indictment and warrant are presented to
me,* read the wire sent to Behan. *Am ready to issue requisition at
once. District Attorney absent at Benson. Have not at present the
proper papers. When it is issued the requisition must go to Prescott for
the Territorial seal. F. A. Tritle.*

By the time Behan had received that message and answered
it by a second demand, Pima County was bidding against him.
Mr. Horton, acting for District Attorney, thus ran the next wire
from Prescott, *asks for the requisition in the name of Sheriff Paul.
F. A. Tritle.*

The race was then on between representatives of the two
counties, armed with the necessary papers, but the man from
Cochise had a longer way to go than his rival. In due course,
therefore, Behan received the following wire:

*John H. Behan: Farley not here. Paul has made application for a
requisition and will leave tomorrow for Denver.*

When he got to this point in his account of the proceedings,
the editor of the *Epitaph* showed signs of having verbal high
blood-pressure, and it can be assumed that if John H. Behan did
not have apoplexy, he was immune to that disorder.

There was one aspect of the case that was not dealt with
by the Tombstone paper, which was in no position to do so.
Governor Tritle could only ask for the return to Arizona of
men actually in the custody of Colorado authorities. The only
member of the special posse of deputy United States Marshals
who was in that category was Doc Holliday. It was, therefore, he
alone that Bob Paul was empowered to bring to trial.

CHAPTER XII

Two teams of attorneys had meanwhile been engaged either by Doc himself, or by those astir on his behalf, these being the legal firms of Deckard and Yonley and Deweese and Naylor. They represented the best in the way of defence counsel that Colorado had to offer. W. S. Deckard, a Federal judge during territorial days, was the dean of Denver's bar. Colonel John T. Deweese, subsequently a prominent lawyer on the coast, was of scarcely inferior standing.

It was not to be expected that such men would neglect their client's interest, although they had to mark time during the period in which an accused but unindicted man could be legally held in jail. When it had elapsed, they pressed for habeas corpus proceedings and secured a hearing, which carried over from May 22 to May 23, at the bench of Judge Victor A. Elliott.

Their aim was to dispose of the flimsily documented charge preferred by Mallen before the extradition writ could arrive from Arizona. How they almost succeeded, as well as why they finally did not, was told in a *Rocky Mountain News* item of May 24.

"The adjourned habeas corpus proceedings in the case of the notorious Doc Holliday were resumed before Judge Elliott at ten o'clock yesterday morning and quickly disposed of. Judge Elliott simply asked to be shown the papers in the case and after carefully scrutinizing them discharged the prisoner on being told there was no further evidence. When the court announced its decision Holliday's face, which had worn a gloomy downcast look since his incarceration, brightened up and a faint smile crept over his features. His joy suddenly vanished, however, when Deputy Sheriff Linton appeared holding a warrant authorizing the arrest of Holliday for the murder of Frank Stillwell."

This was issued on the basis of notification from Prescott that a formal request for the State of Colorado to turn John H. Holliday over to Arizona Territory was finally in transit. The effort to pry Doc loose from durance had to begin all over again, and this, as the *News* reported, was doggedly undertaken. "Holliday's counsel, Decker & Yonley and Deweese & Naylor, immediately applied for another writ of habeas corpus. . . . The trial of the new proceeding will come off on Friday." As that fell on May 26, it meant three more days of trying suspense for Doc.

Worse yet, there was by then little hope that he could be liberated before the arrival of the extradition papers. They did indeed reach Denver before the case was called, but he was given a reprieve for a reason outside the jurisdiction of Judge Elliott's court. In the case of extradition proceedings the man with the final word was not His Honour but His Excellency, and the latter had found business elsewhere. "Owing to the absence from the city of Governor Pitkin," the *Republican* pointed out, "the hearing of the case was postponed to Monday."

So then Doc had three days to worry about what the governor was going to do. Meanwhile, Pitkin fretted over the same problem. He wanted to please the forces, groups and individuals driving for Doc's release, but he did not want to cut his own political throat. The newspaper clamour resulting from Doc's capture had popularized the notion that Doc was America's number one genius of crime. The politico who undertook to give him his liberty might easily run out of explanations satisfactory to voters at the next election. Then he had the newspapers themselves to think about.

They had played the story big and showed no unwillingness to let it drop. In particular, the highly influential *Rocky Mountain News* was growling for Doc's life and insisting on the propriety of co-operating with Arizona in the matter of bringing malefactors to justice.

In the end, however, it was a newspaper, or a representative of one, that turned the nicely balanced scales in Doc's favour. Yet this in turn was due to the influence of Wyatt Earp, acting through his tireless emissary, Bat Masterson. As the crucial hearing approached, Doc's allies decided to transfer emphasis from the merits of the case to the probable inability of Arizona authorities to protect Doc from assassination or lynching at the hands of the surviving Cochise County outlaws. The extradition hearing was scheduled for May 30. Learning that Pitkin had returned to Denver the evening of May 29, Bat went to see

E. D. Cowen that night. Cowen covered the Capitol for the *Denver Tribune* and Masterson had reason to believe that his word would carry weight with the Governor.

"Bat Masterson . . . made a plea for assistance in the *Tribune* editorial rooms," Cowen recalled in the course of a Chicago newspaper article dealing with his experience in the Far West. "He submitted proof of the criminal design upon Holliday's life. Late as the hour was, I called upon Pitkin."

Having heard it before, the Governor was not as impressed by the point itself as by the nature of the new advocate. Cowen represented the *Tribune*, guaranteeing Pitkin that he would have at least one paper to speak up for him, if he bucked public opinion as represented by the *News*. When a man is fence-walking, it doesn't take too much of a wind to blow him down on one side or the other; and this midnight appeal was seemingly the deciding factor. At all events Cowen stated that Pitkin was favourably influenced, and events bore the newspaperman out.

"Helping Holliday" was the indignant heading over the grumpy report on the extradition hearing published by the *News*. The three subheads were as explicit as they were bitter. "Governor Pitkin Assists the Alleged Murderer", howled the first. "By Refusing to Honour the Arizona Requisition", groaned the second. "Kept to Aid the Army of Bunko Steerers", the third accused.

Although various dispatches mentioned that the Governor was distrustful of a territorial penchant for lynch law, Pitkin was not so undiplomatic as to emphasize that point at the hearing. His main argument was that the extradition papers were not properly drawn up and that no court of law would be justified in honouring them. If he had a good reason, the *News* did not give it. As far as can be determined from that journal's report, the Governor simply dropped the ball there, confident that nobody could override his authority. There is, of course, the possibility that the Governor of Arizona deliberately turned in a faulty writ as part of the deal between them.

Pitkin's subsidiary reason had a legal wrapping, but in producing it he must have had a hard time keeping his grin safely hid in his whiskers. "In the second place it was the custom in cases where the person charged with an offence in one State was arrested for another offence in the State in which he lived the trial of the offence committed in the State in which he lived must precede his delivery to the authorities of the other State."

What the Governor had done then was to pick up the phony charge Bat had cooked up in collusion with the Pueblo authorities and act as though he was convinced it was bona fide. In the presence of a flock of newspapermen, who knew the true score as well as he did, that took some gall. As Governor, however, he was the man with the brass earrings, so he was not challenged.

Nevertheless, the *News* did let him know that it was aware of what was going on. "The excuse upon which he allowed the alleged murderer to go free has not impressed the Sheriff's force with a high opinion of his candour, they claiming to know of a case in which a requisition from the same Territory, with the same defect, was honoured by him. Neither does the expression of opinion that 'Doc' should be taken to Pueblo for trial give general satisfaction. . . . There does not appear to be any doubt that the Pueblo charge was trumped up solely for the purpose of taking 'Doc' out of the hands of the Denver Sheriff's force. . . . On the whole, it is held by the officers that Governor Pitkin has not covered himself with any very heavy mantle of glory in refusing to honour the requisition."

His Excellency's action opened the way for another habeas corpus hearing, at which Doc's battery of attorneys carried the day without difficulty. Thereafter Holliday was served with a warrant charging him with fracturing the peace of Colorado. Still in custody but no longer in jeopardy, he promptly fared south. "Doc Holliday was taken to Pueblo last evening," the *News* sourly reported on May 31, "to be tried on the charge of bunko-steering a man out of one hundred dollars. Doc did not appear to have any dark fears for the result."

Bob Paul had also left Denver to resume his normal duties as sheriff of Pima County. He had been authorized only to bring John H. Holliday back to Arizona. As he was given no papers dealing with Wyatt Earp, he made no motion to find the man who actually killed Frank Stilwell. Served with his own type of political deal, Sheriff Behan had been cold-decked and euchred, so the slaying of Florentino Cruz never got a billing. Certain citizens of Tombstone and its environs might and did complain to unjust gods that they had been robbed. Otherwise the story of Cochise County's feud was a completed fact. The case was closed.

Before conceding that fact, as far as Denver was concerned, some notice must be taken of the man who had initiated Doc Holliday's trial. As it progressed, Sheriff-Police Officer Perry M. Mallen slipped more and more into the background. Once the hero of the city, he was all but ignored after Paul arrived. Bat Masterson was partly responsible for his eclipse. Mallen had sung small when Bat had publicly accused him of being the tool of the rustlers, and observant reporters had decided that he was perhaps not such a terror as they had first announced him to be. He also lost out on his blood money when Behan lost his bid to have Doc requisitioned for Cochise County, but his grief was given no mention in the mounting interest in the struggle between the pro-Holliday and anti-Holliday pressure groups.

Even Mallen's departure from Denver went unnoticed and so remained until a couple of days after Doc himself had left. It was then that a reporter for the *Republican* found something in newspaper exchange that he pounced upon with unholy but thoroughly justified delight. What he had spotted was a by-line feature article in the Cincinnati, Ohio, *Enquirer*. After taking the time to check on local angles, he published the sum of his findings in the *Republican's* issue of June 2.

"For a genuine romance of crime with detectives, bloody avengers, bull-dogs and dark lanterns thrown in, the country has never produced anything half as good as the Doc Holliday case. It has been written up so much that the *Republican* would not impose another article on the subject were it not for several facts which have come out of late. These facts round off the hideous tale with a burst of laughter and turn what was nearly a tragedy into a roaring farce. The villain of the first act becomes the hero of the second. The avenger and detective in one, the man who has devoted his life to his dead comrade, and has been shot so often he has trouble in retaining his food, proves to be a petty swindler. In order to understand the affair it is necessary to print an article from the *Cincinnati Enquirer*, which is the funniest part of the whole affair. The entire article betrays the fine Italian hand of Perry Mallen, the alleged avenger, who, as 'Winston' has blown his own bazoo in a very loud and boisterous manner. Perry played it low down in the *Enquirer*, which is a paper very rarely taken in."

The *Enquirer* dispatch, which was then given in full, had a

Denver date-line of May 23, 1882. Ignoring the preamble, whose purport was that Jesse James had died just in time to avoid being overshadowed, the part quoted here will commence with a description of the new national king-pin of crime.

"Doc Holliday, so called because of a peculiar dexterity he possesses in the care and cure of gun-shot wounds, is a tall, dark-looking man of about forty years of age, with a form herculean in its activity and strength. . . . The exact spot of his birth is, and perhaps will remain, a mystery, as he never spoke of his child-hood to anyone unless, perhaps, to his confederates in villainy and crime. It is supposed that he originally came from Georgia, but be this as it may, he first turned up in Missouri some ten years ago as a cowboy, with very strict ideas of honour and the like for one in such a position as his."

Having introduced his character in the manner of Ned Buntline, from whom, perhaps, he was borrowed, the author of the *Enquirer's* bit of fiction had Doc kill a man who was rude enough to accuse him of rustling. In consequence he was chased out of Missouri and into the life of Perry M. Mallen.

From the articles printed in Denver at the time of Doc's arrest it was clear that Mallen had given Holliday quite a career, but the exact nature of it was hinted at rather than described. The *Enquirer* told all, including some special touches for the dudes back East which a Western editor wouldn't have swallowed.

"It is evident that Doc escaped, for he next turned up in St. George, Utah, as the proprietor of a faro table. This was in the spring of 1875. . . . Holladay soon made himself known as a man who would stand no trifling, and with whom contradiction meant 'gore' every time. He gave a practical illustration of his naturally savage propensities by shooting down in cold blood a young man named Harry White of Cleveland, Ohio."

Right there, as the Uncle Remus of Holliday's native State would say, is where Doc dropped his money purse. His act of careless viciousness drew nemesis on his trail in the form of the dead White's faithful and unforgiving pal, Perry M. Mallen. The latter, incidentally, was described in the article as being the Sheriff of Los Angeles, California.

"For the killing of his friend Mallen swore an oath of ven-geance to track down his murderer and bring him to justice." Failing to make good in St. George, he doggedly followed

Holliday when "Doc packed up his traps and emigrated to Fort Yuma, on the Colorado River, where he began the lucrative business of stealing cattle".

It was then that the faithful Mallen received the first of a series of wounds that would have discouraged a less intrepid man. When a sheriff's posse undertook to pursue Doc into the nearby Calico Range, it was asking for, and got, big trouble.

"Three men bit the dust through Holladay who showed his dare-devil courage by riding to the front of his men and boldly shooting them down. Mallen was severely wounded in the combat, but this only strengthened his determination to bring the desperado to his just desserts."

After tracking Doc to Los Angeles and other points in Southern California, Mallen learned that he had gone to "Fort Dodge, Kansas". There he was shocked to discover that Doc had shot a magistrate named Judge Benson, who had handed down a decision unfavourable to a couple of Holliday's chums.

Having planted the judge in Boot Hill, Doc "went to the Indian Territory, where he became the leader of a gang of thieves and cut-throats. One year he spent here practicing all sorts of rascality, when suddenly in '77 the mining fever broke out at Tucson, Arizona". After Tucson came Tombstone where Doc "became identified with the rougher element of that wild place, and as usual his indomitable will and reckless courage soon placed him at the head of the murderous gang of cowboys which has since proved the great terror of that country. His record of shameless murders and robbery during this time throws the deeds of Jesse James, Billy the Kid or any other desperado entirely in the shade. Fearing neither God nor man he became a devil incarnate."

It should not be inferred that Harry White's tried and true friend wasn't giving it the old college try every time he convalesced enough to feel up to it. "Mallen during all this time was on his track, but it seemed fate was against him, for just as the fruit was ripe for the plucking Holliday escaped, always leaving behind him a memento in the shape of a knife wound or an ounce of cold lead. Six bullets from Holliday's pistol perforated Mallen's body, yet he did not despair."

Did the Horatio Alger team of determination and pluck win out? They did, by cracky. "After seven years of pursuit and perseverance he got the 'drop' on Doc and brought him 'dead to rights', May 15, 1882."

The author of the article next proceeded to tell how he secured all this inside information. "Determined to gain news for the *Enquirer*, your correspondent repaired to the room of the American Hotel, where he was shown to the room of Perry Mallen." He was courteously received by that hero, who needed little urging to give a lurid character sketch of Doc. "When on a cattle raid he seldom succeeded without shedding human blood and that in the most dastardly fashion. When on murder bent, he never failed and many are the poor fellows whose bones now lie bleaching on Arizona soil. He has not one germ of true manhood, he is as vain as vanity itself, and his heart is as stone. No cry of anguish or suffering deterred him from his purpose, and like a savage wild beast he gloried in his deeds of blood!"

Asked just how many lives Doc had taken, Mallen was frank to admit that he didn't exactly know. "That is a hard question to answer, but they approach close to fifty. . . . While in Tucson he shot and killed six men within two weeks, all of whom he killed without cause or reason."

Feeling it necessary to leave Tucson after this orgy of blood, the Holliday of this article made for the Indian Territory via Denver. There his nemesis finally accomplished his purpose, avenging the dastardly murder of Harry White by turning Doc over to the law.

"In all probability," the story concluded, "the Earps band will burst, since their leader is in durance vile. He will be taken to Arizona as soon as the requisition arrives, there to answer for his many crimes. From all quarters is his capture hailed with delight, now that the thorn has been made to stick inwardly, there's no doubt that the future welfare and prosperity of Arizona is assured.

"Winston"

So much for what the *Denver Republican's* happy reporter found in the *Cincinnati Enquirer*. Having followed it through to the magnificent *non sequitur* just above the signature, he then began to marshal his reasons for believing that Mallen and Winston were one and the same.

After first pointing out that nobody from Los Angeles had heard of such a peace officer, the article dealt with the great detective's activities in Denver above and beyond his arrest of Doc. "Mallen came with a flourish of trumpets and put up at the Great West Hotel . . . where he met a man called Julius Schweigardt, to whom he presented letters of introduction from Schweigardt's friends in California. Mallen became a guest at the house and cultivated Schweigardt who had just sold his half ownership in the house.

"Mallen then began to work a systematic scheme to beat his friend. He filled him with frightful stories of his escapes by flood and field in his detective work, and of the enormous sums he made off rewards. . . . After Perry had thus seduced his friend he borrowed $310 of him upon the following scheme:

"Mallen called his friend upstairs, and after locking the door and hanging a towel over the keyhole, he confided to him in a stage whisper the fearful information that he knew of a terrible murderer who was living in Kansas City under an assumed name. Mallen proposed to get him. There was a reward of $1500 for him and several bucketfuls of glory. He did not often make such propositions, but if Schweigardt would pay the expense he would take him in as partner.

"Mallen held to his agreement. He did take him in as a partner. He took him in for $310. . . . The two men started for Kansas City about a week ago. Arriving there they held a consultation with the police, and Mallen told his companion that he must go over to Wyandotte to spot his man, who was running a gambling house there. Schweigardt was to remain. Mallen never returned. He may be hunting his man yet and have forgotten all about Schweigardt and the matter of $310. All that is really known is that he has gone."

The *Republican's* reporter had learned what happened, because the demon sleuth's partner finally got tired of his Kansas City vigil. "Schweigardt returned yesterday and found a companion in sorrow. This other victim is Charles Morgan, also a boarder at the Great West, from whom Mallen obtained a loan of $130 on the strength of his notoriety."

In the course of giving his pay-off line the reporter tossed in a reference to still another one of Winston's exploits. "These two cases, in addition to the Omaha case, where Mallen was obliged to return $50, out of which he had swindled a man on a patent-right swindle, will cause Perry's forcible return to Denver should he be found anywhere, but it is probable that his face will never be seen here again. What is our gain is someone else's loss."

The exposure of Perry Mallen was the true conclusion of the Holliday extradition episode and a more beautifully fitting one could not be imagined. It leaves the story a miracle of unedifying perfection, in which every professional defender of law and order acted in disregard of the proprieties and only the notorious malefactor conducted himself with decorum.

This proposition can easily be proved by reviewing the actions of the sworn upholders of the peace. Wyatt Earp started it off by an act of personal vengeance. For this he might be allowed to have ample provocation, without granting that he had the right to sport a United States Marshal's badge when attending to a clan blood feud. The two Arizona sheriffs were similarly out of order. Behan duplicated Earp's conduct by utilizing his office to even personal accounts, while Paul used his authority to pay back his obligation to a former political ally. A deputy sheriff, Masterson went on record as whitewashing a man he later identified as about the worst outlaw in his wide experience. He also implemented a scheme by which the law was used to defeat its own purposes.

All the foregoing were pilgrims of the circuit, nor can their actions be called inconsistent with its peculiar code. Yet the representatives of a more conservative social order did no better. Sheriff Spangler of Denver played fox and geese with Wyatt's foe, John Behan, so as to put the power to act in the hands of the friendly Bob Paul. In this he was aided and abetted by the chief magistrate of a territory, Governor Tritle. Governor Pitkin, the chief magistrate of a State, did not scruple to pocket the hoax Masterson handed him, although it had been freely exposed in the press.

Behind all this—you can smell it but not see it—was the influence of that arch foe of crime, the old Wells, Fargo Express Company, while backstage but still visible stood General Dave Cook and other upholders of the law. They did not uphold it, they juggled with it; and when a for-once innocent man was finally freed, it was not a triumph of justice but of duplicity.

The acknowledged enemy of society, on the other hand, bore himself in a manner above reproach. Obedient to the law of the land, he had not even been a witness to wrongdoing in the case before the courts. Keeping faith, even in the face of extreme adversity, he had not complained when falsely accused of killing Frank Stilwell, nor had he tried to shift the blame to quarters where it could comfortably have rested.

For these decencies he got no credit from the *Rocky Mountain News*, which still growled about Colorado's tolerance for "such cattle" as Holliday, even after he had left Denver; nor were they appreciated even by the better disposed *Republican*. "Holladay," the latter reported, "is resting quietly in Pueblo in the bosom of his constituency; a hard lot, to be sure, but not half as bad as Mallen."

Realizing the worst fears of the *News*, the charge of bunco-steering had not resulted in any trouble for Doc. The only real result, as one newspaperman noted, was "the coining of a new word in Colorado—'Hollidaying' "—for people who used phony indictments to avoid difficulties with the law.

Meanwhile, the rest of the deputy marshal's posse had come to Pueblo to celebrate Doc's release. The fact that they then went separate ways was probably in part due to considerations of policy. Doc and Wyatt hitting any town together would revive the myth of the Earp Gang, which both were anxious to kill. For the rest, they were individualists used to going their own ways unless accident or emergency decreed otherwise.

Where the rest went is a matter of some doubt, though old-timers of Gunnison recalled that Wyatt and several associates ran a gambling hall there during the winter of 1882–83. Doc, however, evidently thought he would do well to give Coloradoans a chance to find a new topic of conversation. He got out of the State and made his way to Deadwood in Dakota Territory.

He seems to have spent the winter there, though there is documentation only for the shooting which marked his arrival. This incident, which was first plucked from its original newspaper sources by Lorenzo Walters, is worth noting for its tone as much as for the nature of the exploit. Following the national publicity distributed out of Tombstone and Denver, Doc was recognized as top-flight journalistic property. The report is thus hopped up with the same brand of corn that newspapermen had slipped into stories about Jim Bowie a half century earlier.

When Doc Holliday arrived in Deadwood in the summer of 1882, he didn't pause for such non-essential details as finding a place to lodge. First things came first and he made for a saloon, there to refresh himself and inquire as to the presence in camp of other circuit paladins. He did not get much information in the almost empty bar, though. The bar-keeper was mean drunk and soon found someone on whom to spend his bad temper.

At that time most of the miners of Deadwood were at the diggings, but one little fellow, for some reason off duty, had come in for a drink. Just one snort was all he wanted, and he stood firm against the bar-tender's urgings that he should have another. Enraged at such temperance or parsimony—a one-drink man in Deadwood was an unheard-of scandal—the bar-keeper changed from arguing to threatening.

Annoyed by the senseless show of rage, Doc had been watching the bar-tender and thus had his eye on him when the fellow climaxed his menaces by reaching in a drawer for a revolver. Holliday had seen too much gun-play not to know the difference between a man bluffing and one that meant business. There was only one way to save the now terrified miner's life, and Doc unlimbered his forty-five. Just as the would-be killer's finger was tightening on the trigger, Holliday's bullet drilled his wrist.

The shot and the uproar made by the anguished bar-keeper drew men on the run. Doc was in trouble again, but he got out of it more easily than was usual for him. What Jim Bowie did in so many stories, he did this one time, standing back with folded arms and withering the opposition simply by introducing himself. "Gentlemen," he is reported to have said, "I am Doc Holliday of Tombstone."

In so far as can be ascertained he had no further difficulties while in Deadwood, nor did he find any challengers for some months after his return to Colorado. That he was still insulated by his awesome reputation is shown by the correspondent for the *New York Sun*, whose article has already been cited with reference to Doc's own report of his Tombstone activities. The item has a date line reading "Silverton, Col., June 1", so Doc must have been sojourning there as of the last of May 1883.

This article ends with Doc pooh-poohing some of the wilder tales of his manslaughtering, but it is obvious that the reporter neither believes these denials himself nor expects his readers to. The opening passages of his dispatch will suffice to give its tone.

"A crowd following a rather good-looking man around, stopping when he stopped, listening as to an oracle when he had anything to say, and all the time gaping at him in open-mouthed wonder, proclaimed the fact that an important personage was in town.

" 'Who is that duck?' an old miner asked.

" 'Sh-h-h!' replied a companion, 'that's Doc Holliday. He's killed thirty men in his day, and there's no telling when he'll turn himself loose again.' "

As it happened, 1883 was Doc's serenest year, being the only one, following his adoption of the career of a professional gambler, in which he had no recorded passage at arms or brush with the law. He prospered amain as a dealer, too, especially after settling in Leadville. That town had finally justified his early expectations of it by becoming one of the circuit's high-flying gambling camps.

Doc's success in Leadville is attested by a correspondent of the *Phoenix Herald*, contributing a report about the activities of former Arizonans which was published on November 15, 1883. Taken altogether it is such a society note as can scarcely be matched in the annals of home-folks journalism.

After first noting that Johnny Meagher was doing well with cards, it carried on with, "Doc Holliday is the chief engineer of three faro games in Leadville, and Johnny Tyler is holding his own in the same city.

"Wyatt Earp is hunting a lively camp in New Mexico or Texas. Virgil is exhibiting his trained tiger to the playfully inclined of the Calico district. Jim is dealing faro bank in Salt Lake City, and Warren is tending bar for his father in Colton."

Doc was thus bracketed in the first paragraph with both an old Tombstone friend and a former Tombstone foe. Johnny Meagher was one of the men who had helped put up bail for him when he was arrested on the bibulous affidavit of Big Nose Kate, while Johnny Tyler had led the expedition which had tried to hoorah the Oriental just after Wyatt had been admitted to partnership.

Doc was not to leave Leadville without first making blood marks on its history, however. That he eventually did so has been generally allowed, although confusion has existed as to just what he accomplished with gun-fire in the two-mile-high silver camp. This has been natural, due to the conflicting state-ments previously encountered by investigators.

One was to the effect that Doc shot it out with a Leadville policeman. Another asserted that the cop's name was Allen. A third positively stated that Doc killed a man in Leadville. A fourth declared that Allen survived.

The resulting conundrum remained without a solution until Joseph Miller—whose paragraph by paragraph studies of frontier newspapers are adding materially to the available stock of infor-mation about the old West—ran across a pick-up which the *Yuma Sentinel* had made from the briefly flourishing *Tombstone Record* on September 3, 1884. This brought to light that in addition to duelling with Allen, Doc had salivated a man named Kelly with hot lead. An early Leadville chronicle contributes the fact that a man named A. J. Kelly doubled in brass as a bartender and constable.

The fight with Allen, who was no less a personage than Leadville's chief of police, took place about the same time, although a little earlier. This encounter and the circumstances leading up to it were described by E. D. Cowen, who was in town at the time and who could have had a ringside seat, courtesy of Doc himself.

"During the three years he lived there," Cowen reported in writing of Doc's Leadville days, "several attempts were made to embroil him, but the local bad men shied away after he spoiled Bill Allen's pistol arm.

"At the time I was engaged on the *Leadville Democrat*, and Holliday, grateful for my perfunctory assistance in the rescue for which the loyalty and energy of Masterson deserved the credit, occasionally called on me. One day he remarked coolly: 'I wish you would do me a favour,' and then, after an assenting word, 'Bill Allen is after me. I want you to come around and see me wing him when the ball comes off. He isn't worth killing.'

"Bill Allen had been chief of police and killed his first man," Cowen went on to say. "His ambition was soaring. Holliday owed him $5.00, which he was unable to pay. Allen served notice that unless the money were forthcoming the following day Holliday would go to his own funeral.

" 'Don't try it on, Bill,' was Doc's gentle suggestion, 'unless you come with both hands full of guns.'

"Holliday had been dealing faro in Hyman's saloon Thirteenth Street, next door to which was Allen's saloon. Nonchalantly leaning against the bar, he awaited the coming of the novel bill collector."

Cowen had not seen fit to put himself in the position of a witness with foreknowledge of the fact in the instance of a possible killing. However, he covered the story, and was able to give the next best thing to a first-hand account.

"I had thankfully, if not gratefully, declined to attend the affair, but the melodrama was performed as the stage manager planned. Allen rushed in through the swinging front doors, six-shooter in hand, caught sight of Holliday standing there at the bar and raised to fire. But he lacked the lightning movement of the Georgian. Holliday's six-shooter barked, and the bite took Allen in the pistol arm, the bullet entering below the wrist, evidently at the instant Allen was lowering. His six-shooter dropped to the floor and he collapsed. The radial bone had been broken and Allen was saved from killing any more men, at least with his right hand."

Constable Kelly was not so fortunate as his chief, whom he may have set out to avenge. All that is known about the engagement which cost him his life is contained in a report picked up by a Tombstone citizen who seemingly knew Doc but not his enemy. The report is especially interesting as showing the Western *code duello* in practice. Ready to slay though he was, Doc took time to make sure that his antagonist was heeled before he reached for his own gun.

As noted above, the account is preserved in the old *Yuma Sentinel*, which owed it to the *Tombstone Record*. "From Charles Bagsby, who recently returned to Tombstone, is gathered the following particulars concerning the reported killing of a man in Leadville by Doc Holliday. It appears that bad blood existed for some time between a policeman there named Kelly, and Holliday. On the evening of the shooting, Kelly had been going about the saloons looking for Holliday, and upon Kelly finally coming into a saloon where the latter was present, Holliday stepped up to him and asked if he was armed. Kelly replied in the affirmative and started to draw his gun. Holliday was too quick for him, however."

A couple of Doc's bullets took effect, though Kelly did not

die until after he had been lugged away from the scene of battle. Doc meanwhile had been trying to finish him off on the spot, but Bagsby declared that he met with interference. "Before he could fire again he was arrested and taken away. At the subsequent examination the testimony showed Holliday entirely in the right, and he was discharged."

If the man who died caused little trouble, even as a post-mortem inconvenience, the one who survived was more of a nuisance. Holliday was indicted for the shooting of Bill Allen and was brought to trial for it on March 28, 1885. Doc beat the rap, newspaper reports showing that he was acquitted on March 30, but Allen scored one point. It was the only time in the history of John Henry Holliday's standing quarrel with the law that any case against him got beyond the stage of indictment or pre-liminary hearing.

CHAPTER XIII

Y<small>ET</small> well before the spring of 1885 Doc had been faced with a matter much more serious than any trouble which the law had been able to cause him. This was the dissolution of the world in which he had flourished.

His difficulty with Allen is a sufficient clue to what was happening. For a top-hand faro dealer to be dunned for a paltry five bucks marked a change in the times. High rollers had always had their sour streaks, but their come-back was taken for granted and their credit was good anywhere in the circuit. By 1884, however, the great days of free-lance gambling in the West had gone.

The uproarious camps had either quieted to talk in whispers, folded entirely, or commenced to turn into humdrum commercial towns. Fort Griffin's Flat was already a legend. Jacksboro was a poky rural trading centre. Deadwood was overshadowed by neighbouring towns, themselves of no particular renown. Las Vegas Old Town was swallowing up New Town. Tombstone's big excitement in 1884 was caused by the activities of a mining union rather than by gun-packing gamblers. Dodge City, which ultimately fell into that state of gracelessness, was preparing to turn bluenose.

In Colorado, Denver had long graduated from a frontier boom town to a full-fledged city, in whose life gambling played only a minor part. Leadville's phenomenal growth—for by 1884 it rivalled Denver in size and had hopes of supplanting it for ever as the State's metropolis—produced a similar effect. When Leadville succumbed to ordinary commercial aspirations and the connected new social outlook, it was all over. Cripple Creek was to come later, but one isolated capital could not revive the empire. The circuit, to use one of its own favourite faro phrases, was played out.

The inevitable result was to shunt those who had been its

leading citizens into the background. Under the new dispensa-
tion gambling had ceased to be something taken for granted, and
its artists were no longer counted among the town's most notable
citizens. Where respectability had become the keynote, they
were not respected. Neither were they capable of inspiring the
old awe by their handiness with guns. Leadville and Denver—as
Bat Masterson discovered when he went on a tear and tried to
hoorah the latter city—were far too big to be treed.

The triumph of commerce finally pushed gambling and
gamblers into the shadow of the underworld where they have
since remained. Dealers no longer had the freedom of the city.
They were relegated to a minor segment of society known as
"the sporting element". To this situation there were two re-
sponsive courses. They could compromise with the new order,
as Wyatt Earp and Masterson eventually did, or they could
stick with the wreckage, as Doc was to do, until the twilight of
the gods deepened into complete night.

There were already signs that he was not to have too long
to wait. His health took a turn for the worse, and his new way
of life did not encourage its betterment. The hours in the gambling saloons were no longer balanced by hours in the saddle.
Civilization was wrapping him in a winding sheet; for rest and
rust are much the same, and now when he moved from one town
to another it was not with the wind in his face. When he shuttled
back and forth between Leadville and Denver, he rode in a train
like any businessman commuter.

By the time Colonel Deweese had successfully defended him
for the winging of Police Chief Allen, Doc had already attained
the status of a museum piece held over from another era. One
newspaperman wrote of him that he was "one of those characters
formerly quite common in the West, but now, like the Indian
and the buffalo becoming quite rare".

His name was still one to evoke recognition, nevertheless,
and men did not cease to tell the things he had done in the realms
of both fact and myth. Except for the closing episode, actuality has
already had its inning here. The legends which have grown up
around Doc will now be briefly treated.

Taking them in the order in which they fit into Doc's career
—it would be impossible to trace the order in which they were
invented—the first few deal with the reasons why Holliday first

ventured into the West. At least one of these is ascribed to his authorship. When young Otero was gauche enough to enquire into his past, Doc said that he had given up the profession of dentistry because he had been jilted by the belle of the Illinois town where he had been practicing. The tale current in Leadville was that Holliday had bolted from Georgia after shooting his uncle in vengeance for the fratricidal murder of Doc's father. Another version floating around Colorado pictured Doc as having run away from home, lured by an uncontrollable lust for adventure, at the age of eleven.

Doc's peculiar sense of humour exhibits itself in the tale of why he found it necessary to leave Dallas. He told this story to Deweese, who passed it on to a Denver reporter. "It was perhaps a little incident connected with his practice of the dental profession that induced the doctor to leave Texas. . . . The doctor at that time had an enemy. He used to tell the story himself and say that he had every desire to kill the man. But the doctor was always a prudent man. He feared he wouldn't be legally protected if he took the man's life. The doctor wanted revenge, but he was in a dilemma. An event occurred, however, which gave the doctor an opportunity he had hardly expected. His enemy came to his office with an aching tooth. The doctor put the patient under laughing-gas, and before his enemy had left the chair the quiet doctor had extracted nearly every tooth he had in his head."

Attached to the Jacksboro period is the statement that Doc was on better than friendly relations with the red-haired Lottie Deno, who in fact is supposed to have been interested in a Back Bay black sheep—possessed of no other known distinction—named Johnny Golden. It has been furthermore adduced that Doc's return to Texas was owing to his vain hope of seeing Lottie again; hence his choice of Fort Griffin, whither La Deno had moved from Jacksboro while Holliday was in Colorado. The story seems to be based on nothing more than legend's commonly encountered effort to bracket unusual personalities.

A tale which might be true, except that it can be traced to no foundation in source material, runs to the effect that Doc got in a big poker game, during his first trip to Colorado, with a mine speculator from San Francisco. The latter lost so heavily that he eventually put up a gold-mine claim—pledged against heavy stakes—which he also lost. It was not until the deed had been signed over that he confessed, to Doc's considerable annoyance, that its true worth was about one white chip. Brooding over this, Holliday used his negotiable winnings to become silent partner in an assay establishment. With samples in the possession of the firm he then salted another old claim, which he sold to the speculator for enough to cover the cost of his partnership and a handsome profit.

Doc's mythical sojourn in southern California—originally a product of Perry M. Mallen's creative powers—has become woven into the body of the Holliday legend. It was not long after the Denver trail that others beside Mallen remembered that they had seen Doc west of the Colorado River.

"I had a brush with the Doc once in the Calico Range back of Fort Yuma," one fellow informed the New York Sun's correspondent at Silverton. "He and twenty-five other horse and cattle thieves were down there, and they sent word to the sheriff they were spoiling for a fight. That made the officer mad, and so he got up a posse and set out, I being one of the party. When we came on the gang we saw that they outnumbered us two to one, and so we concluded not to fight. As soon as the Doc saw that we were sloping he got mad, and, jumping out in front of his party he yelled that he could whip us single-handed.

"He hadn't any more than said the word when he began firing, and we ran like cowards. He killed three of our party before we got to cover, though, and we didn't have any anxiety to interview him again. A little while after that he left the country, greatly to the relief of the sheriff, who said he never could be chief while Doc was around."

Not all the tall tales were told by men who professed to stand in awe of Doc, of course. As in the case of Billy the Kid, there lacked not men who recalled—after he was safely dead—that they had trampled all over him. One such was a character who dubbed himself "Arizona Bill" in his published reminiscences. The Arizona Rangers were not formed until 1901; but Bill was a soon man, and he had already worked his way up to a sergeancy in the territorial police force when he rode into Tombstone one evening in 1882. To the best of his recollection—the same one that enabled him to see Wild Bill Hickok several years after that worthy had drawn the dead man's hand in the Black

Hills—he spent the bulk of his time cuffing Doc around and telling him where to get off.

Another tale—of which Ike Clanton was the would-be robber in the original version—portrays John Slaughter as scaring Doc away from an attempted hold-up by remarking that he, too, was armed. As this incident was supposed to have taken place on the same night as the Benson stage murders, it can be dismissed on the strength of the evidence which found him dealing cards in Tombstone throughout the entire period.

Doc's quarrel with Frank McLowry over the latter's rude remarks about Nellie Cashman's food should probably likewise be classed as legendary. The story is basically a stock Western yarn, which has found a niche in the annals of a number of camps. In Dodge City, for instance, the lead is played by Stink-finger Jack. Chivalrous, if smelly of digit, Jack persuaded a cad to show *bon appetit* for a Mrs. Kelly's viands by shooting under the table.

A legend which arouses admiration through its sheer and indelicate ingenuity has also arranged for Doc to gaze once more upon Big Nose Kate, after her departure from Tombstone. This found its way into print no longer ago than 1952, when it was published in a hobby periodical called *Guns*. Like all good tall tales it points to first-hand experience for authority. The supposed original teller of this yarn was a collector of firearms, who was electrified to run across a revolver with a tag identifying it as the six-shooter which had killed Big Nose Kate. Anxious to verify the statement, the collector hopped by 'plane from his native Middle West to Tombstone, where he put himself in the hands of a knowledgeable old-timer. His confidence was not misplaced, for the veteran took him to the old copper mining town of Bisbee, where another grey-beard recognized the revolver in a moment.

There was no question about it. This was the weapon which had done for Kate in a saloon located in Bisbee's famous Brewery Gulch. A crazy drunk had come into the place shooting at random. Everybody dropped to the floor as usual, but when the man had run out of ammunition, Kate did not get up. She was dead, yet nobody could find anything the matter with her. They peeled off her duds, but could discover no indication that she had been wounded. Finally somebody suggested that it would be well to send for Doc Holliday.

In answer to summons by telegraph Doc galloped the twenty-odd miles from Tombstone to Bisbee, and was in Brewery Gulch by dawn. Examining the nude corpse, his keen eye saw what the others had missed. On one of the buttocks of Big Nose Kate was an infinitesimal fleck of blood. Calling for a razor, Doc performed an autopsy with cool dexterity and was rewarded by finding the cause of Kate's demise. When the gun-happy drunk entered the saloon, she had hit the floor with her stern oriented in his direction. One of the bullets had found this target, scoring such a precision hit on her rectum that it gained admittance at the cost of no blood except the tiny spot which Doc alone had observed. With his extraction of the spent slug from his former mistress's entrails, the way was paved for ballistics to show that the gun located by the collector was indeed the one which had fired the fatal shot.

The legends stemming from Doc's Colorado years largely cluster about his death in Glenwood Springs. One man remembered having been told as a boy that it wasn't tuberculosis that had done for Doc, it was syphilis. Why he had come to a place dedicated to curing respiratory diseases was not explained, but in any case he had promptly caught pneumonia and died. An amplified version of this tale finds another youth actually present in a doctor's office when Doc was brought in—a day or so short of death—by Wyatt Earp.

But other lads, whose memory also never failed them in after years, had been present in Glenwood Springs while Doc was there. Far from being in the last stages of dissolution, he was well enough to tend bar for weeks before a sudden illness made away with him. In another tale Doc was a guest. That was remembered by a man who claimed to have served as a bell-hop in the hotel where Doc was staying. Holliday had apparently not come there for his health at all, but rather because—like Billy Bones—he was seeking a quiet place where he hoped his enemies wouldn't think to look for him. When giving Doc room service, the bell-hop was always careful to announce himself, and even then he always found Holliday sitting with two revolvers aimed at the door. Precisely whom he feared was a thing never established, as he at length foiled all pursuit by dying.

To refer back to the subject of Wyatt Earp, he did not create any Holliday legends; but he was unwittingly responsible for misinformation with regard to Doc's death. In his article published in 1896, Wyatt gave the impression that it was written just after Doc's demise. This led Earp's biographer to postulate that Holiday had died more than a decade after the exodus from Tombstone, with a kick-off date of 1895 or '96. Examining the same item, Walter Noble Burns, author of *Tombstone: An Iliad of the Southwest*, stumbled into a similar error. So, come to think of it, did a fellow named Myers in his chronicle of the old silver camp called *The Last Chance*.

Actually Doc died in 1887, though Wyatt knew nothing about it at the time. This should be no cause for astonishment. In a restless effort to find again the world that had gone, Earp wandered all over the West, but ended by becoming more or less of a fixture in California. It is the rediscovery of the fact that Wyatt had been interviewed by a Denver paper in 1895—after what was patently a considerable absence from Colorado—which tells what happened. Doc and Wyatt had no more inclination to correspond with each other than do the average foot-loose males. Eventually they had lost track of each other, and it was not until he returned to Colorado after a lapse of years that Wyatt learned Doc had long been dead.

Wishing to pay some tribute to his friend, in part for auld lang syne and in part out of realization that Doc's like was not commonly encountered, Earp drafted the article which was published by the *San Francisco Weekly Examiner* in August 1896. In its total effect it was the crude output of an amateur; but Wyatt squeezed one epigram out of emotion remembered in tranquillity which was pretty good.

"Doc was," Earp wrote, "a dentist whom necessity had made a gambler; a gentleman whom disease had made a frontier vagabond; a philosopher whom life had made a caustic wit; a long, lean ash-blond fellow nearly dead with consumption, and at the same time the most skilful gambler and the nerviest, speediest, deadliest man with a six-gun I ever knew." Let that stand as Doc's epitaph, written by a man who prized him

Yet John Holliday had no immediate need of an epitaph, after he succeeded in proving to the court that he had shot Bill Allen in self-defence. Times were bad and his health was worse, but he somehow made it on his own for another two years. Yet even his differences with the law reflected waning strength. As one newspaperman wrote when dealing with this sundown period, "He figured, though rather indirectly, in one or two little scrimmages between sporting men, was arrested for vagrancy but released."

City directories show that he was betimes a resident of both Denver and Leadville during most of his last two years. It was from that latter city that he ultimately bought a one-way ticket to Glenwood Springs.

By then consumption so wracked him that he could hardly keep on his feet. As a realist, Doc was not one to believe in miraculous cures, but as a man of action he refused to stop in his tracks while there was a chance of going on. The sulphur vapours at Glenwood were ballyhooed as being medicine's final answer to the evil challenge of tuberculosis. On the off-chance that this was true, Doc went to the health resort to play his last chip. This was in May 1887.

It was all that was left for him to do, but for once that was not enough. His lungs were too far gone, and the sulphur fumes destroyed what remained of them instead of effecting any cure. As he himself expected no better results, he wrapped himself in a chrysalis of fatalism as he moved courteously among peaceful people.

All this was made plain in an obituary which was written for him six months later. The fact that the only known copy is in a scrap-book of clippings prevents positive newspaper ascription. As the article has been generally identified as the work of James L. Riland, it is believed to have appeared in a sheet published in Riland's home town of Meeker. It is evident that either Riland did not know Doc well enough to be sure of his name or the composing-room couldn't read Riland's writing well enough to tell an "A" from an "H."

"Death of J. A. Holliday," ran the scarehead. "Died in Glenwood Springs, Colo., Tuesday Nov. 8, 1887," the lower bank announced. "About 10 o'clock a.m. of consumption.

"J. A. Holliday, or Doc Holliday as he was better known, came to Glenwood Springs from Leadville last May, and by his quiet and gentlemanly demeanour during his short stay . . . made many friends. . . . Since he took up his residence at the Springs the evil effects of the sulphurous vapours arising from the hot springs on his weak lungs could readily be detected and for the last few months it was seen that dissolution was only the question of a little time, hence his death was not entirely unexpected."

The mortuary notice next made it apparent that legend had gone to bat for Doc in a community where fact might not have served him so well. "Holliday was born in Georgia. . . . Twenty-five years ago, when but eleven years of age, he started for the West, and since that time he had probably been in every State and territory west of the Mississippi River. He served as sheriff in one of the counties of Arizona during the troublesome times in that region, and served in other official capacities in different parts of the West."

This seems to be an echo of Bat Masterson's foreswearing when he was trying to save Doc from being extradited. Bat himself would have blinked at the follow-up sentence, however. "Of him it can be said that he represented law and order at all times and places."

Nobody would have enjoyed that joke as much as John H. Holliday, had he lived to read of his virtues. But he did not, having succumbed to absolute consumption. The shredded walls of his lungs could no longer keep the water from rising in them, until he drowned where he lay helpless in bed.

Unlike the mythical pneumonia attacks which did for him overnight, it was not a rapid process, however. "For the past two months," Riland wrote, "his death was expected at any time; during the past 57 days he had only been out of bed twice; the past two weeks he was delirious."

Yet witnesses said that one step short of eternity, Holliday emerged from coma to perform three conscious acts and to speak twice. Towards ten o'clock on the morning of November 8, he astonished those gathered at his bedside by opening clear eyes and asking for a tumbler of whiskey. An attendant officiating, he drank the liquor with deliberate satisfaction. Leaving no heel-taps, he gave the man an appreciative smile before he spoke once more. "This is funny," he said, and closed his eyes for ever.

All veterans of the circuit who heard of his pronouncement knew what he had meant. For nearly fifteen years, it had been common knowledge that Doc had a standing bet with the odds. Up until the time he had resigned himself to being a patient at Glenwood Springs, he always believed that somebody would

o

manage to finish him with a bullet before tuberculosis could put him under grass.

The editor of a Colorado publication called *Field and Farm* was clearly aware of Doc's fatalistic wager, for he included a quaint reference to it in the periodical's obituary. "It was reported this week that Doc Holiday died. . . . He always expected to die with his boots on, and his demise at Glenwood Springs must have been a considerable surprise to him."

To investigators of his past life, however, the great surprise was the disclosure of the preparation he had made for the one to come. "He was baptized," Riland stated, "in the Catholic Church."

The astonishment created by this statement has nothing to do with sectarian bias, pro or con. What startles, by its apparent inconsistency, is the indication that Doc had sufficient interest in the gifts and forfeits of Heaven to feel that any declaration of religious intent would be worth while. In a word, if he felt it necessary to take off into the hereafter from some spiritual stance, why did he shift from his family's hereditary Presbyterianism?

It is Riland's obituary that gives the clue. "He had only one correspondent among his relatives—a cousin, a Sister of Charity, in Atlanta. She will be notified of his death."

The nun referred to was Miss Mattie Holliday, whose entrance into a convent followed hard upon the exit of Dr. John Henry Holliday from Georgia. Whatever she may or may not have meant to him in other ways, she remained his one contact with different values from those cherished by followers of the circuit. Yet it would be unwarranted to infer that his gesture stood for any effort to ensure a mystical meeting beyond middle earth. All that it is necessary to believe is that he knew it would please her for him to show an interest in a future state of salvation, especially if he acknowledged faith in the rituals to which she herself was dedicated. Once he had conceived that it would mean a great deal to her—a point she was no doubt urging from her post near the altar—he did not boggle at it. The proclivity which gave unity to a life which would otherwise have been without it was his compulsion to pay all debts faithfully, to friends as well as to foes.

Appropriately for a town which derived much of its revenue from the last-ditch hopes of the incurable, no great to-do was made over the disposition of the remains. As a corpse is discouraging to the paying guests, that of Doc was hustled into the earth before it could gain the full benefits of his conversion. To take up Riland's statement on a note of repetition, "He was baptized in the Catholic Church, but Father Ed. Downey being absent, Rev. W. S. Rudolph delivered the funeral address, and the remains were consigned to their final resting place in Linwood cemetery at four o'clock in the afternoon of November 8th, in the presence of many friends."

Not mentioned were his enemies, of whom an appreciable number had been blasted across the Styx by his .45. Exactly how many had stepped off into eternity, prompted by his revolver or sheath-knife, is a matter of some dispute. Estimates scale down from thirty-five to about half that. Lorenzo Walters, who had the advantage of talking with a number of men who had known Doc, placed the figure at twenty-three. A Denver newspaperman who took an interest in this problem six weeks after Doc's death reported that, "The best authorities say he had killed sixteen." That checks with the number of finished-off victims cited in this chronicle, although several more are noted on the basis of dubious authority.

E. D. Cowen, however, made mention of "thirty duels to the death", and he knew more about Doc than anybody else who has expressed himself on this particular subject. It is a subject, too, on which more returns may eventually be available. Wyoming investigators, for instance, believe that a man calling himself Charles McKee, who fractured the skull of a Fort Laramie soldier named Robert Wyatt in the fall of 1876—presumably by buffaloing—may have been John Holliday. The evidence to date is inconclusive, though.

That Doc had not gone through these wars unscathed is proved by the obituary notice published in the *Denver Republican* on November 10, 1887. This item noted that "his body was full of wounds received in bloody encounters". One was given him by the last shot fired by Frank McLowry. There is no record as to by whom and under what circumstances he at other times was tapped for the blood which his ever-ailing body could ill spare.

But the *Republican's* death notice makes other statements about Doc which are pertinent here. For one thing, they should have some further influence in modifying the legend of the morose misanthrope whom most people heartily disliked.

"Doc Holladay is dead," was the lead to an item which showed that the newspaper had changed its original opinion of Doc, but not its ideas about spelling his name. "Few men have been better known to a certain class of sporting people, and few men of his character had more friends or stronger champions. He represented a class of men who are fast disappearing in the New West. He had the reputation of being a bunco-man, desperado and bad man generally; yet he was a very mild-mannered man; was genial and companionable and had many excellent qualities. . . . He was a rather good-looking man and his coolness and courage, his affable ways and his fund of interesting experiences won him many admirers. He was a strong friend, a cool and determined enemy and a man of quite strong character."

Surely that last phrase is truth's Siamese twin. What can be said of John Henry Holliday more than anything else is that he had an abundance of character, which he used as the drives of his will and the whims of necessity directed. To an all but absolute degree he seems to have walked with himself, and his response to social pressures was negative, except for one thing. He retained the manners which had been inculcated in him in his youth, together with certain selected standards of his patrician class, where these bore upon individual conduct. Of group morality he was not scornful; there is nothing to show that he cared that much. He was rather congenitally indifferent to it.

He himself let that be known at least once. Those who enjoyed his company were not limited to what the *Republican's* correspondent referred to as "sporting people". Colonel John T. Deweese, for one, was fascinated by Doc's odd assortment of characteristics and used to dine out on Holliday anecdotes. Unfortunately he did not write them down for the entertainment of posterity, but one has been preserved, because it was told to the Denver newspaperman who undertook to write a post-mortem feature about Doc.

"The Doctor," says Colonel Deweese, "had just as lief kill a man as not. All he looked for usually was to have the law on his side. I said to him one day: 'Doctor, don't your conscience ever trouble you?' 'No,' he replied, with that peculiar cough of his, 'I coughed that up with my lungs long ago.'"

ACKNOWLEDGMENTS

Sᴘᴇᴄɪᴀʟ thanks for assistance indispensable to the compilation of this work are extended to:

Miss Lillian McKey and Mr. W. H. McKey of Valdosta, Georgia—cousins of Dr. John Henry Holliday—for their great courtesy in supplying information concerning their kinsman's youth and family background.

Joseph Miller of Phoenix, Arizona, for his generosity in sharing the fruits of his long and laborious investigations of Western frontier newspapers.

Mrs. Alys Freeze of the Denver Public Library and Miss Frances Shea of the State Historical Society of Colorado, both alike unsparing of their time, for furnishing a wealth of source material which would have been overlooked but for their knowledge and co-operative spirit.

Messrs. Maurice Frink of the University of Colorado and Dean Krakel of the University of Wyoming, for taking time off from their own researches to give a hand to a stranger.

Harold Batchelor, librarian of Arizona State College at Tempe, for granting use of library exchange service to a layman, and Robert Jones for implementing it with efficiency and dispatch.

Others to whom I am greatly indebted for supplying information, leads and bibliographical advice are:

Miss Lilla M. Hawes of the Georgia Historical Society, Savannah; Mr. Mulford Winsor and Mrs. Alice Good of the Arizona State Department of Library and Archives, Phoenix; Miss Llerena Friend of the Barkley Historical Centre, Austin, Texas; Mr. Will G. Robinson of the South Dakota State Historical Society, Pierre; Miss Eleanor B. Sloan of the Arizona Pioneers Historical Society, Tucson; Mr. T. B. Converse of the Lowndes County Court House, Valdosta, Georgia; Mrs. Olive B. Corwin of the Museum of New Mexico Library,

Santa Fe; Mr. Fred Shelly of the Maryland Historical Society, Baltimore; Mrs. Ida L. Huckabay, Jacksboro, Texas; Mr. Ken Williams of the Spalding County and Griffin Chamber of Commerce; Miss Helen McFarland of the Kansas State Historical Society, Topeka; Mr. Thomas M. Bogie of the Dallas Public Library; Miss Lillian Henderson of the Department of Confederate Pensions and Records, Atlanta, Georgia; Mr. Don Rickey of the University of Oklahoma Library, Norman; Miss Irene Simpson, Director of the Wells, Fargo Bank History Room, San Francisco; F. Stanley of Canadian, Texas; Mrs. Breed Robinson, Librarian of the Baltimore College of Dental Surgery; Mrs. Allan R. Ottley of the California State Library, Sacramento; Miss Lola M. Homsher of the Wyoming State Historical Department, Cheyenne; Mr. L. P. Goodrich of Griffin, Georgia; and John Barr Tompkins of the Bancroft Library, Berkeley, California.

BIBLIOGRAPHY

Adams, Andy, *Log of a Cowboy*, Boston, 1903.

Arnold, Oren, *Thunder in the West*, Norman, Okla., 1952.

Asbury, Herbert, *Sucker's Progress*, New York, 1938.

Bakarich, Sarah Grace, *Gun Smoke*, Tombstone, Ariz., 1947.

Barnes, Will C., and Raine, William McLeod, *Cattle*, Garden City, N. Y., 1930.

Beadle, J. H., *Western Wilds and the Men Who Redeem Them*, Cincinnati, 1878.

Bechdolt, Frederick R., *When the West Was Young*, New York, 1922.

Beebe, Lucius, and Clegg, Charles, *The Saga of Wells Fargo*, New York, 1949.

Bennett, Estelline, *Old Deadwood Days*, New York, 1928.

Breakenridge, William M., *Helldorado*, Boston, 1929.

Brophy, Frank, *Arizona Sketches*, Phoenix, 1952.

Burns, Walter Noble, *Tombstone: An Iliad of the Southwest*, Garden City, N. Y., 1927.

Chisholm, Joe, *Brewery Gulch*, San Antonio, 1949.

Clum, John P., "It All Happened in Tombstone", *Arizona Historical Quarterly*, October, 1929.

Conard, Howard Louis, *Uncle Dick Wootton*, Chicago, 1890.

Cowen, E. D., "Happy Bad Men of the West", *Chicago Chronicle* 1898 (clipped article; day and month not noted).

Crumbine, Samuel J., *Frontier Doctor*, Philadelphia, 1948.

Cunningham, Eugene, *Triggernometry*, Caldwell, Ida., 1934.

Dixon, Olive K., *Life of Billy Dixon*, Dallas, 1914.

Dobie, J. Frank, *A Vaquero of the Brush Country*, Dallas, 1929.

Dunn, Frank A., "Celebrating a Holliday", *Oral Hygiene*, September, 1933.

Earp, Wyatt Stapley, Article signed "Wyatt S. Earp" in *San Francisco Examiner*, Aug. 6, 1896 (title missing in copy inspected).

Foy, Eddie, and Harlow, Alvin, *Clowning Through Life*, New York, 1928.

Gard, Wayne, *Frontier Justice*, Norman, Okla., 1949.

Gardner, Raymond Hatfield, *Adventures of Arizona Bill*, San Antonio, 1949.

General James Jackson Chapter, D. A. R., *History of Lowndes County, Ga.*, Valdosta, Ga., n. d.

Hayes, A. A., Jr, *New Colorado and the Santa Fe Trail*, New York, 1880.

Hendricks, George D., *Bad Men of the West*, San Antonio, 1942.

Hill, Alice Polk, *Tales of the Colorado Pioneers*, Denver, 1884.

Holloway, Carroll C., *Texas Gun Lore*, San Antonio, 1952.

Hough, Emerson, *The Story of the Outlaw*, New York, 1907.

Hume, James B., and Thacker, John N., *Report of James B. Hume and John N. Thacker, Special Officers, Wells, Fargo & Co.'s Express*, San Francisco, 1885.

Hunter, J. Marvin, and Rose, Norah H., *The Album of Gun-fighters*, Bandera, Tex., 1951.

Keleher, William A., *The Fabulous Frontier*, Sante Fe, 1948.

King, Frank P., *Wranglin' the Past*, Pasadena, 1935.

Lake, Stuart, *Wyatt Earp: Frontier Marshal*, Boston, 1931.

Lowther, Charles C., *Dodge City*, Philadelphia, 1940.

McClintock, James H., *Arizona, the Youngest State*, 3 vols., Chicago, 1916.

McNeal, T. A., *When Kansas was Young*, New York, 1922.

Manning, Jay F., and others, *Leadville, Lake County and the Gold Belt*, Denver, 1895.

Martin, Douglas D., *Tombstone's Epitaph*, Albuquerque, 1951.

Masterson, William Barclay, Article about Doc Holliday in series entitled "Famous Gunfighters of the Western Frontier", *Human Life*, May, 1907.

Myers, John Myers, *The Last Chance: Tombstone's Early Years*, New York, 1950.

Otero, Miguel Antonio, *My Life on the Frontier*, 2 vols., New York, 1935.

Parsons, George W., *Private Journal of George Whitwell Parsons*, Phoenix, 1934.

Quiett, Glenn Chesney, *They Built the West: An Epic of Rails and Cities*, New York, 1934.

Raine, William McLeod, *Famous Sheriffs and Western Outlaws*, New York, 1929.

——, *Guns of the Frontier*, Boston, 1940.

Richardson, R. N., and Rister, C. C., *The Greater Southwest*, Glendale, Calif., 1934.

Rister, Carl Coke, *The Southwestern Frontier*, Cleveland, 1928.

Rogers, John Williams, *The Lusty Texans of Dallas*, New York, 1951.

Rye, Edgar, *The Quirt and the Spur*, Chicago, 1909.

Scullin, George, "The Killer", *Holiday*, Aug., 1954.

Siringo, Charles A., *Riata and Spur*, Boston, 1912.

Smiley, Jerome C., *History of Denver*, Denver, 1901.

Sonnichsen, Charles L., *Billy King's Tombstone*, Caldwell, Ida., 1942.

Spring, Agnes Wright, *Cheyenne and Black Hills Stage Route*, Glendale, Calif., 1949.

Stanley, F., *Desperadoes of New Mexico*, Denver, 1953.

——, *The Las Vegas Story*, Denver, 1951.

Thompson, George C., *Bat Masterson: The Dodge City Years*, Topeka, 1943.

Tilghman, Zoe A., *Marshal of the Last Frontier*, Glendale, Calif., 1951.

Van Denmark, Harry, "Looking-for-Trouble Holliday", *Texas Monthly*, vol. 3.

Vestal, Stanley, *Queen of Cow Towns, Dodge City*, New York, 1952.

Wallace, Earnest, and Hoebel, F. Adamson, *The Comanches*, Norman, Okla., 1952.

Walters, Lorenzo D., *Tombstone's Yesterdays*, Tucson, 1928.

Wellman, Paul I., *The Trampling Herd*, New York, 1939.

Willson, Neil V., *Treasure Express: Epic Days of Wells, Fargo*, New York, 1939.

Wright, Robert M., *Dodge City, the Cowboy Capital*, Wichita, Kan., 1913.

INDEX